IRON FIST

PHANTOM LIMB

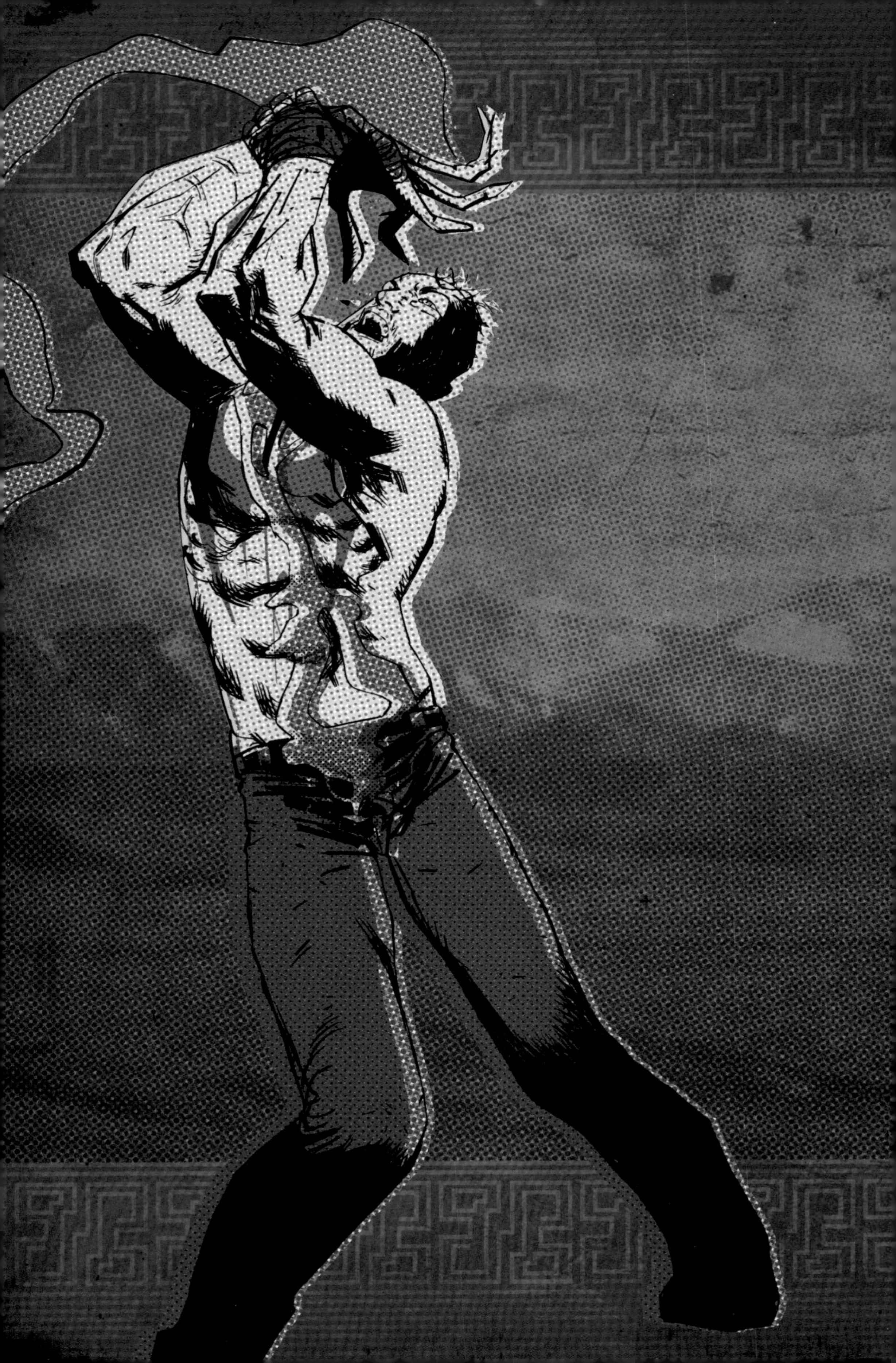

IRON FIST
PHANTOM LIMB

WRITER CLAY McLEOD CHAPMAN
ARTIST GUILLERMO SANNA
COLOR ARTIST LEE LOUGHRIDGE

LETTERER VC'S TRAVIS LANHAM
COVER ARTISTS KHOI PHAM & CHRIS SOTOMAYOR

ASSISTANT EDITOR LAUREN AMARO
EDITOR DEVIN LEWIS
EXECUTIVE EDITOR NICK LOWE

COLLECTION EDITOR MARK D. BEAZLEY - ASSISTANT EDITOR CAITLIN O'CONNELL - ASSOCIATE MANAGING EDITOR KATERI WOODY
SENIOR EDITOR, SPECIAL PROJECTS JENNIFER GRÜNWALD - VP PRODUCTION & SPECIAL PROJECTS JEFF YOUNGQUIST
SVP PRINT, SALES & MARKETING DAVID GABRIEL - BOOK DESIGNER JAY BOWEN

EDITOR IN CHIEF C.B. CEBULSKI - CHIEF CREATIVE OFFICER JOE QUESADA - PRESIDENT DAN BUCKLEY - EXECUTIVE PRODUCER ALAN FINE

IRON FIST: PHANTOM LIMB. First printing 2018. ISBN 978-1-302-91467-7. Published by MARVEL WORLDWIDE, INC., a subsidiary of MARVEL ENTERTAINMENT, LLC. OFFICE OF PUBLICATION: 135 West 50th Street, New York, NY 10020. **Printed in Canada.** DAN BUCKLEY, President, Marvel Entertainment; JOHN NEE, Publisher; JOE QUESADA, Chief Creative Officer; TOM BREVOORT, SVP of Publishing; DAVID BOGART, SVP of Business Affairs & Operations, Publishing & Partnership; DAVID GABRIEL, SVP of Sales & Marketing, Publishing; JEFF YOUNGQUIST, VP of Production & Special Projects; DAN CARR, Executive Director of Publishing Technology; ALEX MORALES, Director of Publishing Operations; DAN EDINGTON, Managing Editor; SUSAN CRESPI, Production Manager; STAN LEE, Chairman Emeritus. For information regarding advertising in Marvel Comics or on Marvel.com, please contact Vit DeBellis, Custom Solutions & Integrated Advertising Manager, at vdebellis@marvel.com. For Marvel subscription inquiries, please call 888-511-5480. **Manufactured between 11/8/2018 and 12/10/2018 by SOLISCO PRINTERS, SCOTT, QC, CANADA.**

10 9 8 7 6 5 4 3 2 1

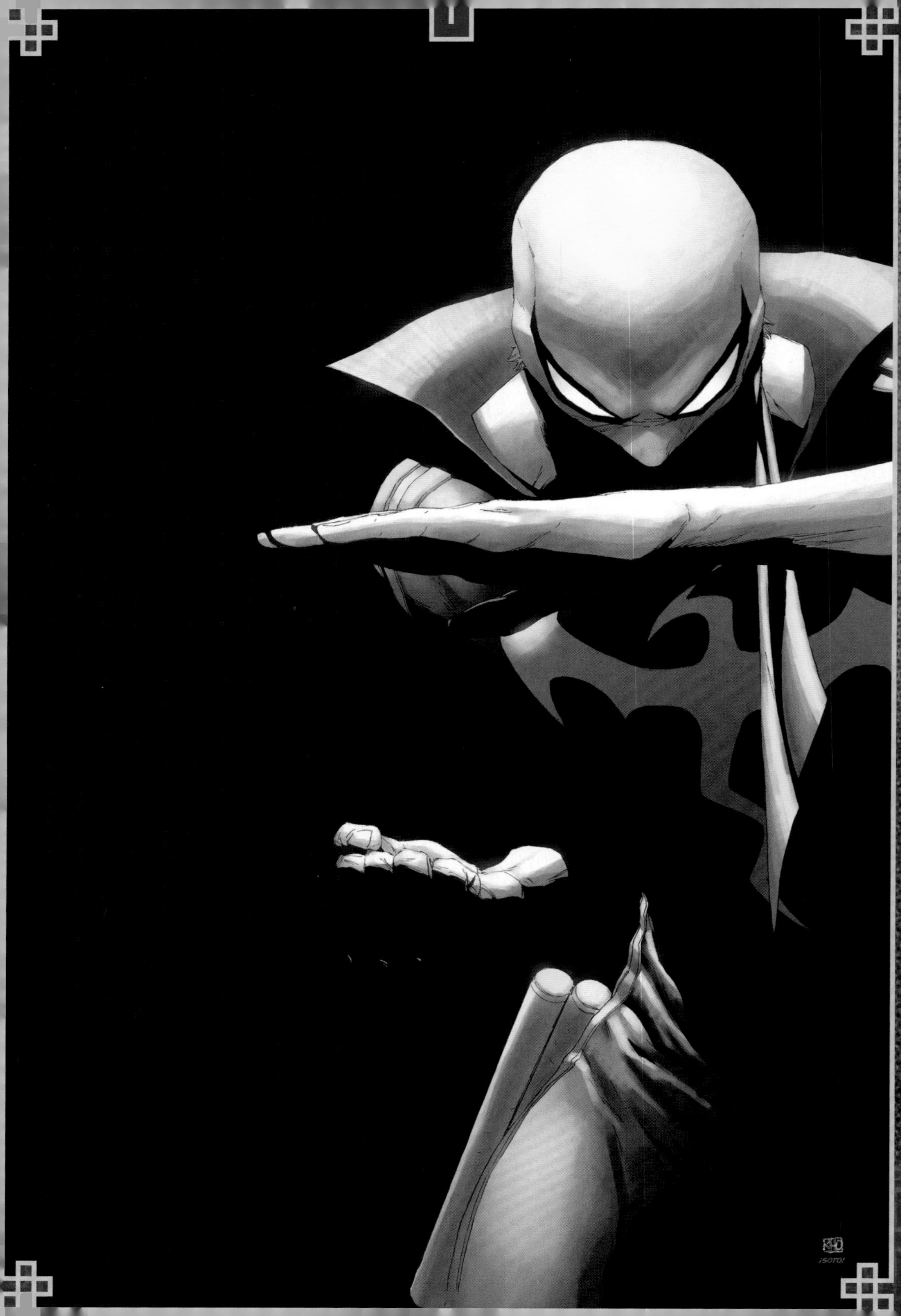

PHANTOM LIMB

CHAPTER 1

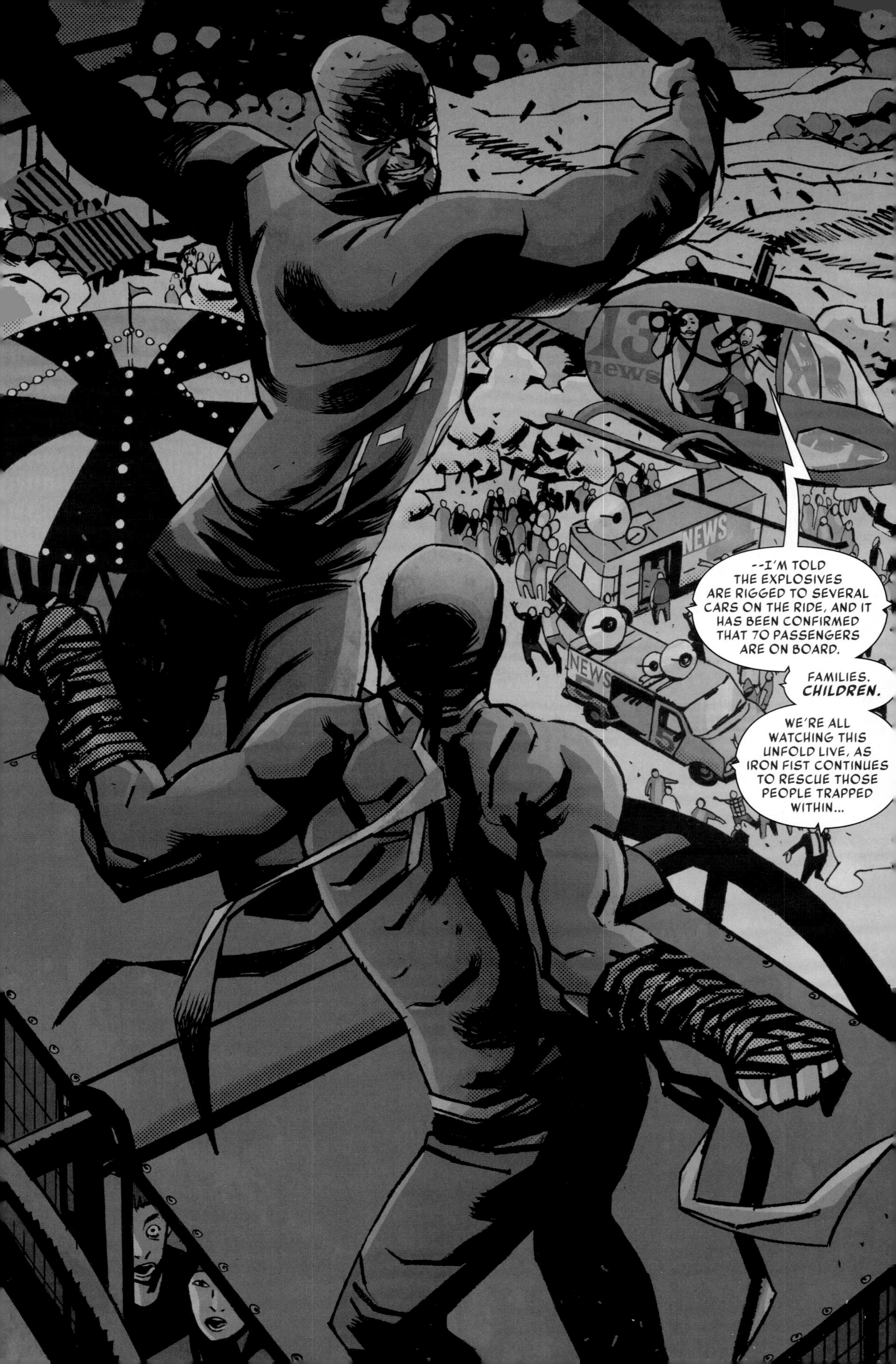
--I'M TOLD THE EXPLOSIVES ARE RIGGED TO SEVERAL CARS ON THE RIDE, AND IT HAS BEEN CONFIRMED THAT 70 PASSENGERS ARE ON BOARD.
FAMILIES. **CHILDREN.**
WE'RE ALL WATCHING THIS UNFOLD LIVE, AS IRON FIST CONTINUES TO RESCUE THOSE PEOPLE TRAPPED WITHIN...
13 news
NEWS
NEWS

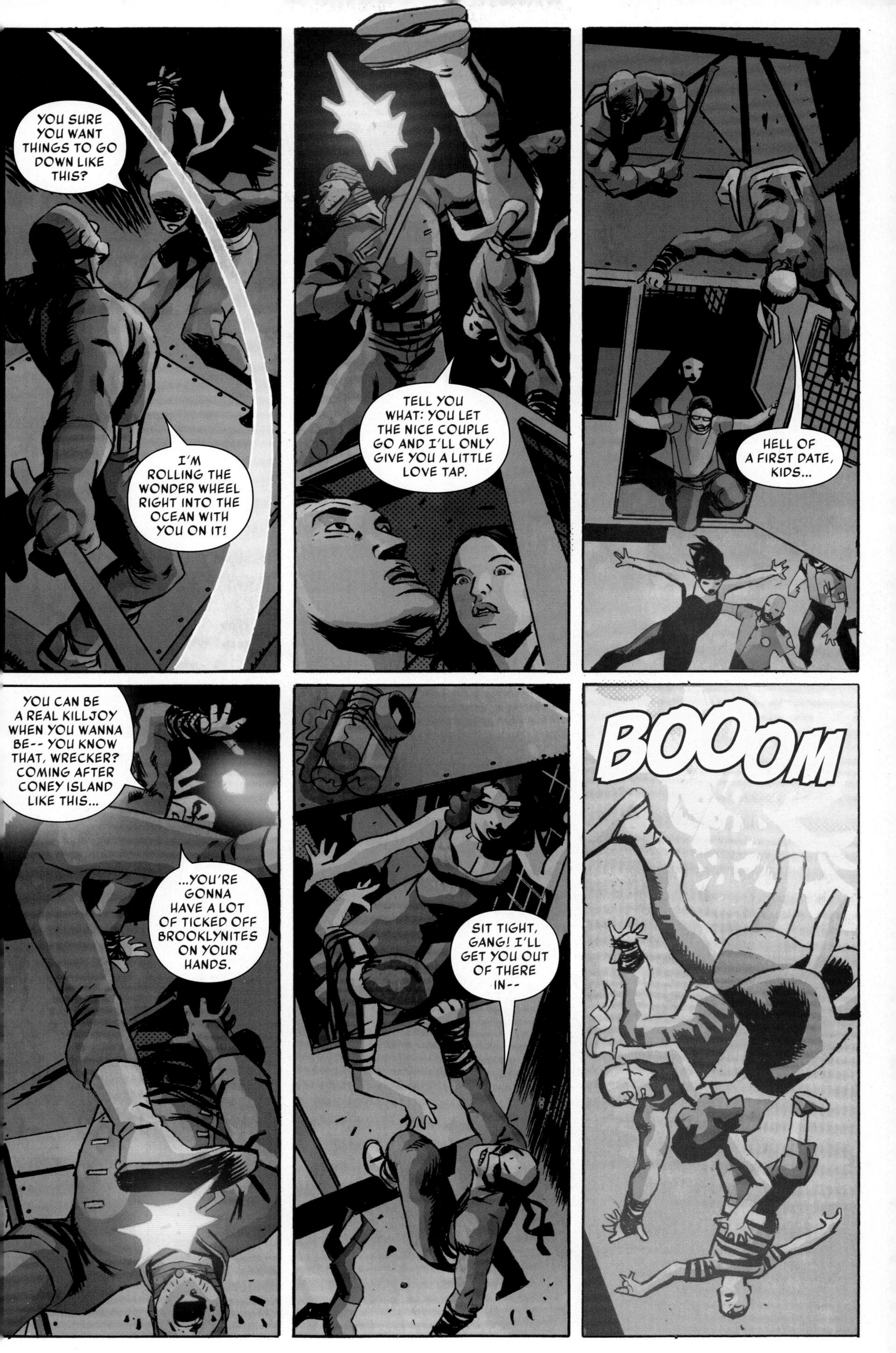
YOU SURE YOU WANT THINGS TO GO DOWN LIKE THIS?
I'M ROLLING THE WONDER WHEEL RIGHT INTO THE OCEAN WITH YOU ON IT!
TELL YOU WHAT: YOU LET THE NICE COUPLE GO AND I'LL ONLY GIVE YOU A LITTLE LOVE TAP.
HELL OF A FIRST DATE, KIDS...
YOU CAN BE A REAL KILLJOY WHEN YOU WANNA BE-- YOU KNOW THAT, WRECKER? COMING AFTER CONEY ISLAND LIKE THIS...
...YOU'RE GONNA HAVE A LOT OF TICKED OFF BROOKLYNITES ON YOUR HANDS.
SIT TIGHT, GANG! I'LL GET YOU OUT OF THERE IN--
BOOOOM

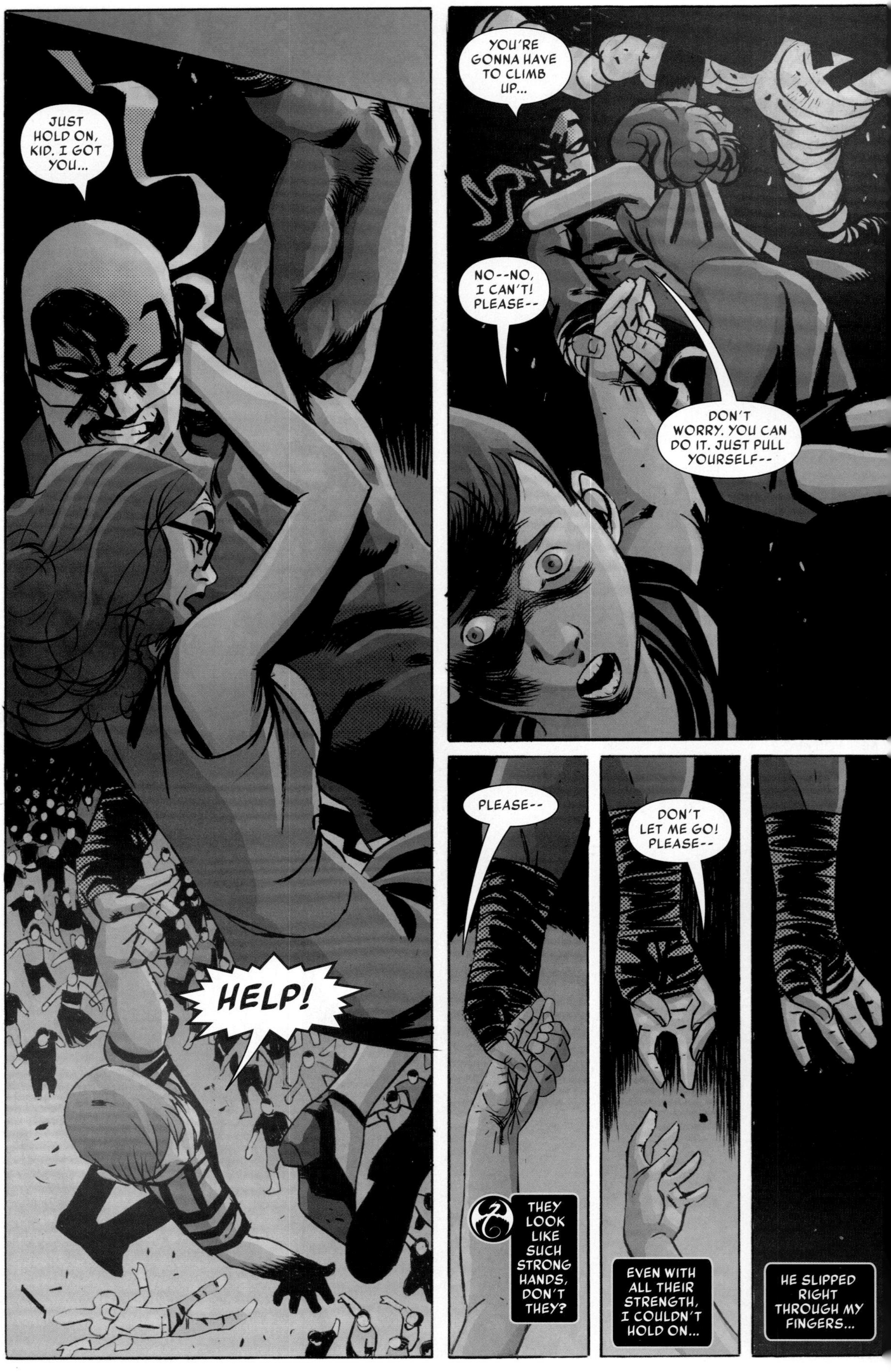
JUST HOLD ON, KID. I GOT YOU...
HELP!
YOU'RE GONNA HAVE TO CLIMB UP...
NO--NO, I CAN'T! PLEASE--
DON'T WORRY. YOU CAN DO IT. JUST PULL YOURSELF--
PLEASE--
THEY LOOK LIKE SUCH STRONG HANDS, DON'T THEY?
DON'T LET ME GO! PLEASE--
EVEN WITH ALL THEIR STRENGTH, I COULDN'T HOLD ON...
HE SLIPPED RIGHT THROUGH MY FINGERS...

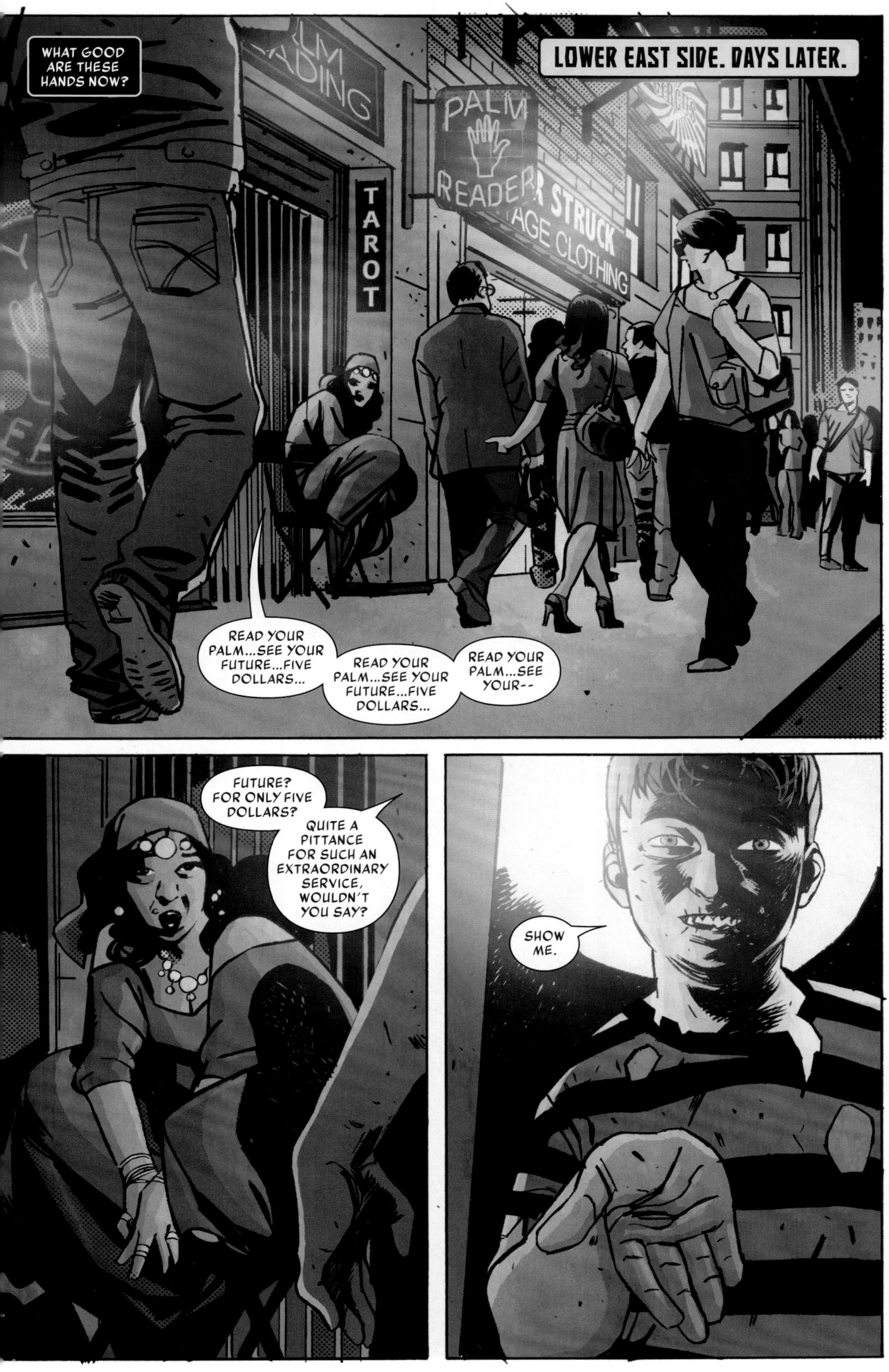
WHAT GOOD ARE THESE HANDS NOW?
LOWER EAST SIDE. DAYS LATER.
PALM READER
TAROT
READ YOUR PALM...SEE YOUR FUTURE...FIVE DOLLARS...
READ YOUR PALM...SEE YOUR FUTURE...FIVE DOLLARS...
READ YOUR PALM...SEE YOUR--
FUTURE? FOR ONLY FIVE DOLLARS?
QUITE A PITTANCE FOR SUCH AN EXTRAORDINARY SERVICE, WOULDN'T YOU SAY?
SHOW ME.

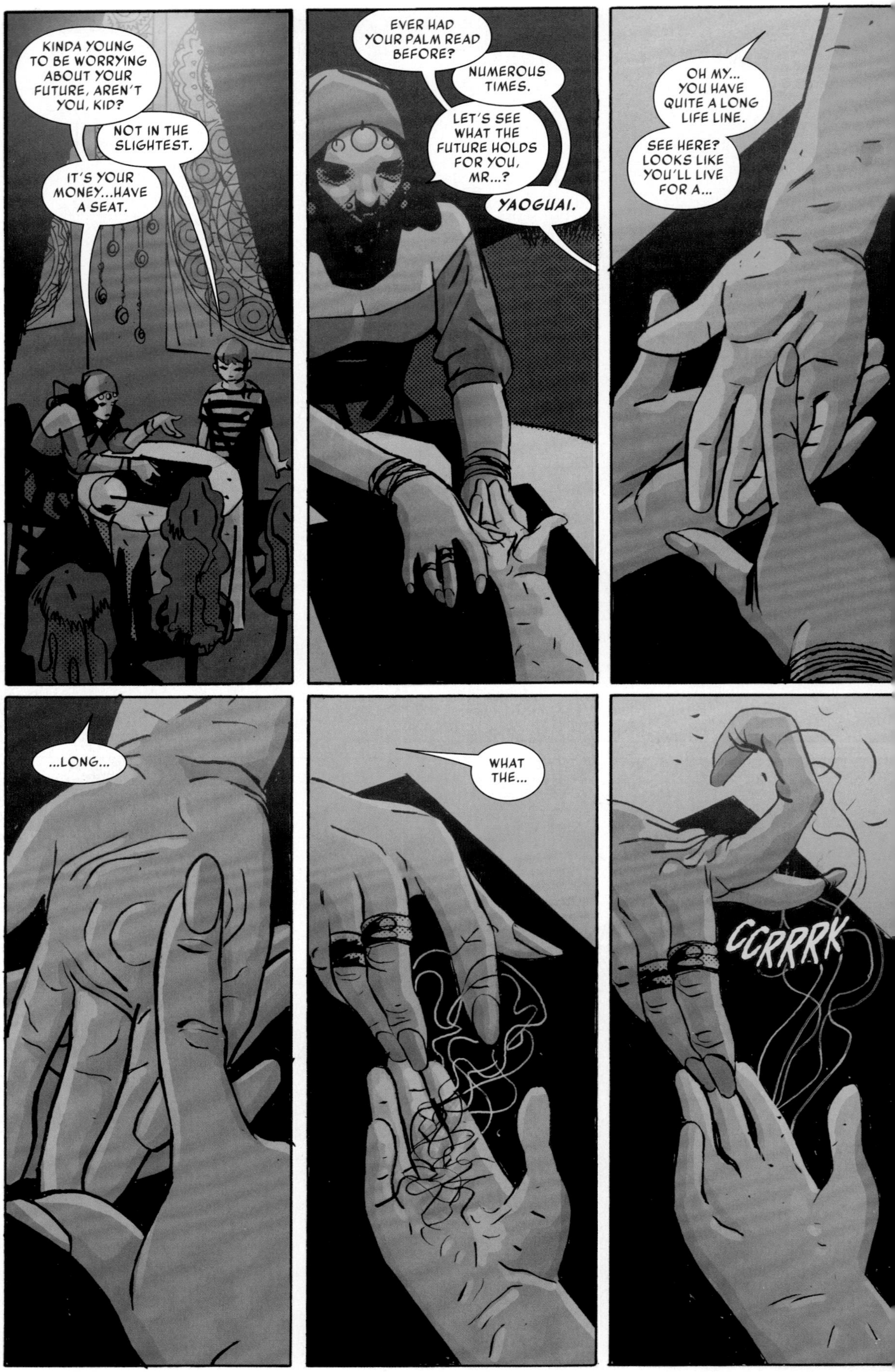
KINDA YOUNG TO BE WORRYING ABOUT YOUR FUTURE, AREN'T YOU, KID?
NOT IN THE SLIGHTEST.
IT'S YOUR MONEY...HAVE A SEAT.
EVER HAD YOUR PALM READ BEFORE?
NUMEROUS TIMES.
LET'S SEE WHAT THE FUTURE HOLDS FOR YOU, MR...?
YAOGUAI.
OH MY... YOU HAVE QUITE A LONG LIFE LINE.
SEE HERE? LOOKS LIKE YOU'LL LIVE FOR A...
...LONG...
WHAT THE...
CCRRRK

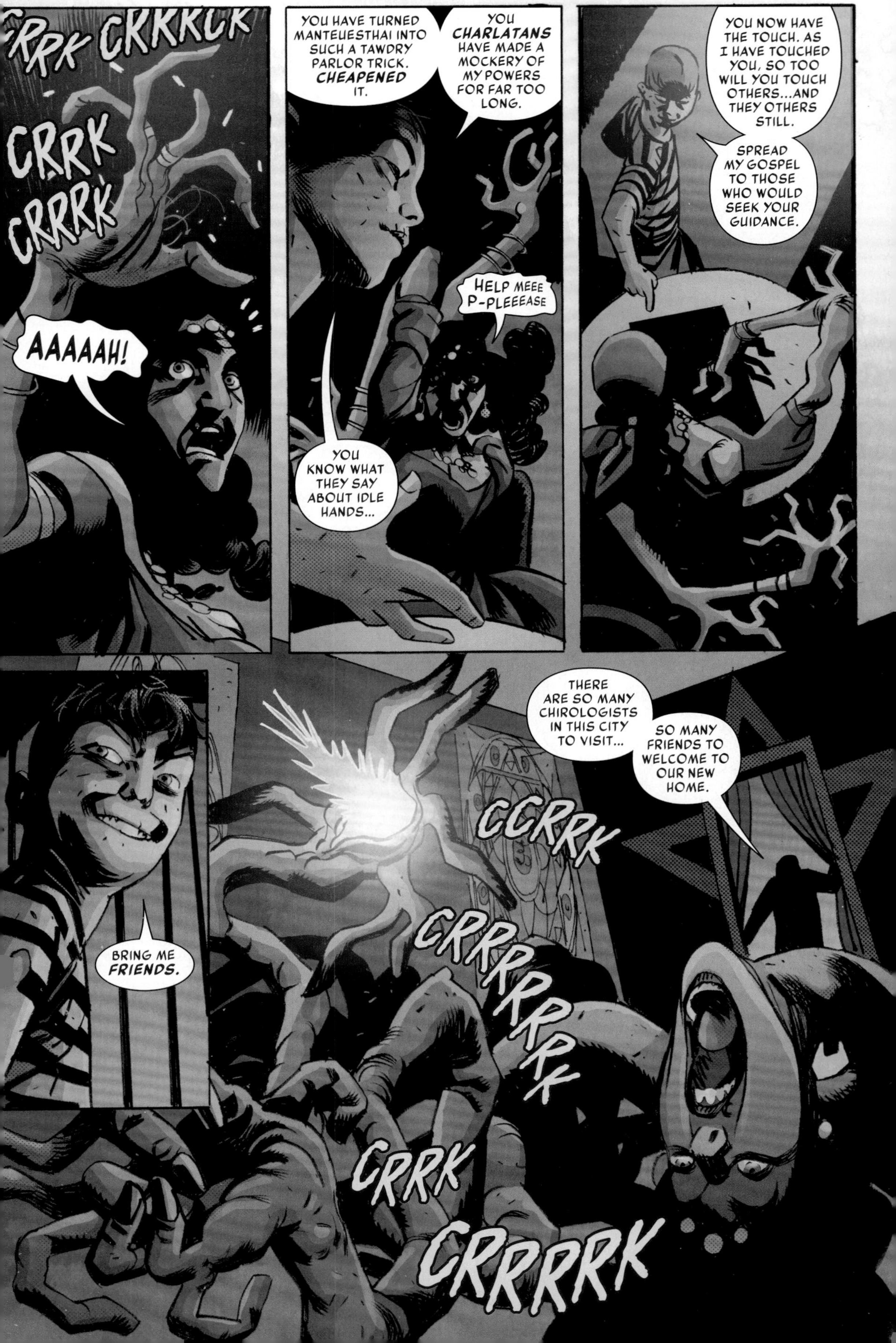
GRRK CKKKCK
CRRK
CRRRK
AAAAAH!
YOU HAVE TURNED MANTEUESTHAI INTO SUCH A TAWDRY PARLOR TRICK. CHEAPENED IT.
YOU CHARLATANS HAVE MADE A MOCKERY OF MY POWERS FOR FAR TOO LONG.
HELP MEEE P-PLEEEASE
YOU KNOW WHAT THEY SAY ABOUT IDLE HANDS...
YOU NOW HAVE THE TOUCH. AS I HAVE TOUCHED YOU, SO TOO WILL YOU TOUCH OTHERS...AND THEY OTHERS STILL.
SPREAD MY GOSPEL TO THOSE WHO WOULD SEEK YOUR GUIDANCE.
BRING ME FRIENDS.
THERE ARE SO MANY CHIROLOGISTS IN THIS CITY TO VISIT...
SO MANY FRIENDS TO WELCOME TO OUR NEW HOME.
CCRRK
CRRRRRRRK
CRRK
CRRRRK

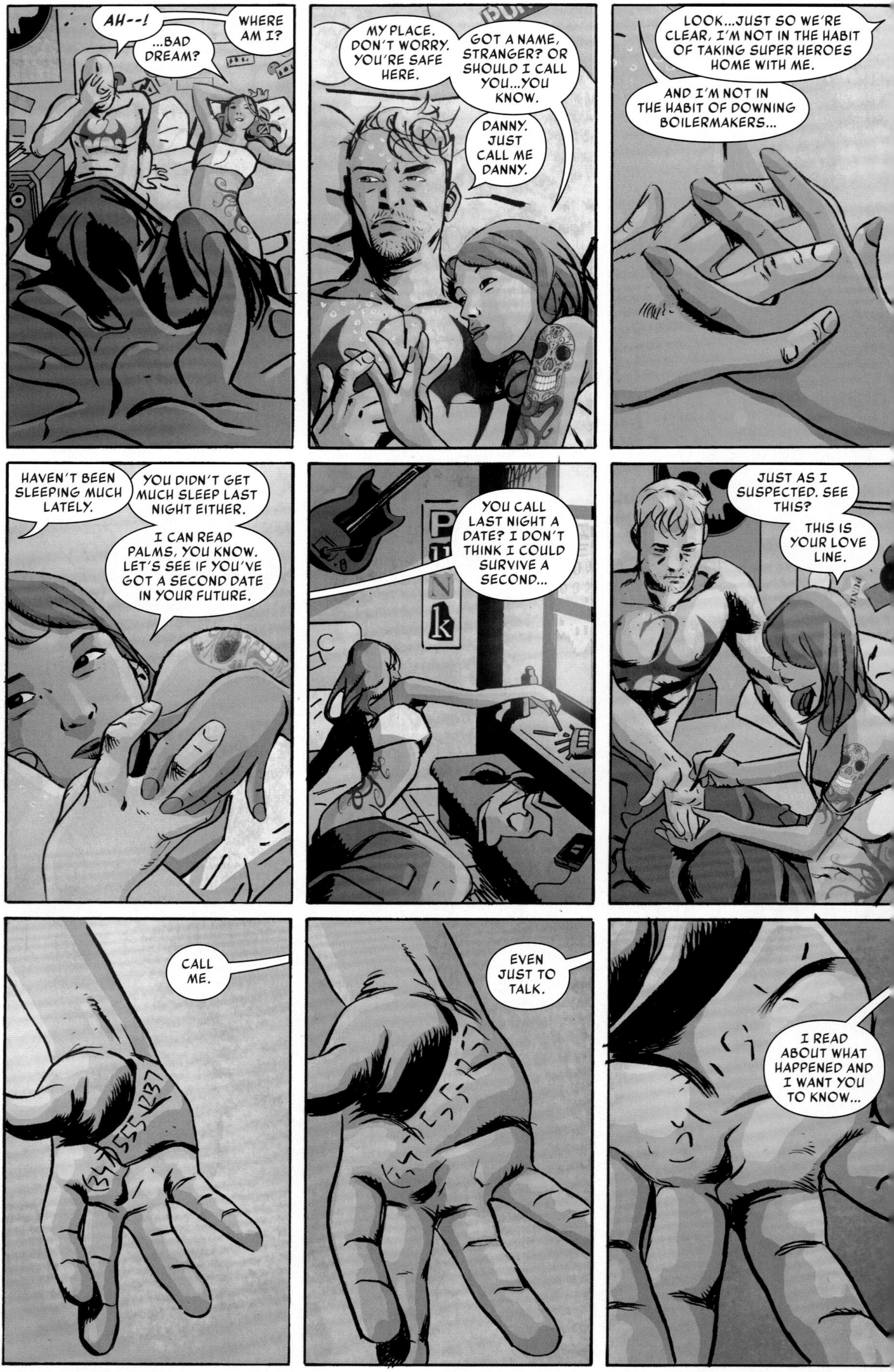
AH--!
...BAD DREAM?
WHERE AM I?
MY PLACE. DON'T WORRY. YOU'RE SAFE HERE.
GOT A NAME, STRANGER? OR SHOULD I CALL YOU...YOU KNOW.
DANNY. JUST CALL ME DANNY.
LOOK...JUST SO WE'RE CLEAR, I'M NOT IN THE HABIT OF TAKING SUPER HEROES HOME WITH ME.
AND I'M NOT IN THE HABIT OF DOWNING BOILERMAKERS...
HAVEN'T BEEN SLEEPING MUCH LATELY.
YOU DIDN'T GET MUCH SLEEP LAST NIGHT EITHER.
I CAN READ PALMS, YOU KNOW. LET'S SEE IF YOU'VE GOT A SECOND DATE IN YOUR FUTURE.
YOU CALL LAST NIGHT A DATE? I DON'T THINK I COULD SURVIVE A SECOND...
PUNK
JUST AS I SUSPECTED. SEE THIS?
THIS IS YOUR LOVE LINE.
CALL ME.
EVEN JUST TO TALK.
I READ ABOUT WHAT HAPPENED AND I WANT YOU TO KNOW...

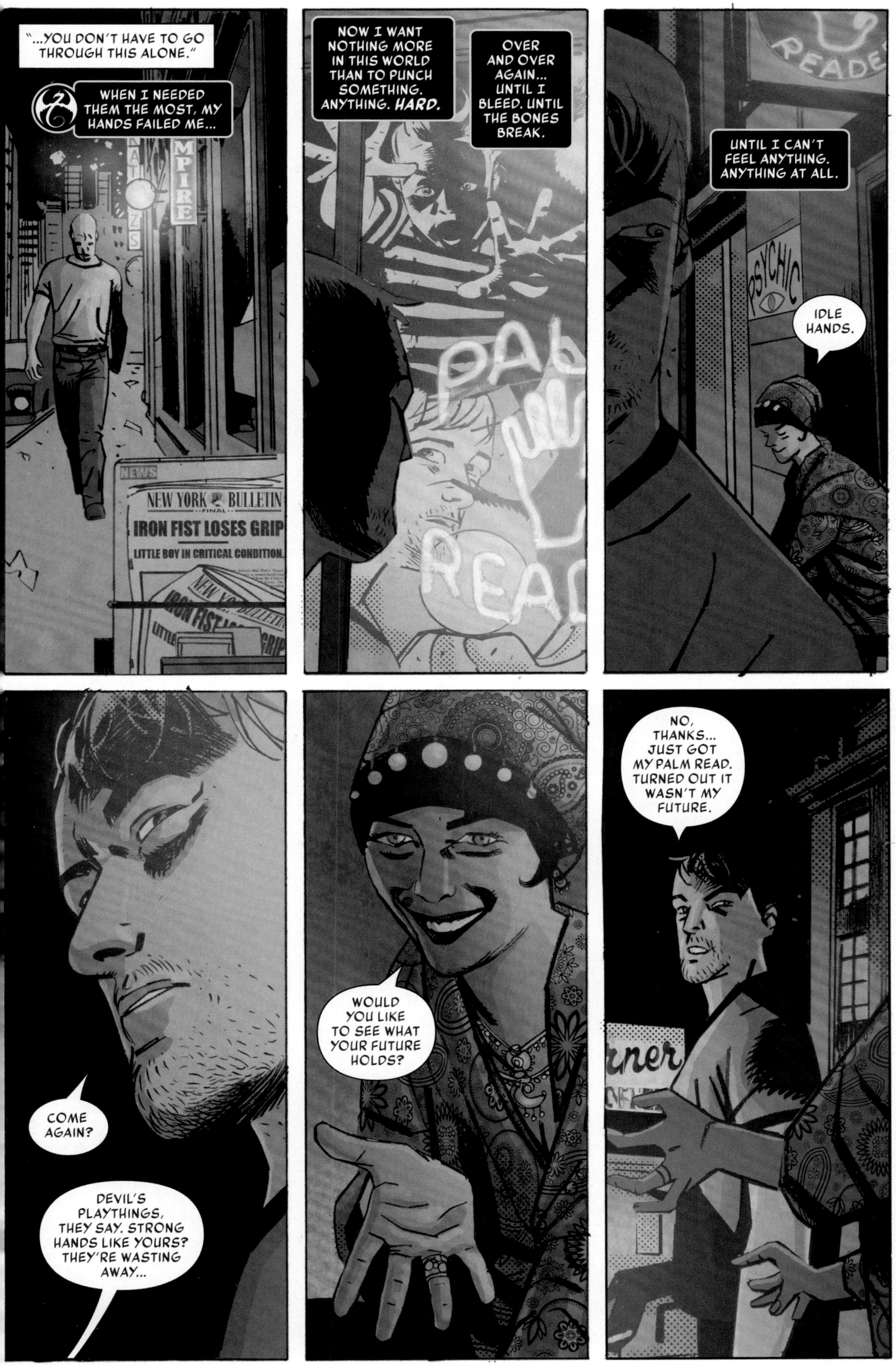

"...YOU DON'T HAVE TO GO THROUGH THIS ALONE."
WHEN I NEEDED THEM THE MOST, MY HANDS FAILED ME...
EMPIRE
NEWS
NEW YORK BULLETIN
FINAL
IRON FIST LOSES GRIP
LITTLE BOY IN CRITICAL CONDITION.
NOW I WANT NOTHING MORE IN THIS WORLD THAN TO PUNCH SOMETHING. ANYTHING. HARD.
OVER AND OVER AGAIN... UNTIL I BLEED. UNTIL THE BONES BREAK.
UNTIL I CAN'T FEEL ANYTHING. ANYTHING AT ALL.
PSYCHIC
IDLE HANDS.
COME AGAIN?
DEVIL'S PLAYTHINGS, THEY SAY. STRONG HANDS LIKE YOURS? THEY'RE WASTING AWAY...
WOULD YOU LIKE TO SEE WHAT YOUR FUTURE HOLDS?
NO, THANKS... JUST GOT MY PALM READ. TURNED OUT IT WASN'T MY FUTURE.

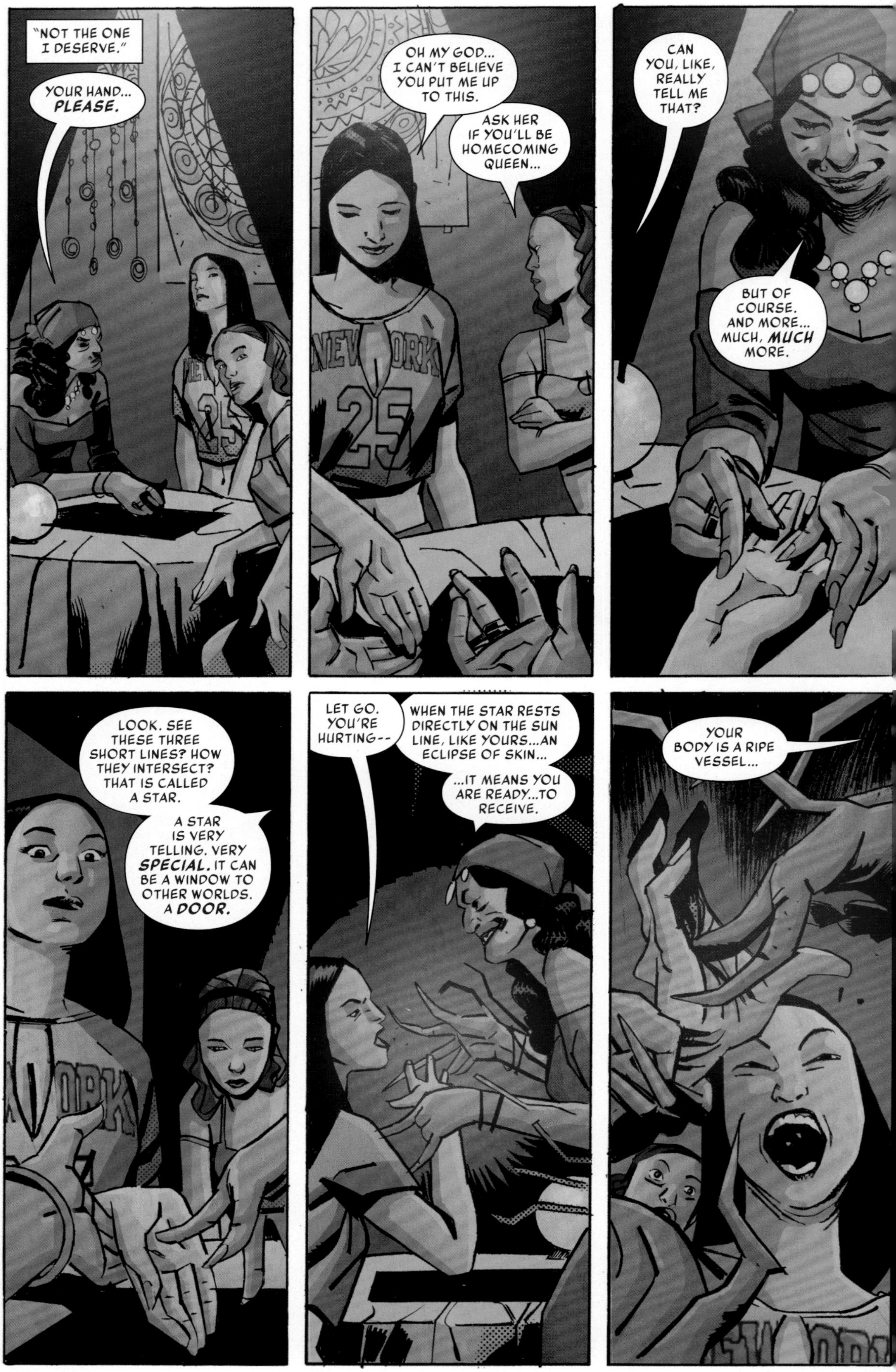
"NOT THE ONE I DESERVE."
YOUR HAND... PLEASE.
OH MY GOD... I CAN'T BELIEVE YOU PUT ME UP TO THIS.
ASK HER IF YOU'LL BE HOMECOMING QUEEN...
CAN YOU, LIKE, REALLY TELL ME THAT?
BUT OF COURSE. AND MORE... MUCH, MUCH MORE.
LOOK. SEE THESE THREE SHORT LINES? HOW THEY INTERSECT? THAT IS CALLED A STAR.
A STAR IS VERY TELLING. VERY SPECIAL. IT CAN BE A WINDOW TO OTHER WORLDS. A DOOR.
LET GO. YOU'RE HURTING--
WHEN THE STAR RESTS DIRECTLY ON THE SUN LINE, LIKE YOURS...AN ECLIPSE OF SKIN...
...IT MEANS YOU ARE READY...TO RECEIVE.
YOUR BODY IS A RIPE VESSEL...

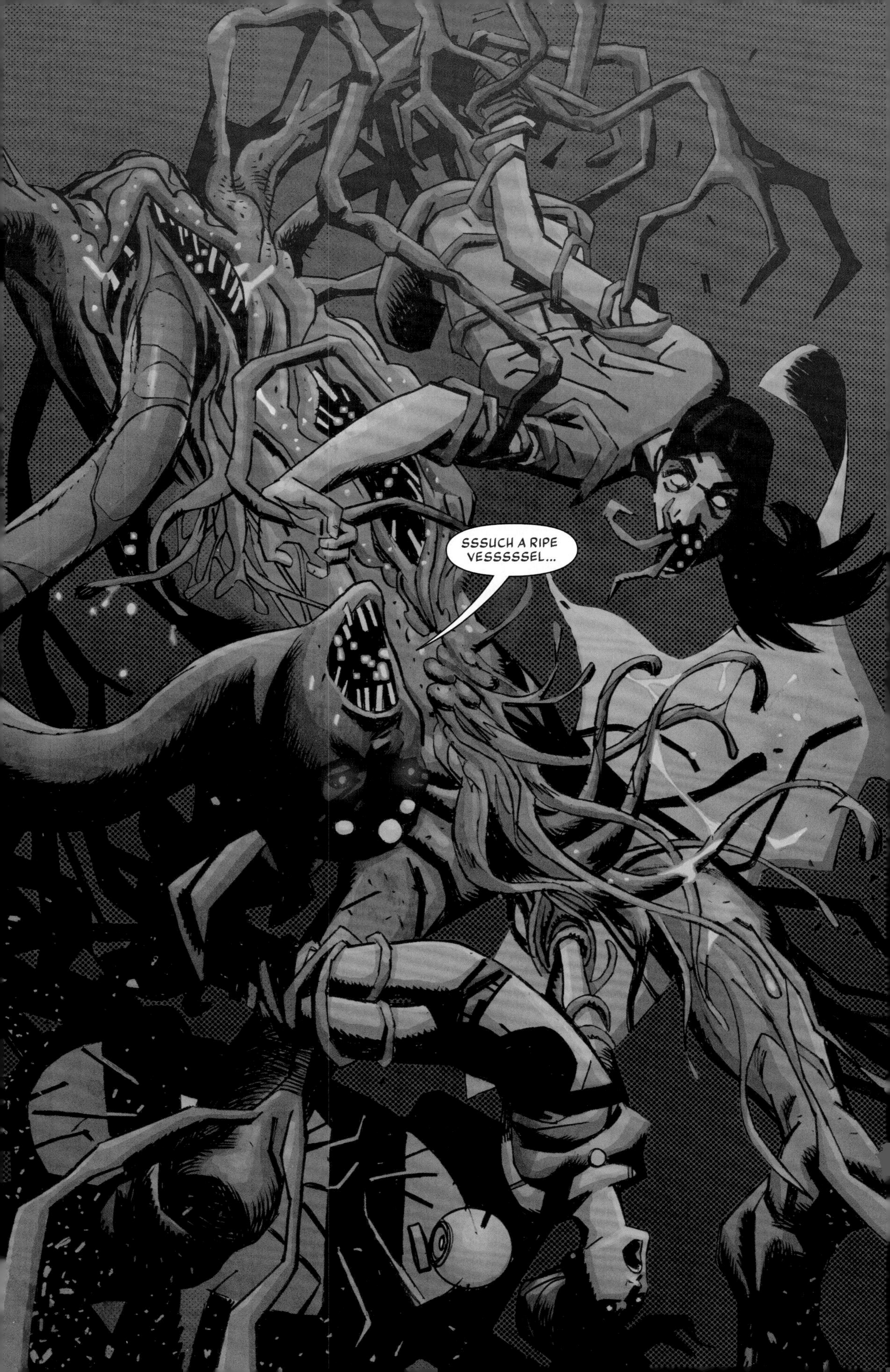
SSSUCH A RIPE VESSSSSEL...

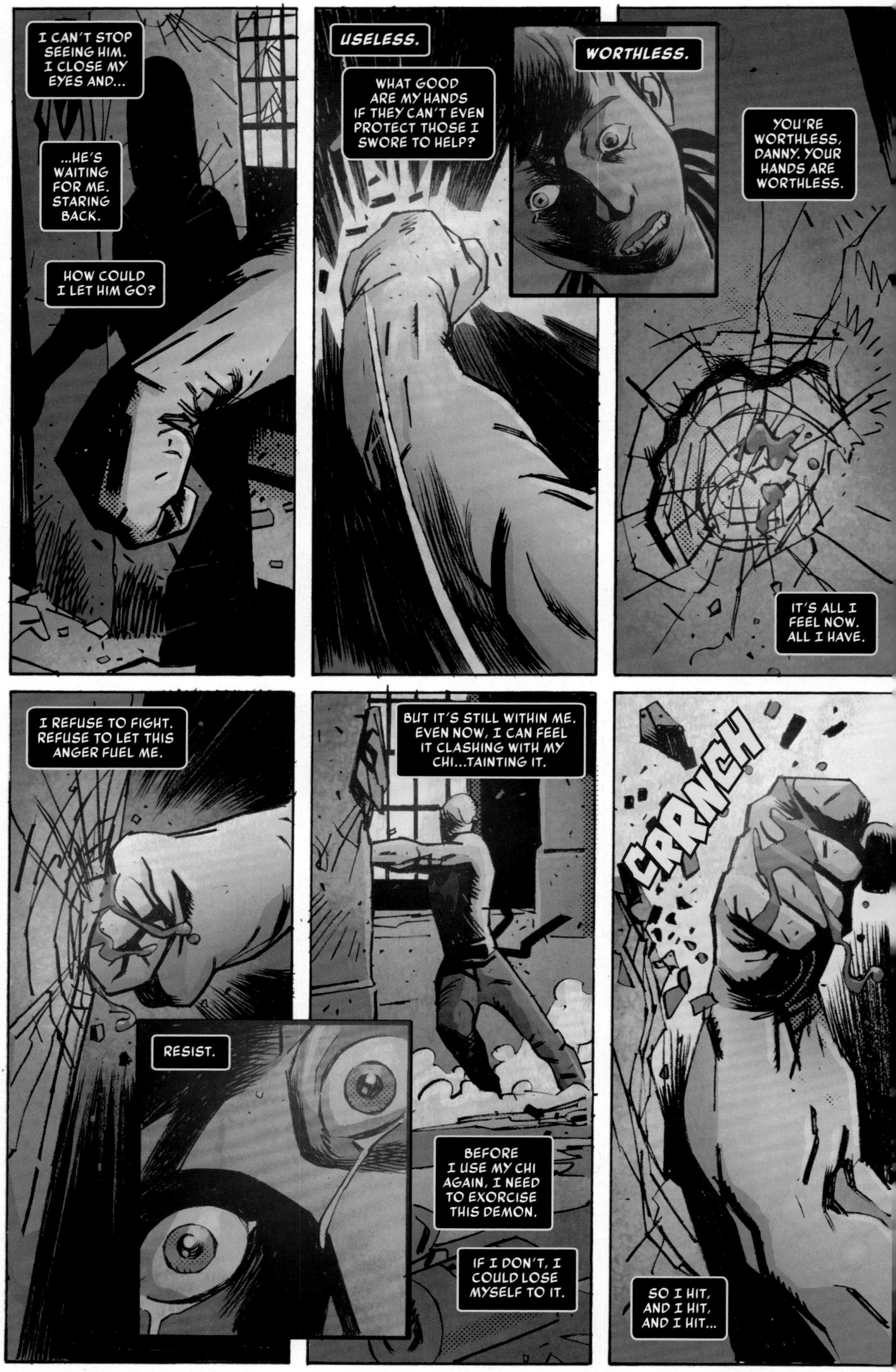
I CAN'T STOP SEEING HIM. I CLOSE MY EYES AND...
...HE'S WAITING FOR ME. STARING BACK.
HOW COULD I LET HIM GO?
USELESS.
WHAT GOOD ARE MY HANDS IF THEY CAN'T EVEN PROTECT THOSE I SWORE TO HELP?
WORTHLESS.
YOU'RE WORTHLESS, DANNY. YOUR HANDS ARE WORTHLESS.
IT'S ALL I FEEL NOW. ALL I HAVE.
I REFUSE TO FIGHT. REFUSE TO LET THIS ANGER FUEL ME.
RESIST.
BUT IT'S STILL WITHIN ME. EVEN NOW, I CAN FEEL IT CLASHING WITH MY CHI...TAINTING IT.
BEFORE I USE MY CHI AGAIN, I NEED TO EXORCISE THIS DEMON.
IF I DON'T, I COULD LOSE MYSELF TO IT.
CRRNCH
SO I HIT, AND I HIT, AND I HIT...

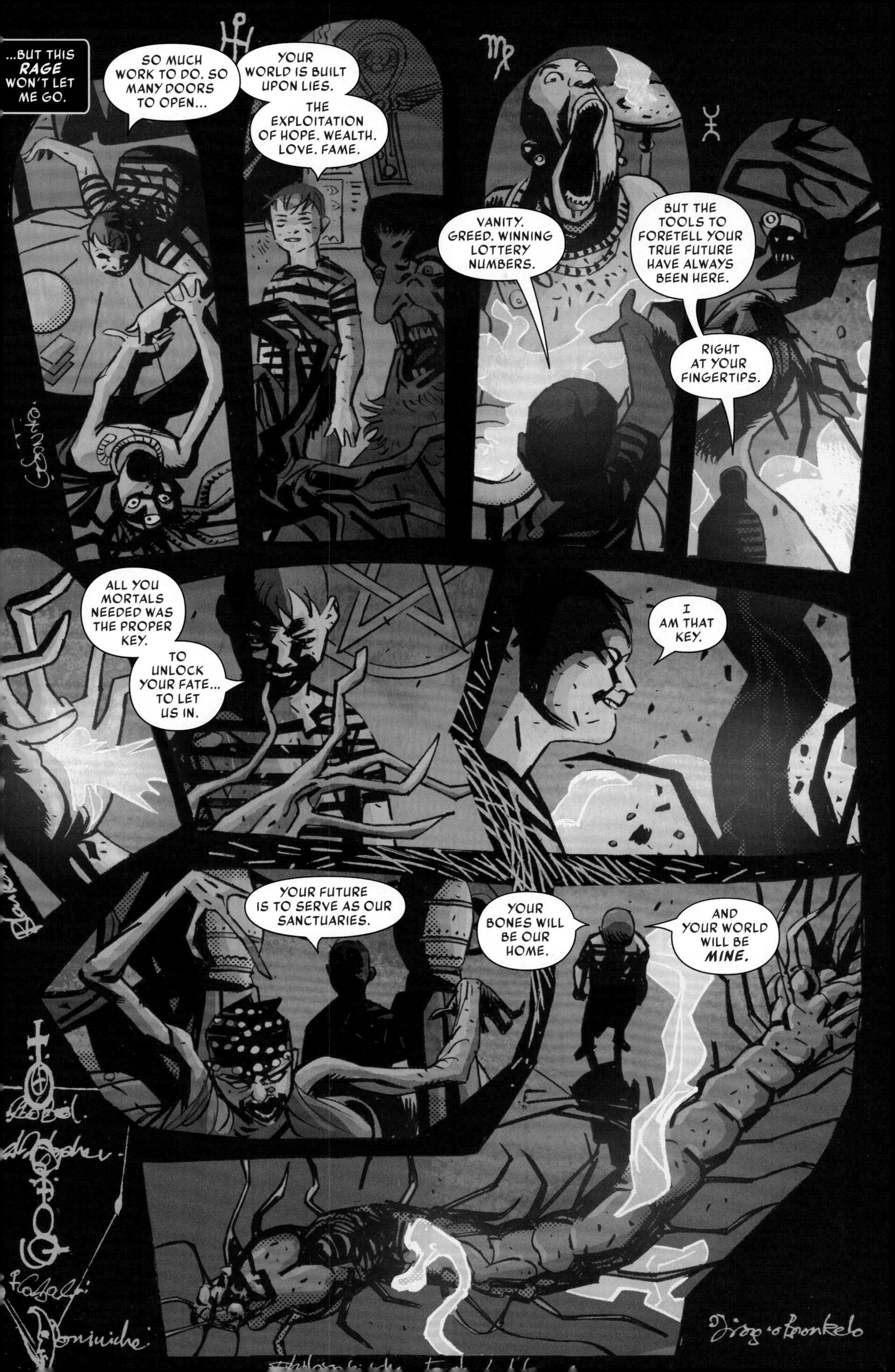
...BUT THIS RAGE WON'T LET ME GO.
SO MUCH WORK TO DO. SO MANY DOORS TO OPEN...
YOUR WORLD IS BUILT UPON LIES.
THE EXPLOITATION OF HOPE. WEALTH. LOVE. FAME.
VANITY. GREED. WINNING LOTTERY NUMBERS.
BUT THE TOOLS TO FORETELL YOUR TRUE FUTURE HAVE ALWAYS BEEN HERE.
RIGHT AT YOUR FINGERTIPS.
ALL YOU MORTALS NEEDED WAS THE PROPER KEY.
TO UNLOCK YOUR FATE... TO LET US IN.
I AM THAT KEY.
YOUR FUTURE IS TO SERVE AS OUR SANCTUARIES.
YOUR BONES WILL BE OUR HOME.
AND YOUR WORLD WILL BE MINE.

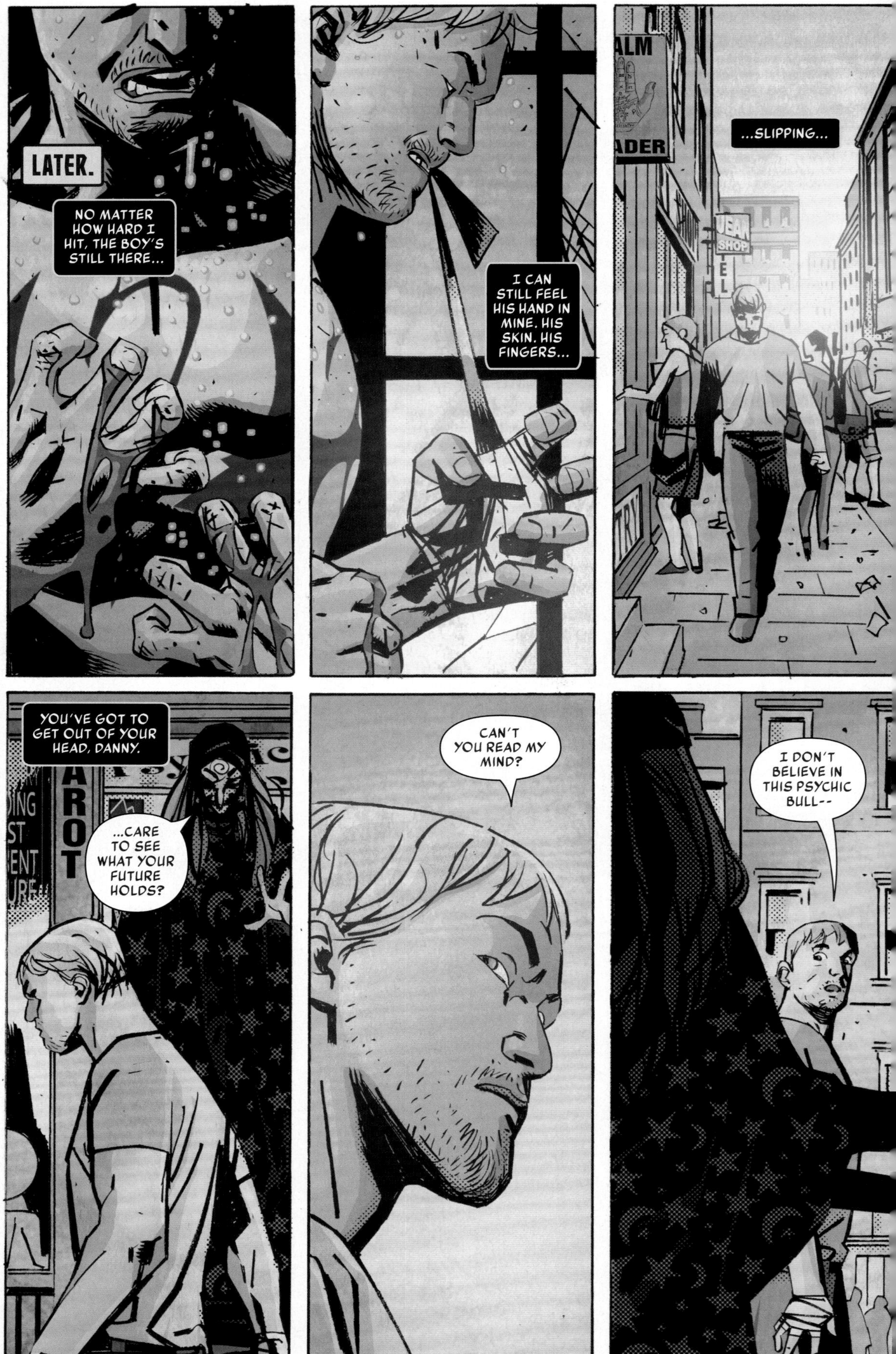
LATER.
NO MATTER HOW HARD I HIT, THE BOY'S STILL THERE...
I CAN STILL FEEL HIS HAND IN MINE. HIS SKIN. HIS FINGERS...
ALM
ADER
...SLIPPING...
YOU'VE GOT TO GET OUT OF YOUR HEAD, DANNY.
AROT
...CARE TO SEE WHAT YOUR FUTURE HOLDS?
CAN'T YOU READ MY MIND?
I DON'T BELIEVE IN THIS PSYCHIC BULL--

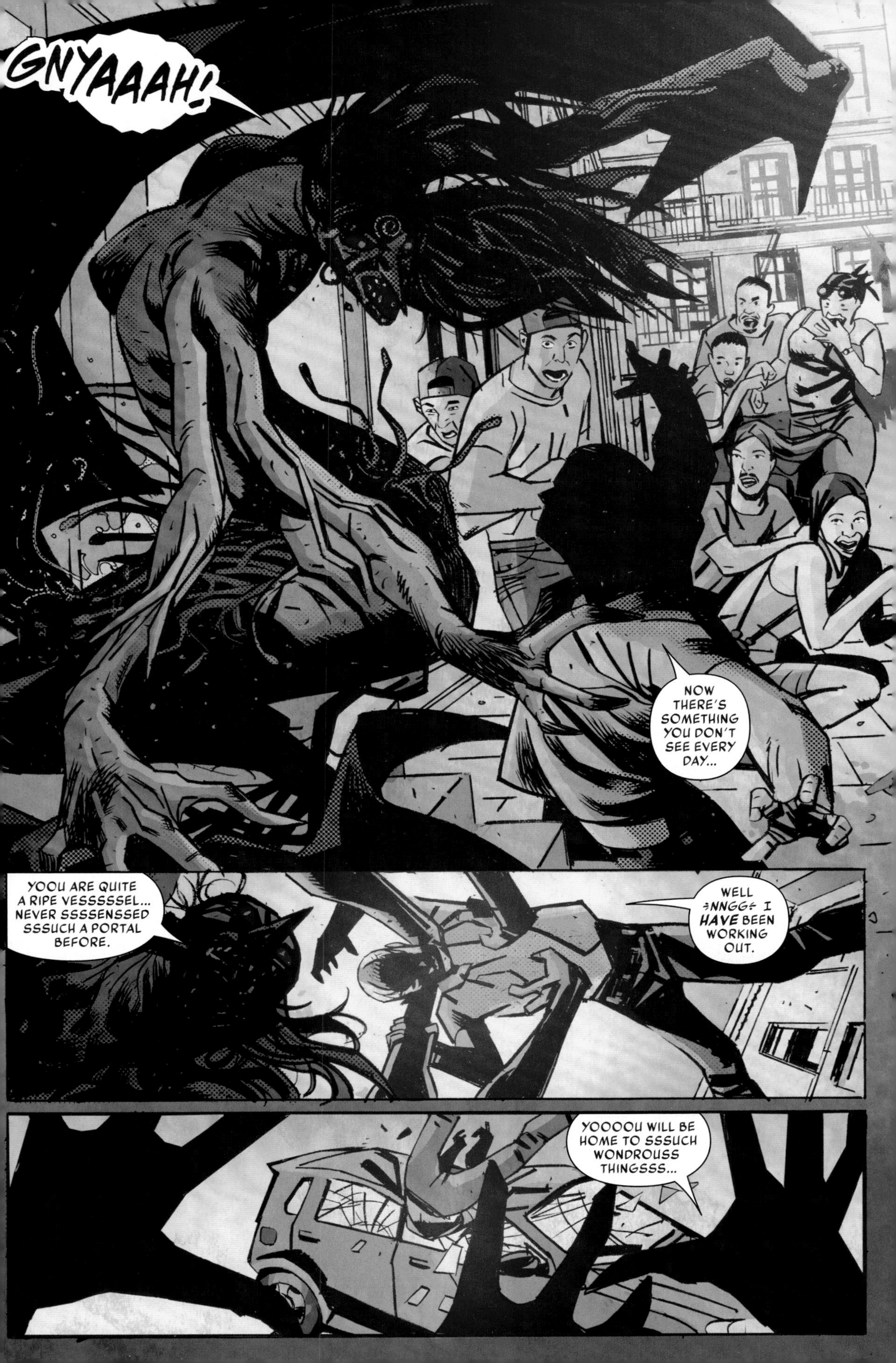
GNYAAAH!
NOW THERE'S SOMETHING YOU DON'T SEE EVERY DAY...
YOOU ARE QUITE A RIPE VESSSSSEL... NEVER SSSSENSSED SSSUCH A PORTAL BEFORE.
WELL ≶NNG≶ I **HAVE** BEEN WORKING OUT.
YOOOOU WILL BE HOME TO SSSUCH WONDROUSS THINGSSS...

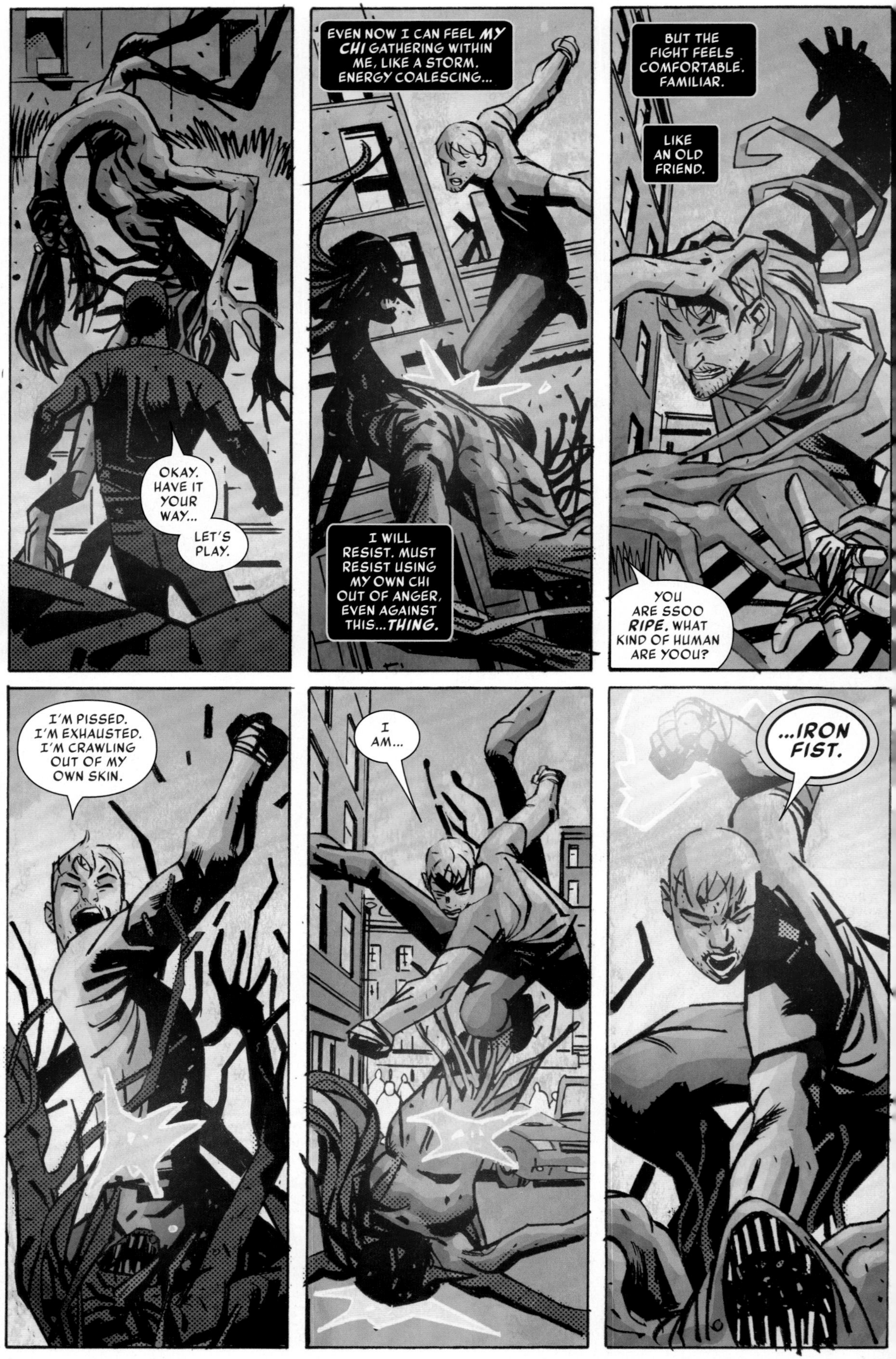
OKAY. HAVE IT YOUR WAY...
LET'S PLAY.
EVEN NOW I CAN FEEL MY CHI GATHERING WITHIN ME, LIKE A STORM. ENERGY COALESCING...
I WILL RESIST. MUST RESIST USING MY OWN CHI OUT OF ANGER, EVEN AGAINST THIS...THING.
BUT THE FIGHT FEELS COMFORTABLE. FAMILIAR.
LIKE AN OLD FRIEND.
YOU ARE SSOO RIPE. WHAT KIND OF HUMAN ARE YOOU?
I'M PISSED. I'M EXHAUSTED. I'M CRAWLING OUT OF MY OWN SKIN.
I AM...
...IRON FIST.

MY, MY... WHAT CHI!

NO. IT... IT CAN'T BE.

IT'S YOU...

HOW...? FORGIVE THE CHEAP COSTUME. FRESH SKIN IS SO HARD TO COME BY.

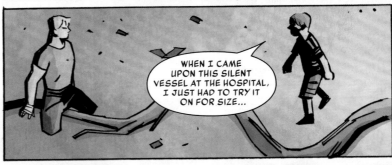

WHEN I CAME UPON THIS SILENT VESSEL AT THE HOSPITAL, I JUST HAD TO TRY IT ON FOR SIZE...

ONCE I DID, I SAW ALL HIS MEMORIES. HIS FALL.

I SAW YOU, DANNY... AND I KNEW I HAD TO HAVE YOU.

YOUR CHI. ALL FOR MYSELF.

PLEASE... WHATEVER YOU ARE, DON'T DO THIS...

MY MANNERS! PARDON.

I AM MO WANG. KING OF YAOGUAI.

YAOGUAI. DEMONS.

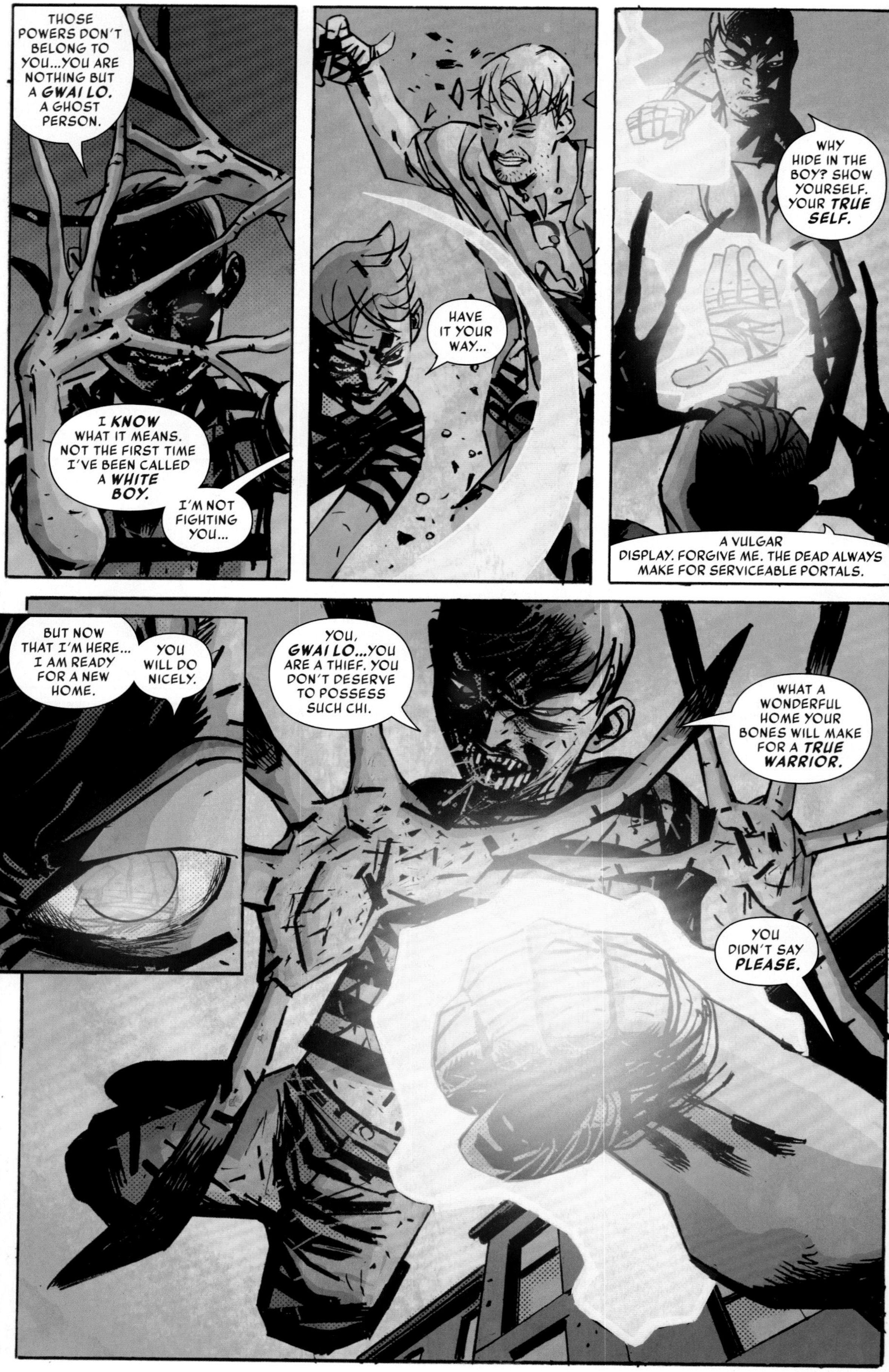
THOSE POWERS DON'T BELONG TO YOU...YOU ARE NOTHING BUT A GWAI LO. A GHOST PERSON.
I KNOW WHAT IT MEANS. NOT THE FIRST TIME I'VE BEEN CALLED A WHITE BOY.
I'M NOT FIGHTING YOU...
HAVE IT YOUR WAY...
WHY HIDE IN THE BOY? SHOW YOURSELF. YOUR TRUE SELF.
A VULGAR DISPLAY. FORGIVE ME. THE DEAD ALWAYS MAKE FOR SERVICEABLE PORTALS.
BUT NOW THAT I'M HERE... I AM READY FOR A NEW HOME.
YOU WILL DO NICELY.
YOU, GWAI LO...YOU ARE A THIEF. YOU DON'T DESERVE TO POSSESS SUCH CHI.
WHAT A WONDERFUL HOME YOUR BONES WILL MAKE FOR A TRUE WARRIOR.
YOU DIDN'T SAY PLEASE.

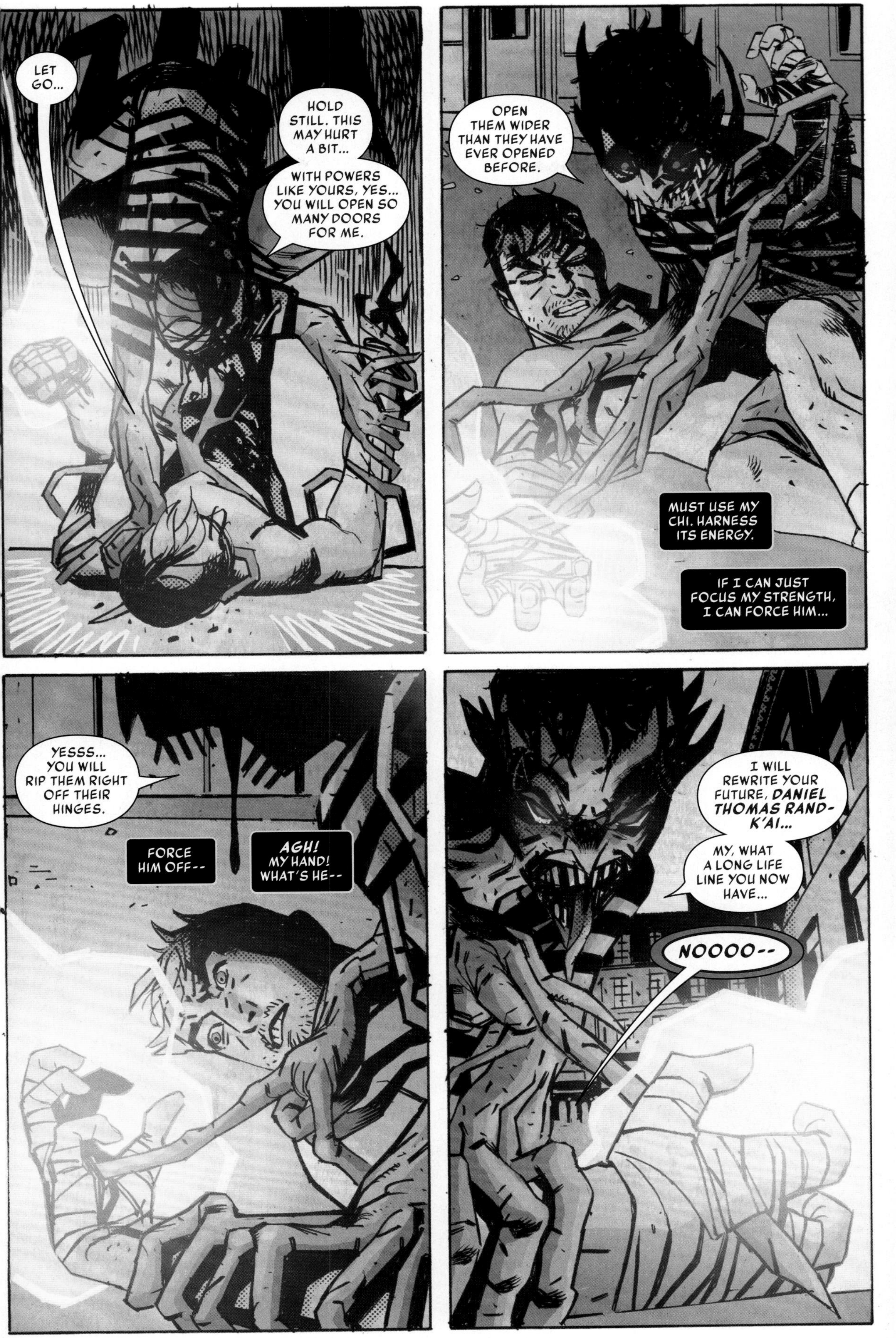
LET GO...
HOLD STILL. THIS MAY HURT A BIT...
WITH POWERS LIKE YOURS, YES... YOU WILL OPEN SO MANY DOORS FOR ME.
OPEN THEM WIDER THAN THEY HAVE EVER OPENED BEFORE.
MUST USE MY CHI. HARNESS ITS ENERGY.
IF I CAN JUST FOCUS MY STRENGTH, I CAN FORCE HIM...
YESSS... YOU WILL RIP THEM RIGHT OFF THEIR HINGES.
FORCE HIM OFF--
AGH! MY HAND! WHAT'S HE--
I WILL REWRITE YOUR FUTURE, DANIEL THOMAS RAND-K'AI...
MY, WHAT A LONG LIFE LINE YOU NOW HAVE...
NOOOO--

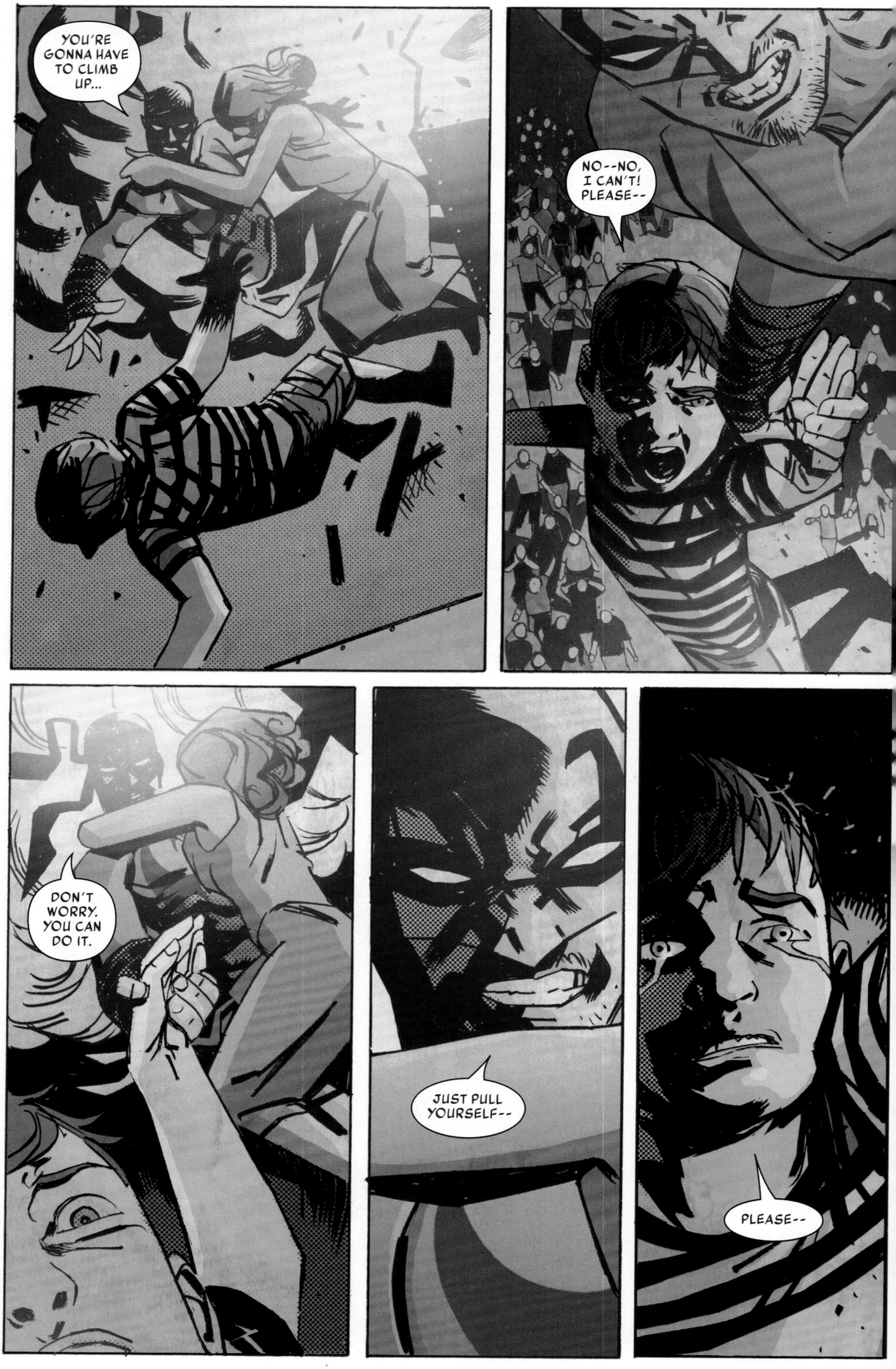
YOU'RE GONNA HAVE TO CLIMB UP...
NO--NO, I CAN'T! PLEASE--
DON'T WORRY. YOU CAN DO IT.
JUST PULL YOURSELF--
PLEASE--

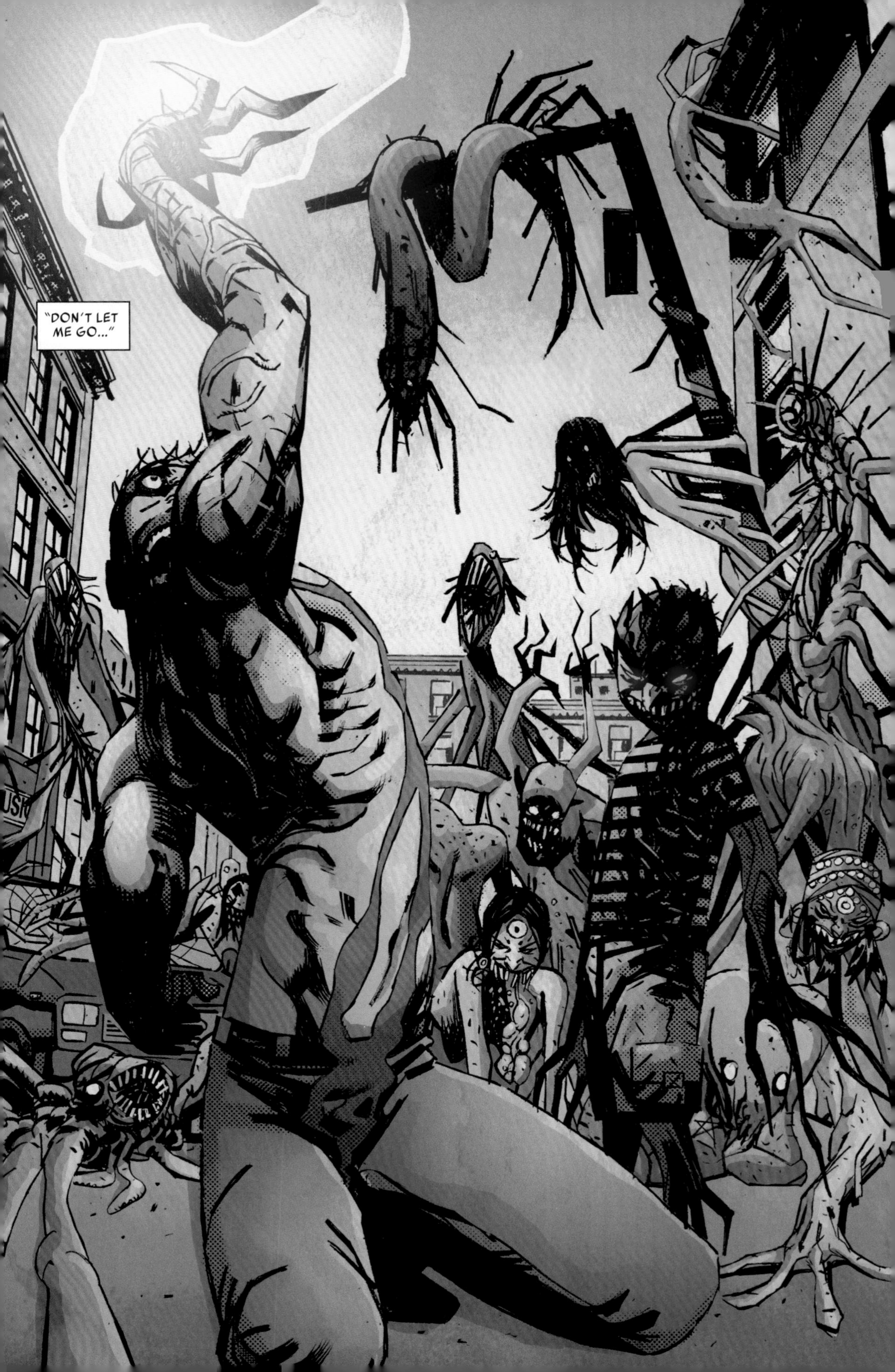
"DON'T LET ME GO..."

PHANTOM LIMB

CHAPTER 2

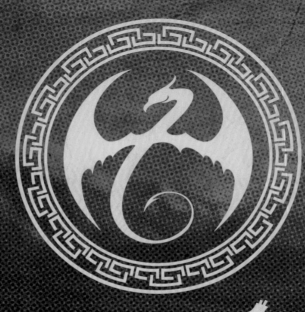

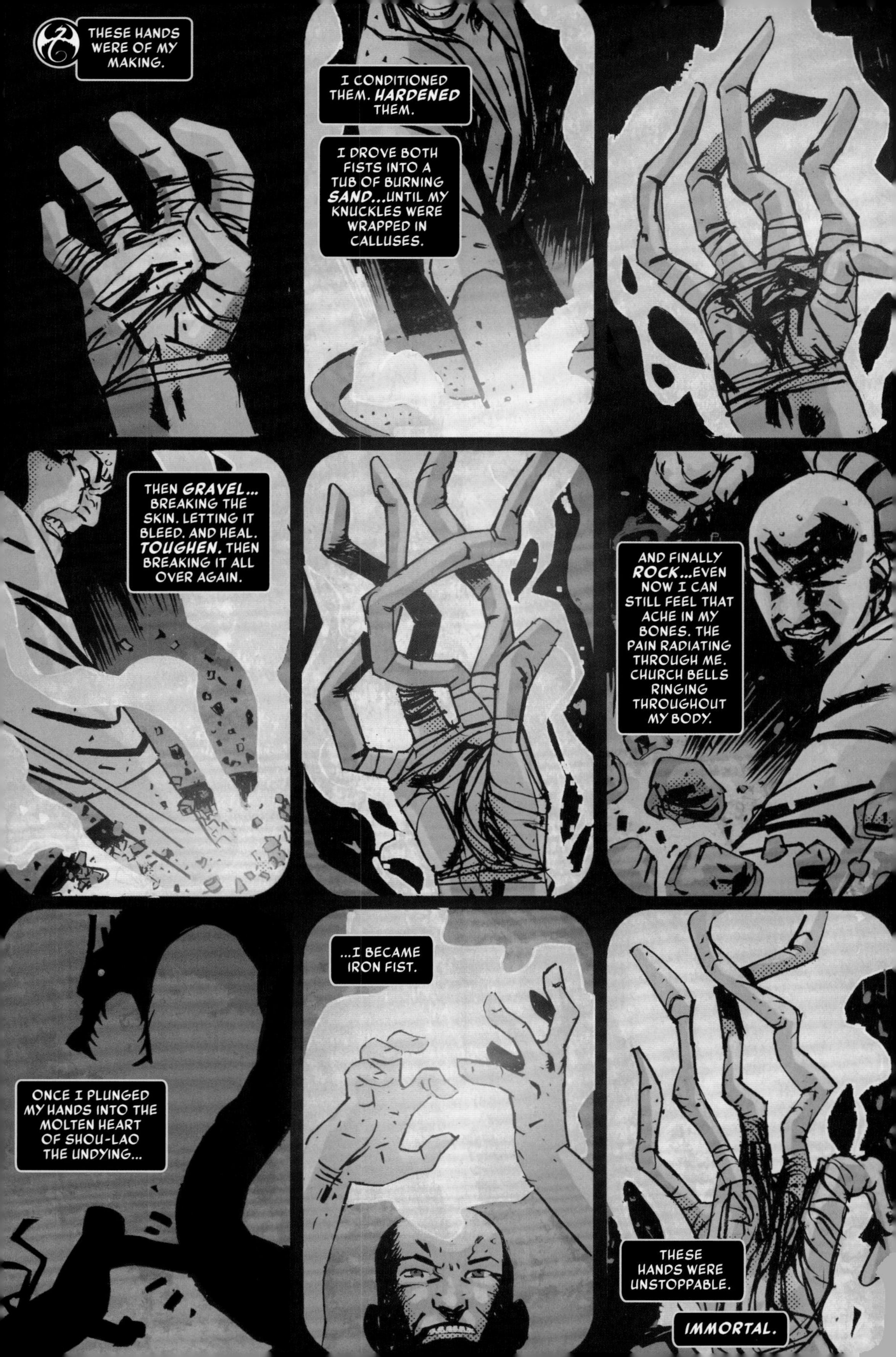
THESE HANDS WERE OF MY MAKING.
I CONDITIONED THEM. HARDENED THEM.
I DROVE BOTH FISTS INTO A TUB OF BURNING SAND...UNTIL MY KNUCKLES WERE WRAPPED IN CALLUSES.
THEN GRAVEL... BREAKING THE SKIN. LETTING IT BLEED. AND HEAL. TOUGHEN. THEN BREAKING IT ALL OVER AGAIN.
AND FINALLY ROCK...EVEN NOW I CAN STILL FEEL THAT ACHE IN MY BONES. THE PAIN RADIATING THROUGH ME. CHURCH BELLS RINGING THROUGHOUT MY BODY.
ONCE I PLUNGED MY HANDS INTO THE MOLTEN HEART OF SHOU-LAO THE UNDYING...
...I BECAME IRON FIST.
THESE HANDS WERE UNSTOPPABLE.
IMMORTAL.

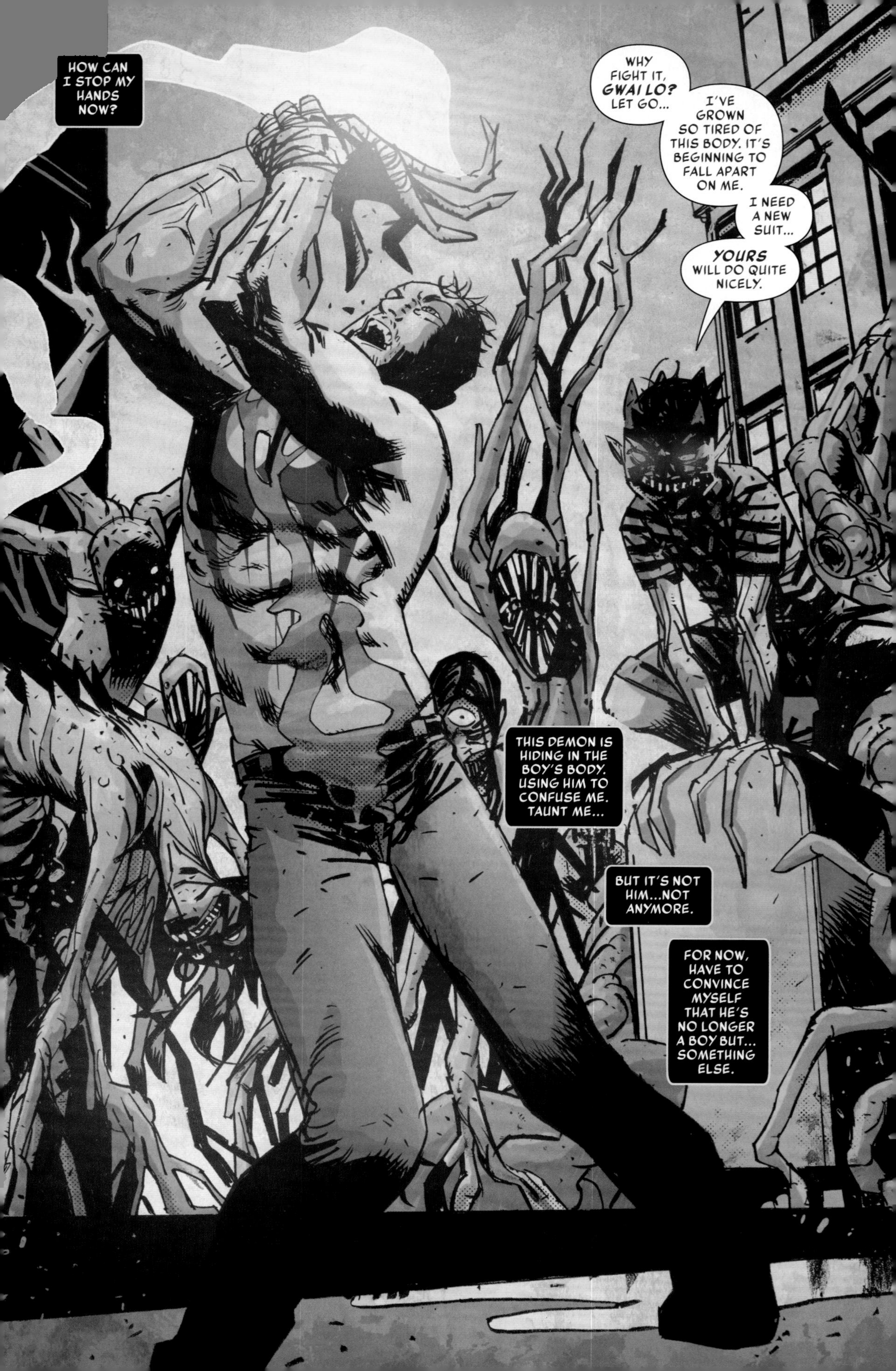
HOW CAN I STOP MY HANDS NOW?
WHY FIGHT IT, GWAI LO? LET GO...
I'VE GROWN SO TIRED OF THIS BODY. IT'S BEGINNING TO FALL APART ON ME.
I NEED A NEW SUIT...
YOURS WILL DO QUITE NICELY.
THIS DEMON IS HIDING IN THE BOY'S BODY. USING HIM TO CONFUSE ME. TAUNT ME...
BUT IT'S NOT HIM...NOT ANYMORE.
FOR NOW, HAVE TO CONVINCE MYSELF THAT HE'S NO LONGER A BOY BUT... SOMETHING ELSE.

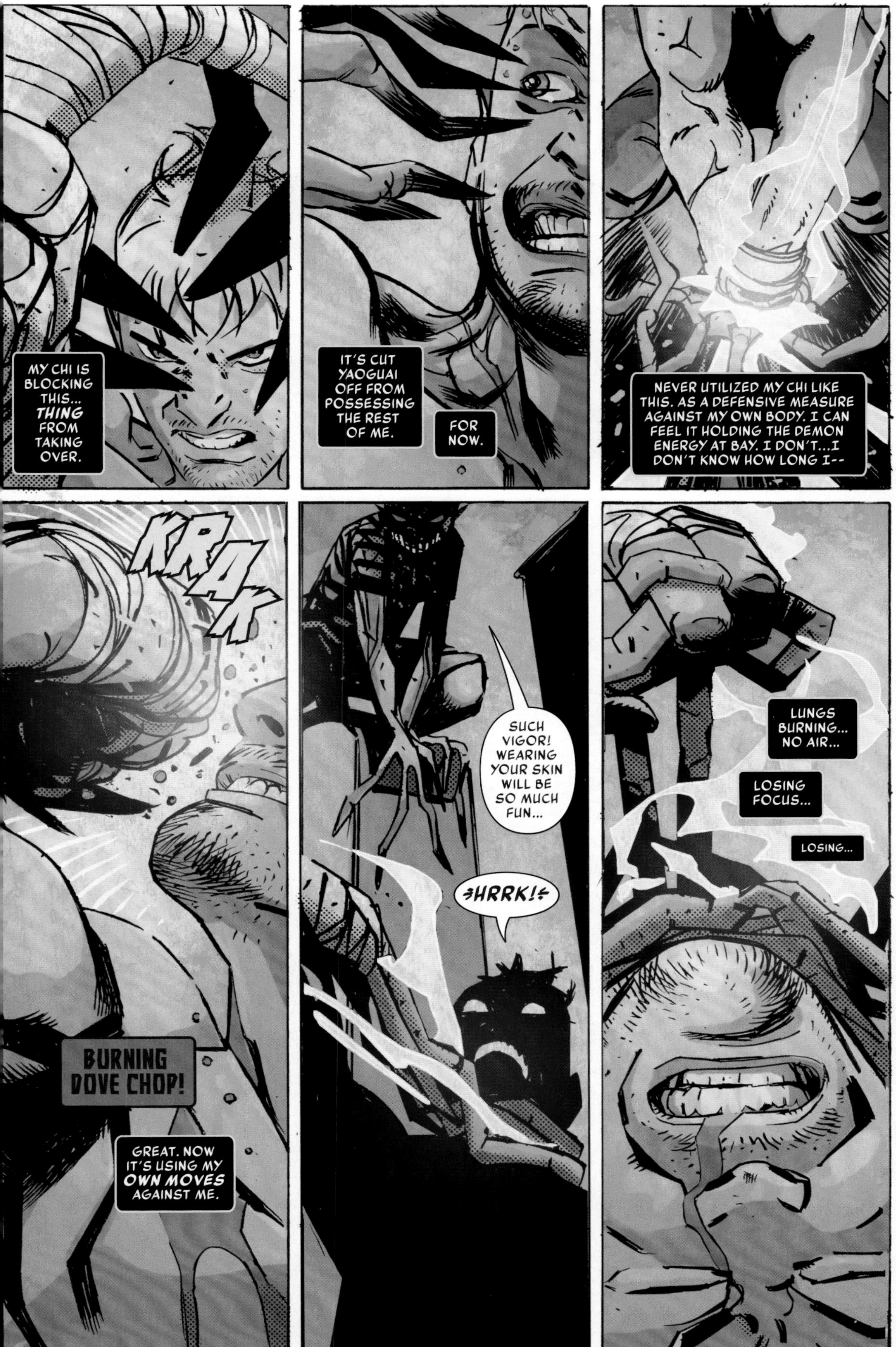

MY CHI IS BLOCKING THIS... THING FROM TAKING OVER.
IT'S CUT YAOGUAI OFF FROM POSSESSING THE REST OF ME.
FOR NOW.
NEVER UTILIZED MY CHI LIKE THIS. AS A DEFENSIVE MEASURE AGAINST MY OWN BODY. I CAN FEEL IT HOLDING THE DEMON ENERGY AT BAY. I DON'T...I DON'T KNOW HOW LONG I--
KRAK
BURNING DOVE CHOP!
GREAT. NOW IT'S USING MY OWN MOVES AGAINST ME.
SUCH VIGOR! WEARING YOUR SKIN WILL BE SO MUCH FUN...
HRRK!
LUNGS BURNING... NO AIR...
LOSING FOCUS...
LOSING...

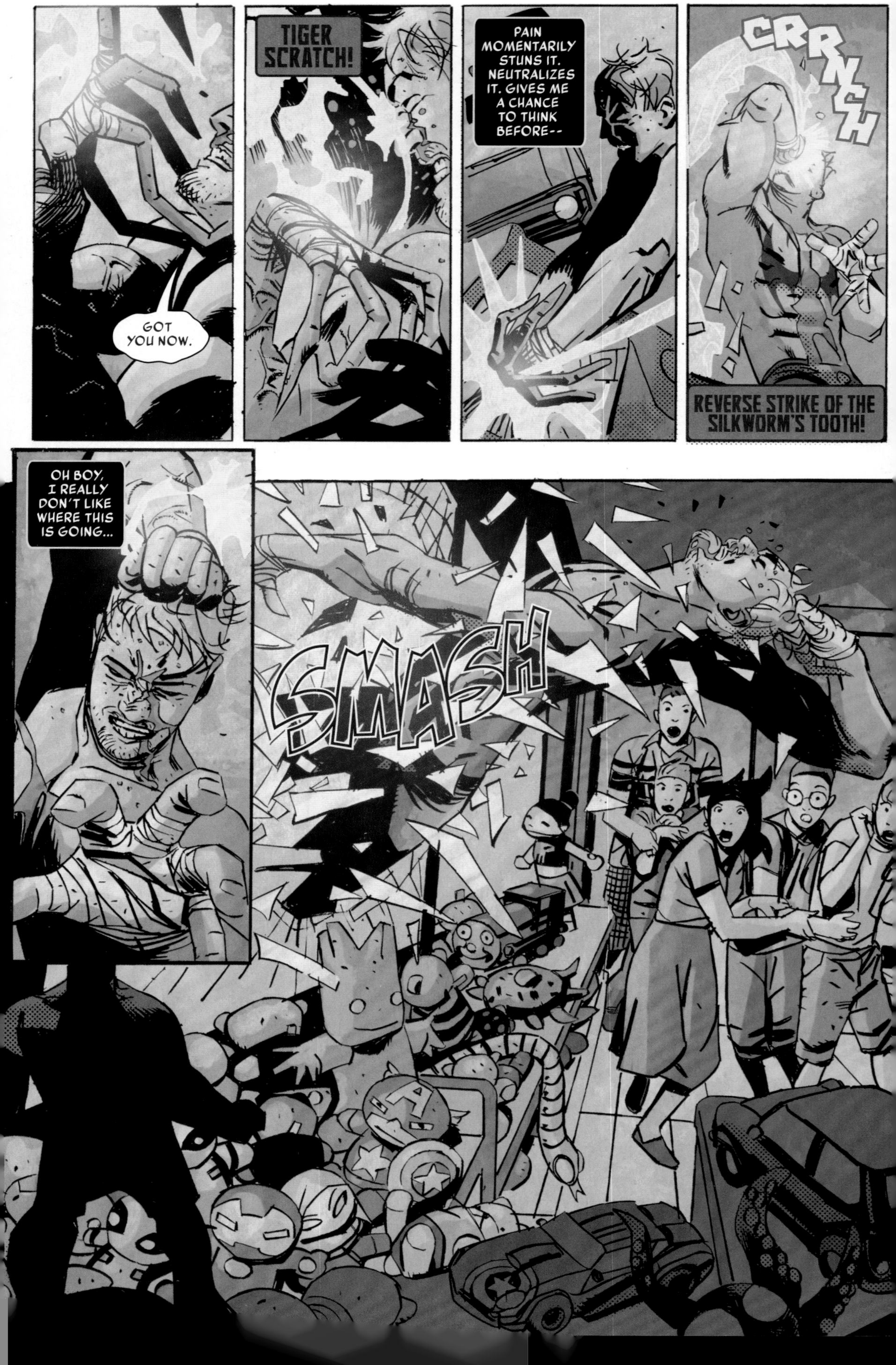
GOT YOU NOW.
TIGER SCRATCH!
PAIN MOMENTARILY STUNS IT. NEUTRALIZES IT. GIVES ME A CHANCE TO THINK BEFORE--
CRRNCH
REVERSE STRIKE OF THE SILKWORM'S TOOTH!
OH BOY, I REALLY DON'T LIKE WHERE THIS IS GOING...
SMASH

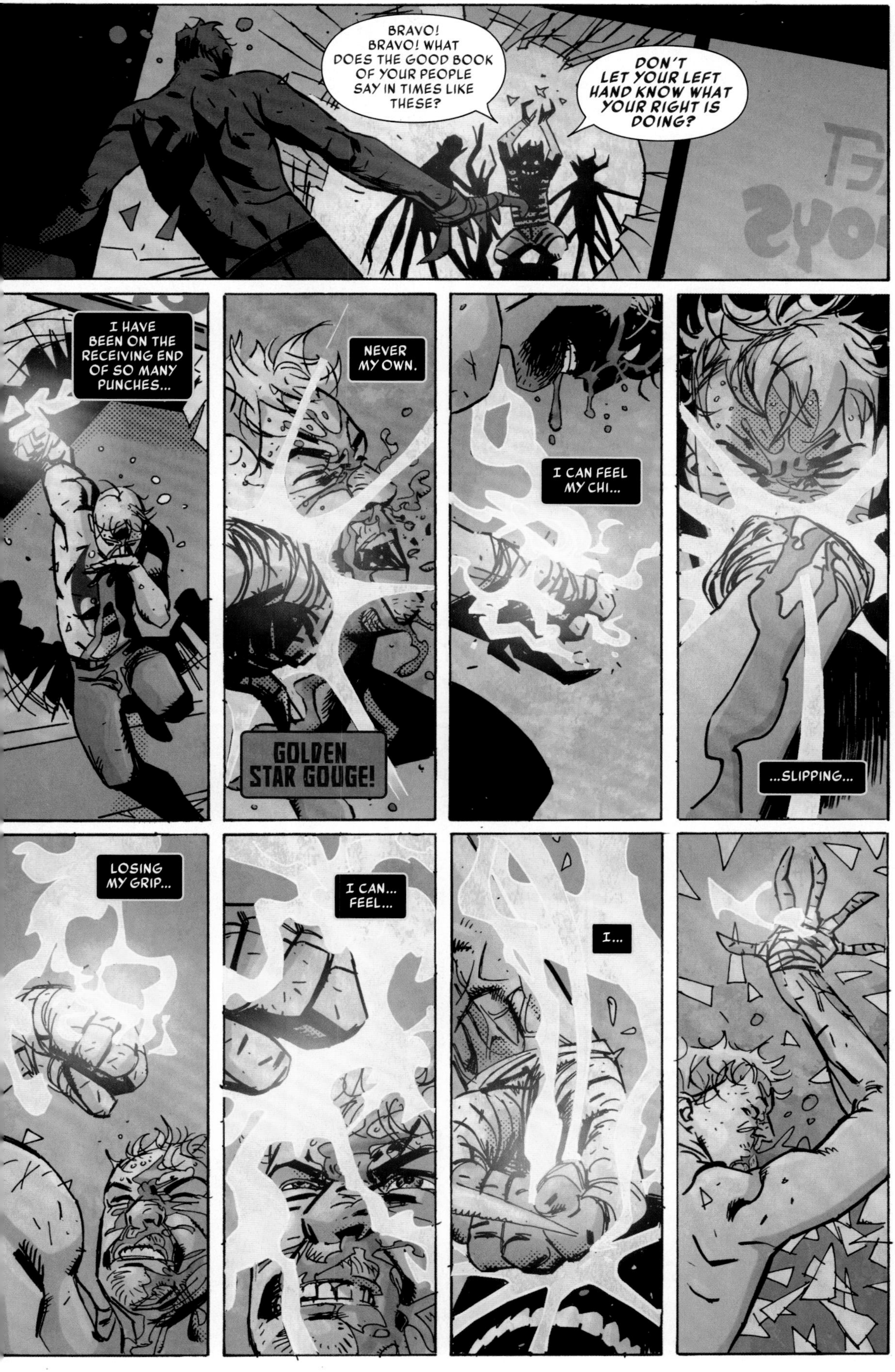

BRAVO! BRAVO! WHAT DOES THE GOOD BOOK OF YOUR PEOPLE SAY IN TIMES LIKE THESE?
DON'T LET YOUR LEFT HAND KNOW WHAT YOUR RIGHT IS DOING?
I HAVE BEEN ON THE RECEIVING END OF SO MANY PUNCHES...
NEVER MY OWN.
GOLDEN STAR GOUGE!
I CAN FEEL MY CHI...
...SLIPPING...
LOSING MY GRIP...
I CAN... FEEL...
I...

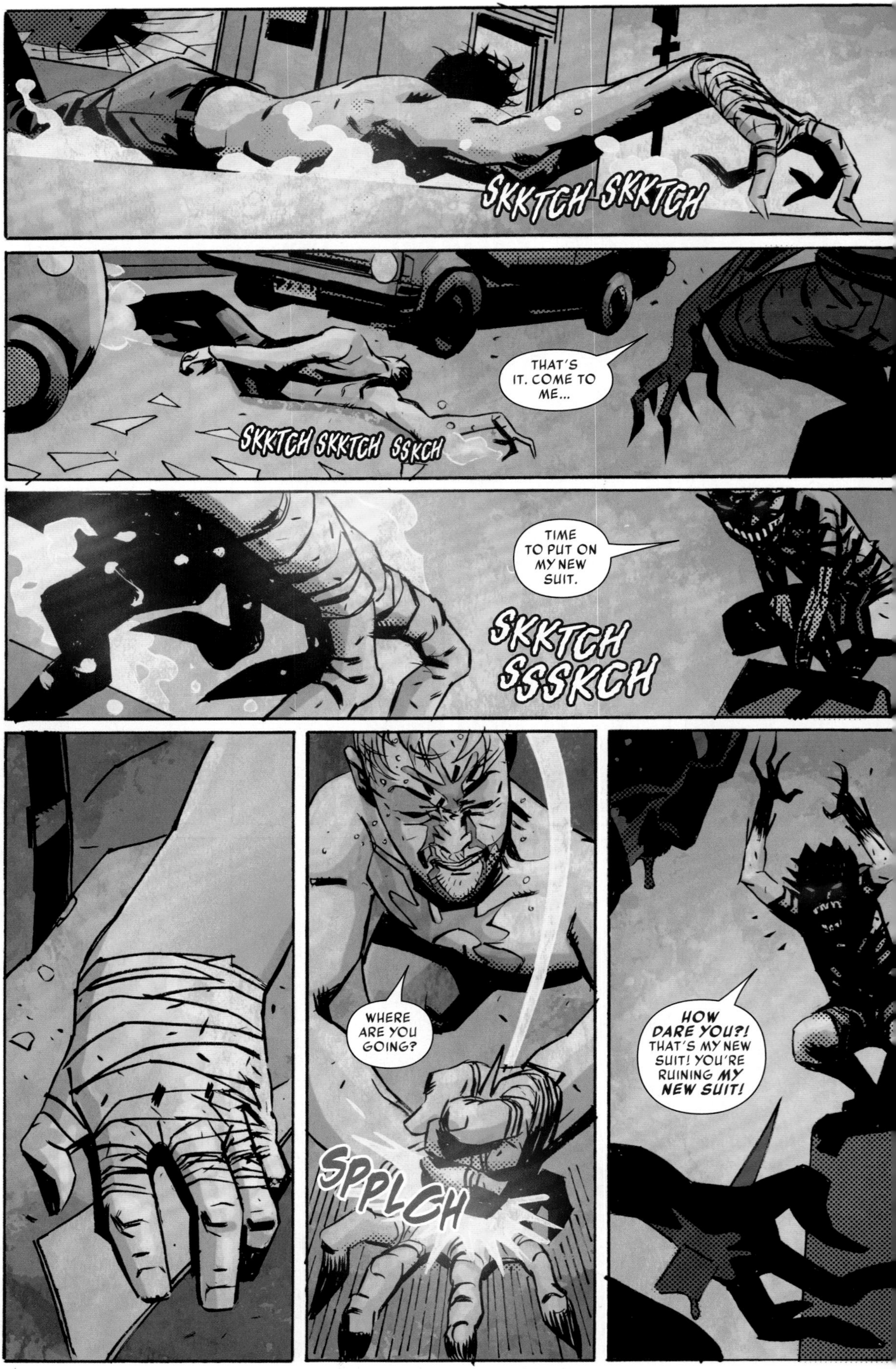
SKKTCH SKKTCH
THAT'S IT. COME TO ME...
SKKTCH SKKTCH SSKCH
TIME TO PUT ON MY NEW SUIT.
SKKTCH SSSKCH
WHERE ARE YOU GOING?
SPPLCH
HOW DARE YOU?! THAT'S MY NEW SUIT! YOU'RE RUINING MY NEW SUIT!

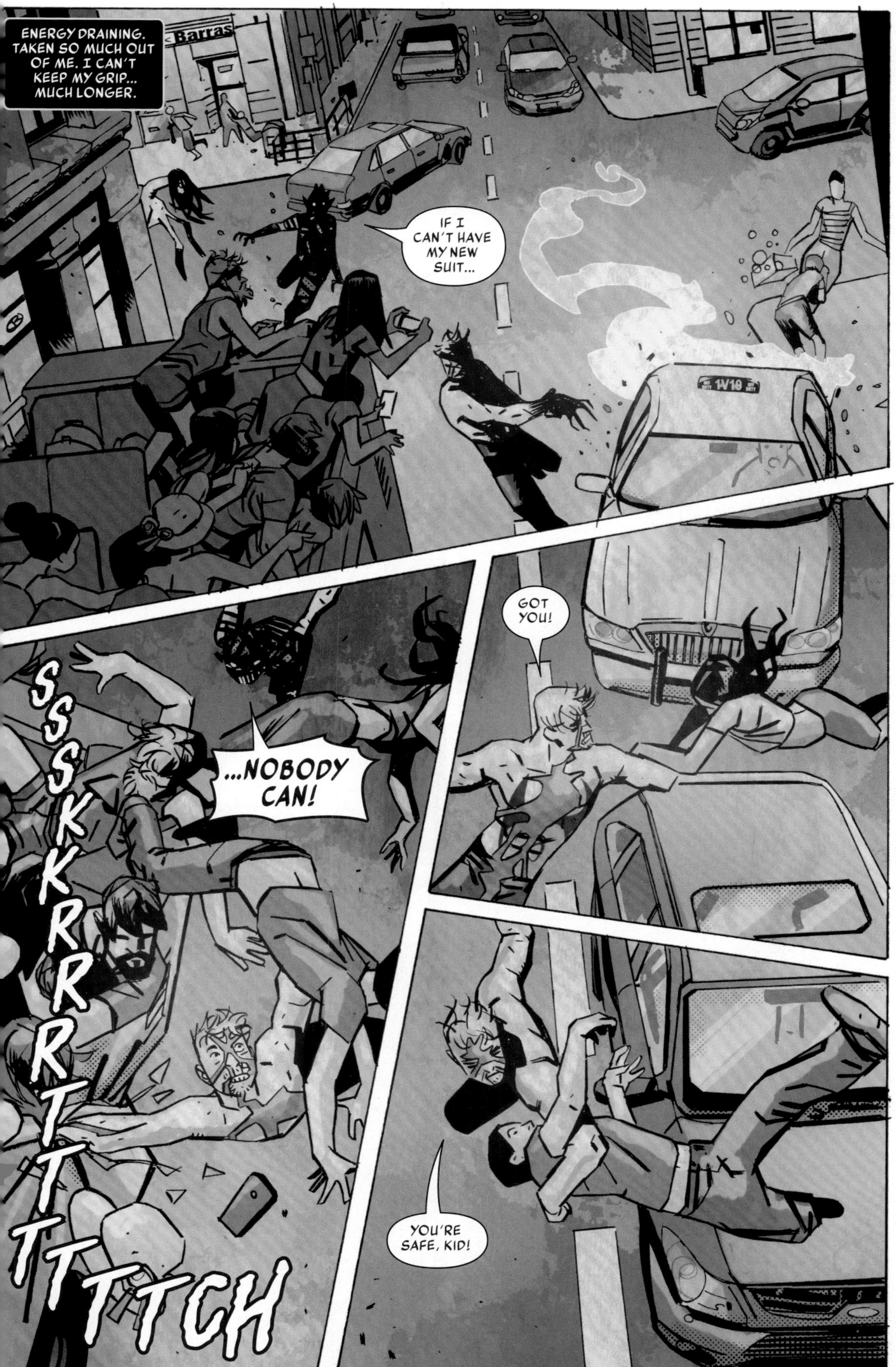
ENERGY DRAINING. TAKEN SO MUCH OUT OF ME. I CAN'T KEEP MY GRIP... MUCH LONGER.
Barras
IF I CAN'T HAVE MY NEW SUIT...
1W10
...NOBODY CAN!
SSSKKRRRRTTTTTTTCH
GOT YOU!
YOU'RE SAFE, KID!

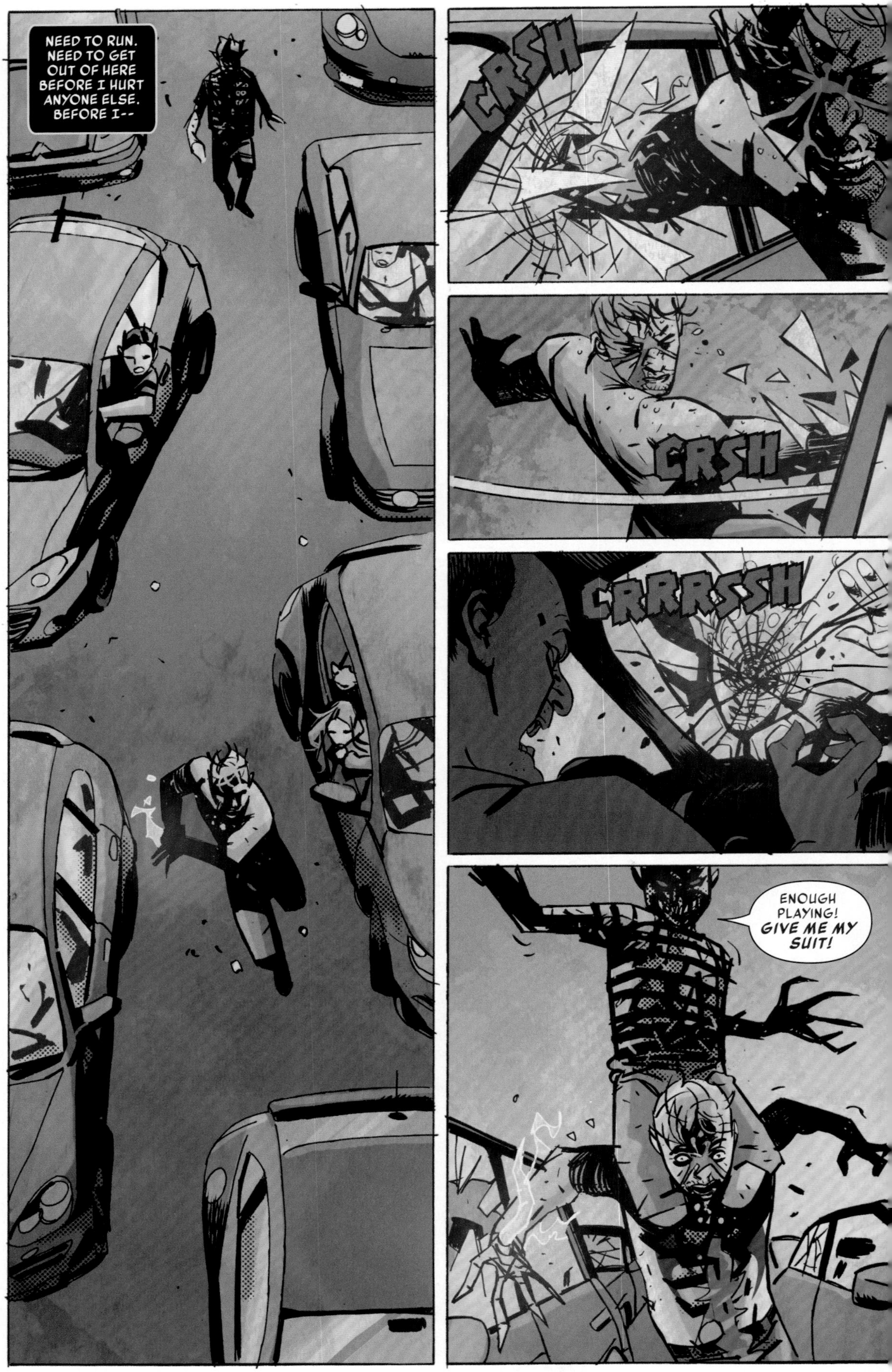
NEED TO RUN. NEED TO GET OUT OF HERE BEFORE I HURT ANYONE ELSE. BEFORE I--
CRSH
CRSH
CRRRSSH
ENOUGH PLAYING! GIVE ME MY SUIT!

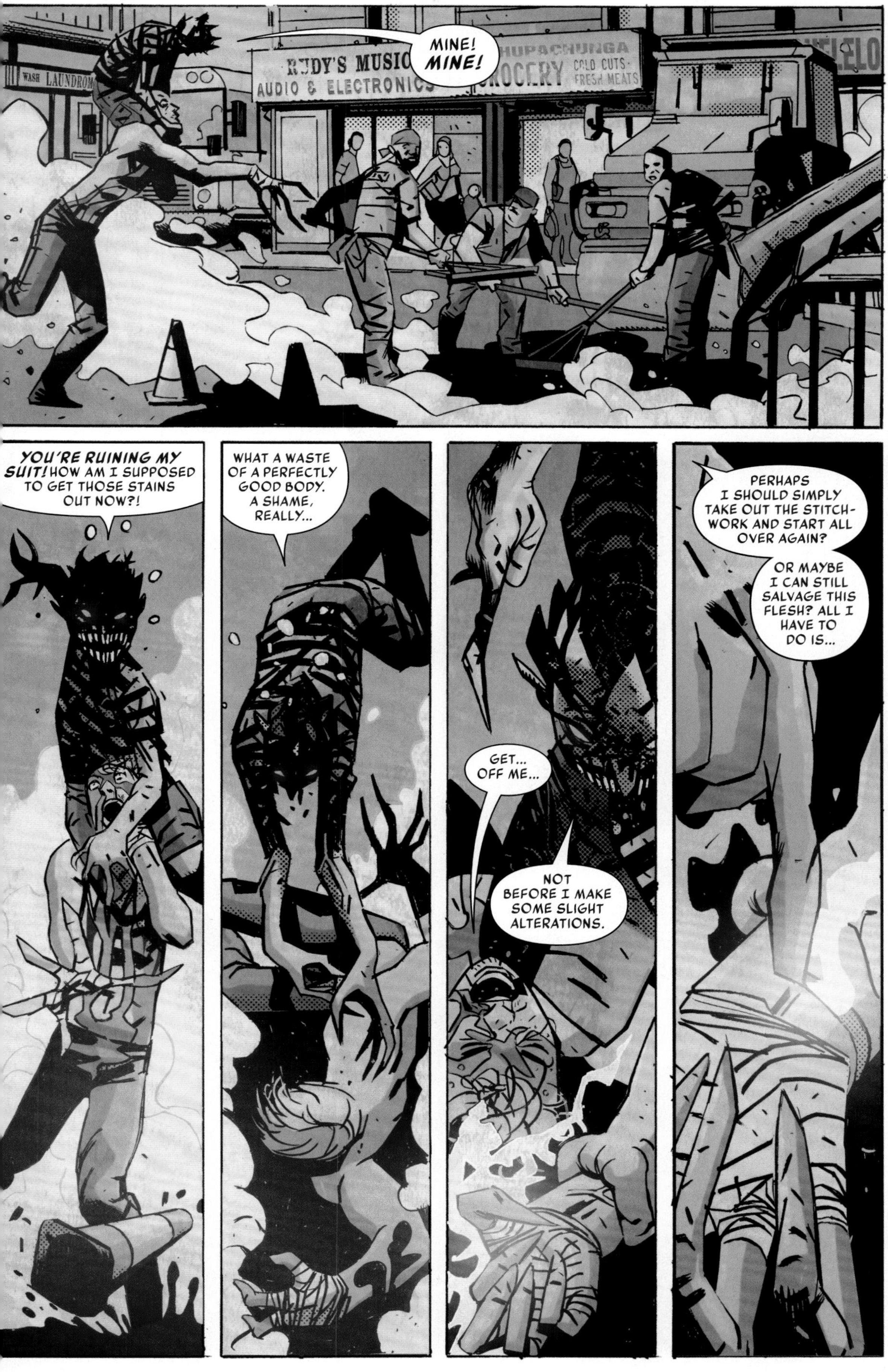
RUDY'S MUSIC
AUDIO & ELECTRONICS
CHUPACHUNGA
GROCERY
COLD CUTS · FRESH MEATS
WASH LAUNDROM
MINE! MINE!
YOU'RE RUINING MY SUIT! HOW AM I SUPPOSED TO GET THOSE STAINS OUT NOW?!
WHAT A WASTE OF A PERFECTLY GOOD BODY. A SHAME, REALLY...
GET... OFF ME...
NOT BEFORE I MAKE SOME SLIGHT ALTERATIONS.
PERHAPS I SHOULD SIMPLY TAKE OUT THE STITCH-WORK AND START ALL OVER AGAIN?
OR MAYBE I CAN STILL SALVAGE THIS FLESH? ALL I HAVE TO DO IS...

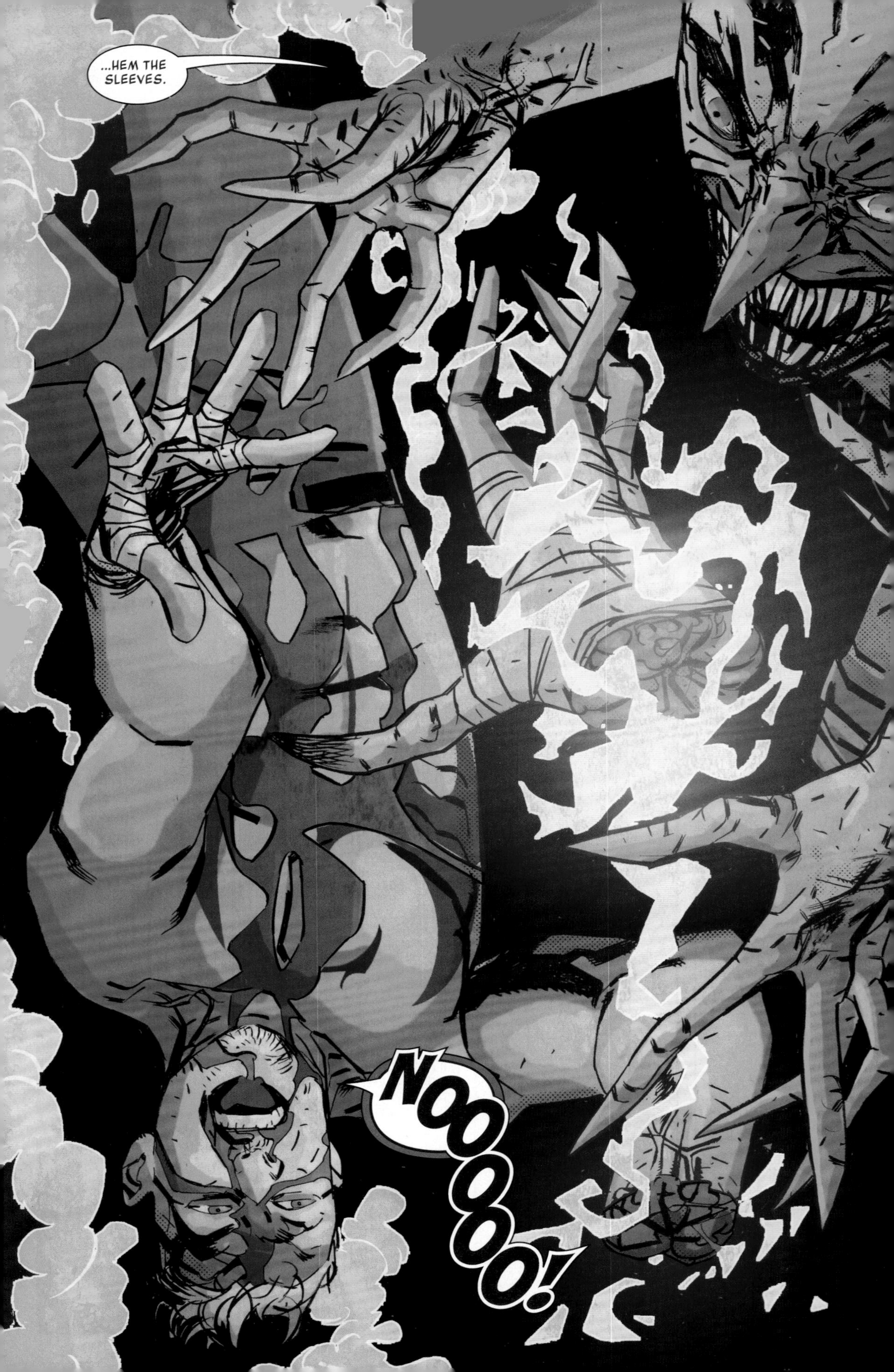
...HEM THE SLEEVES.
NOOOOOO!

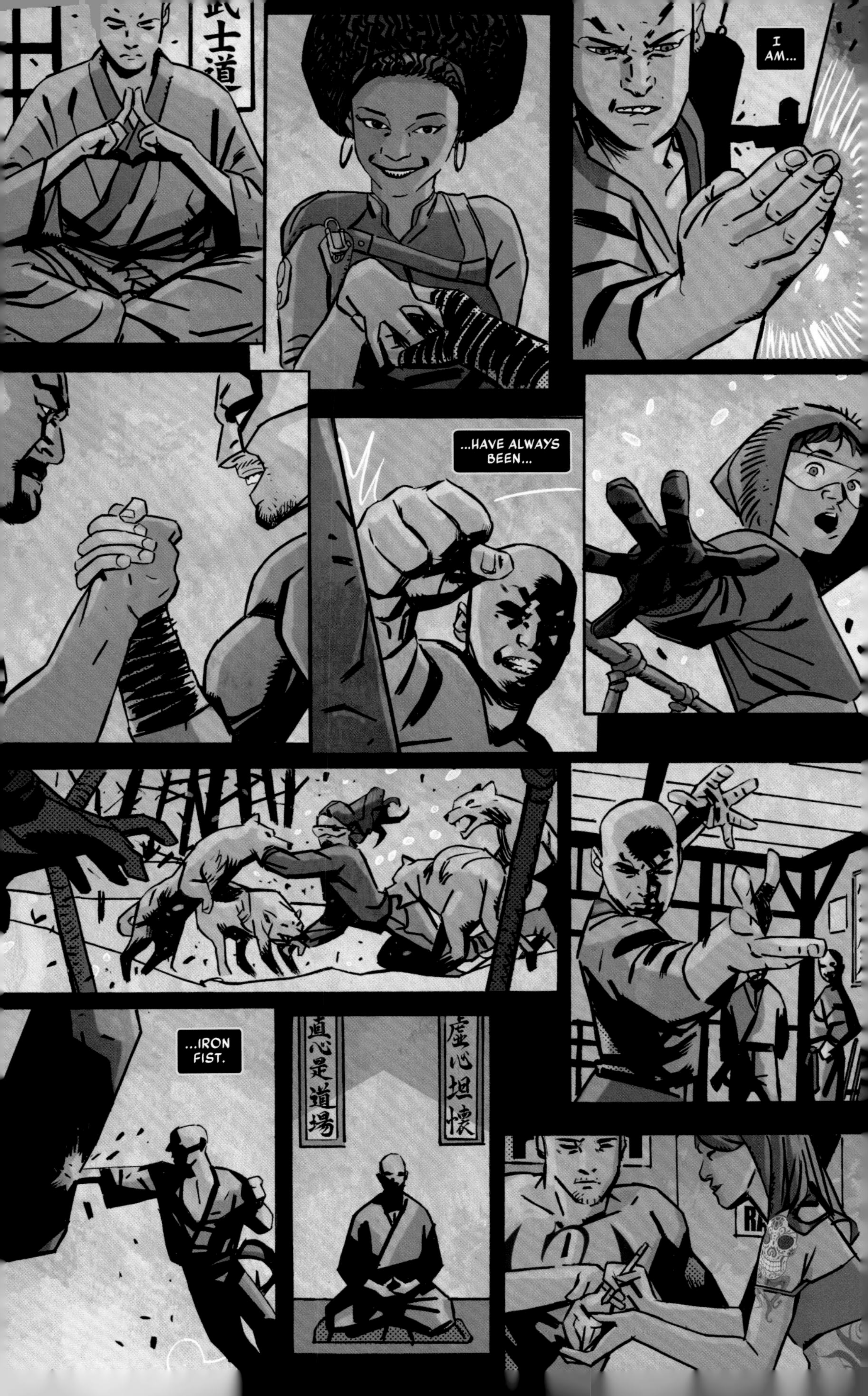
武士道
I AM...
...HAVE ALWAYS BEEN...
...IRON FIST.
直心是道場
虛心坦懷

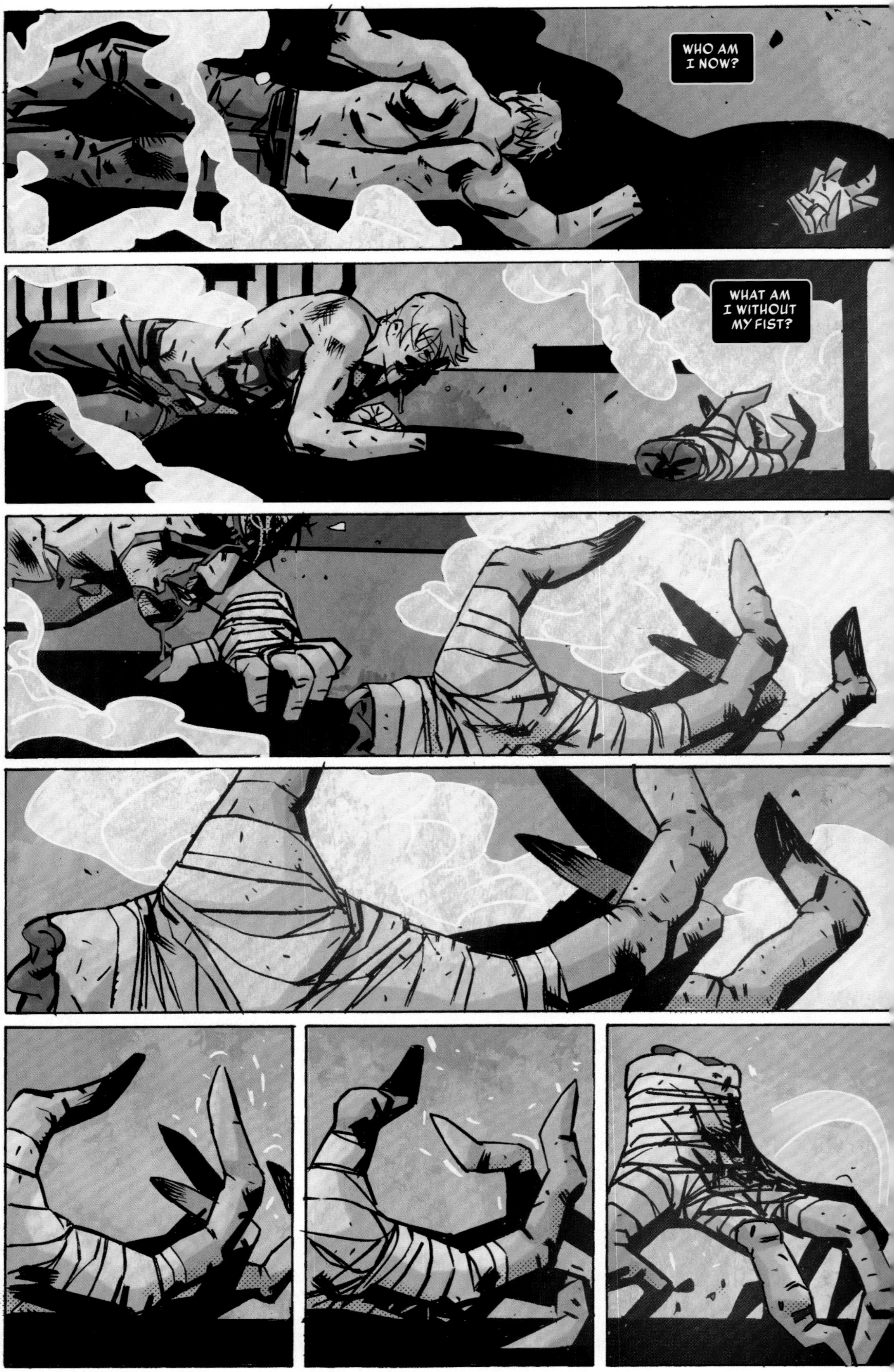
WHO AM I NOW?
WHAT AM I WITHOUT MY FIST?

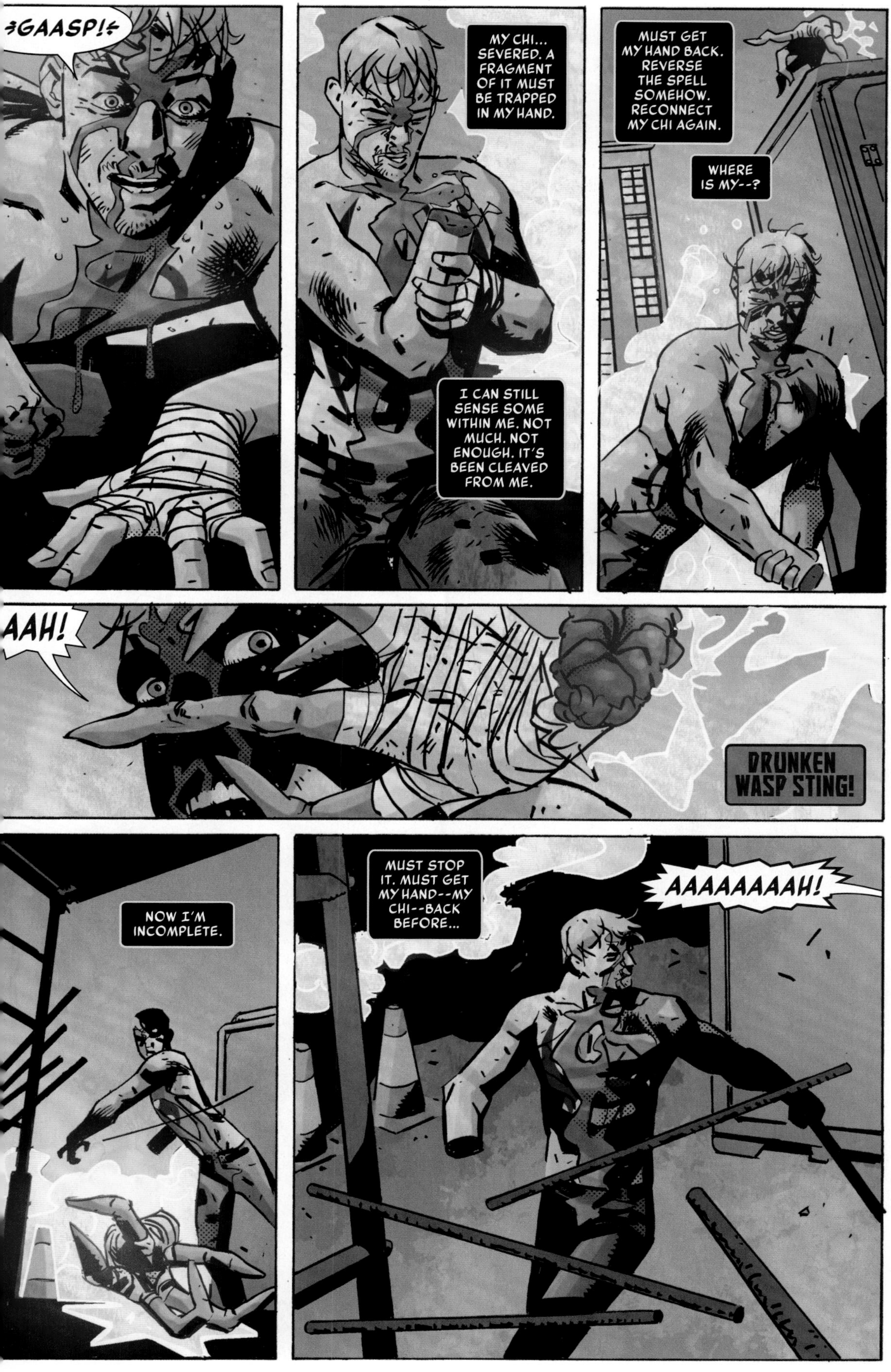

GAASP!
MY CHI... SEVERED. A FRAGMENT OF IT MUST BE TRAPPED IN MY HAND.
I CAN STILL SENSE SOME WITHIN ME. NOT MUCH. NOT ENOUGH. IT'S BEEN CLEAVED FROM ME.
MUST GET MY HAND BACK. REVERSE THE SPELL SOMEHOW. RECONNECT MY CHI AGAIN.
WHERE IS MY--?
AAH!
DRUNKEN WASP STING!
NOW I'M INCOMPLETE.
MUST STOP IT. MUST GET MY HAND--MY CHI--BACK BEFORE...
AAAAAAAAH!

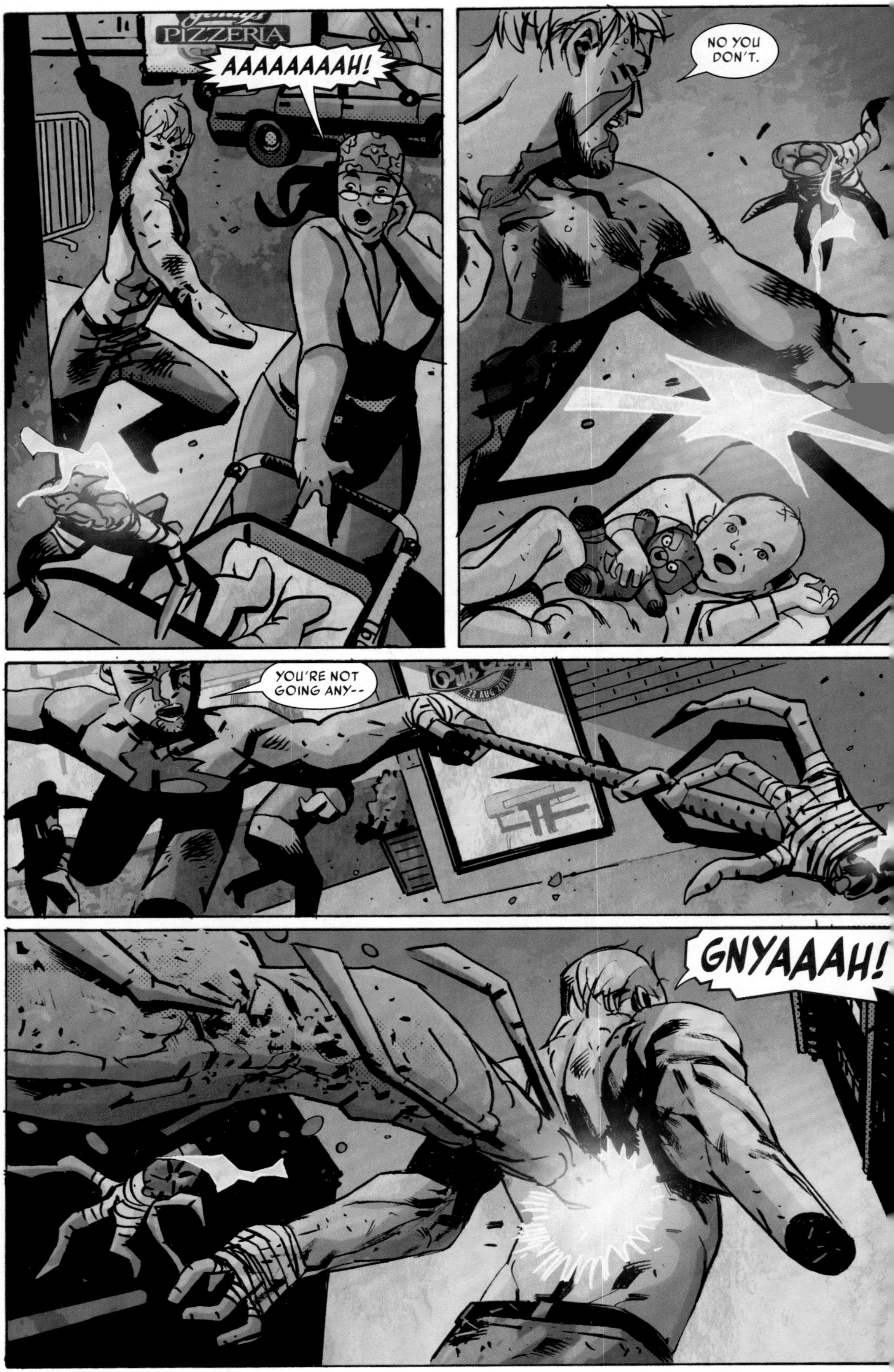
PIZZERIA
AAAAAAAAH!
NO YOU DON'T.
YOU'RE NOT GOING ANY--
GNYAAAH!

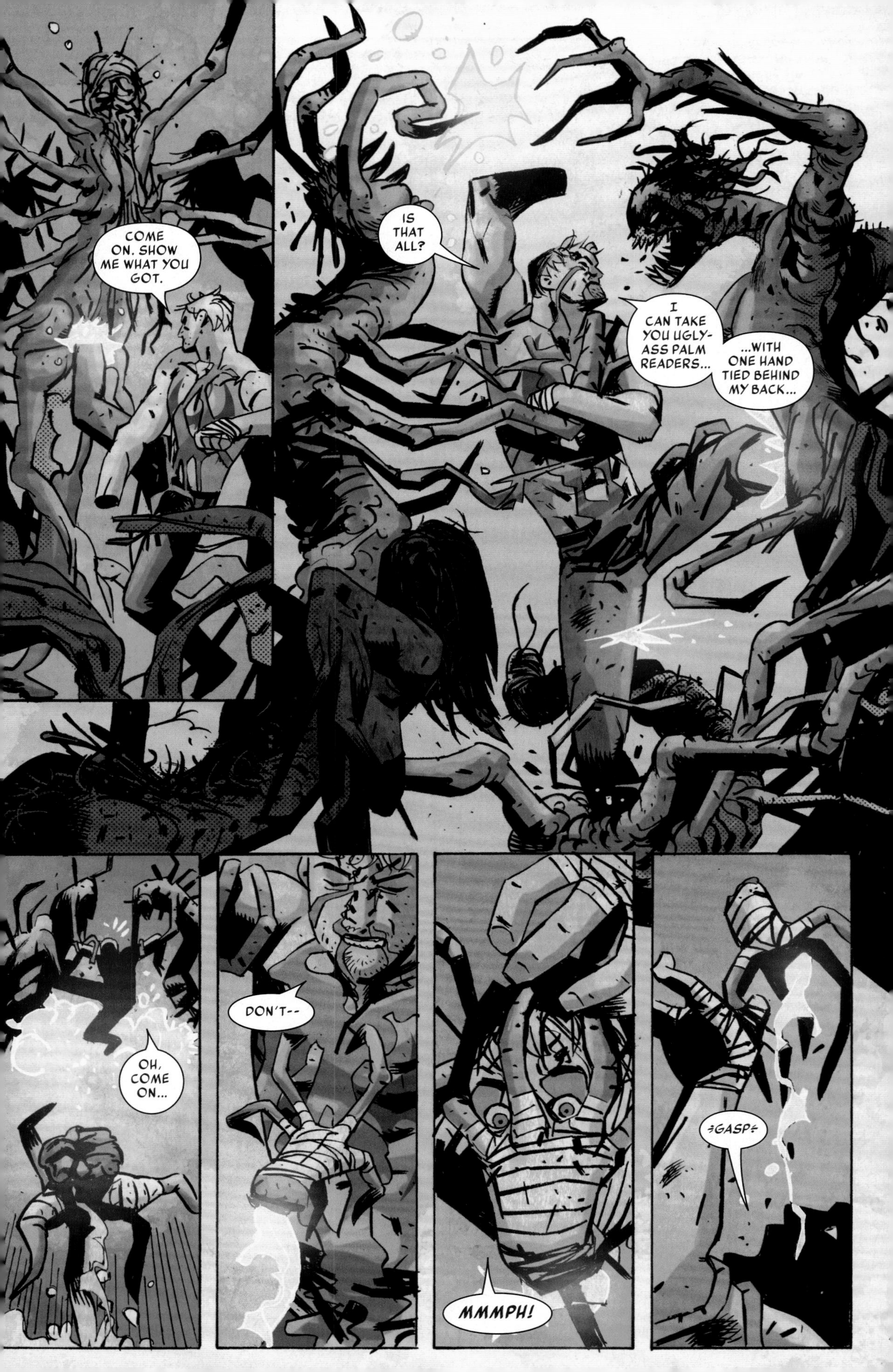
COME ON. SHOW ME WHAT YOU GOT.
IS THAT ALL?
I CAN TAKE YOU UGLY-ASS PALM READERS...
...WITH ONE HAND TIED BEHIND MY BACK...
OH, COME ON...
DON'T--
MMMPH!
GASP

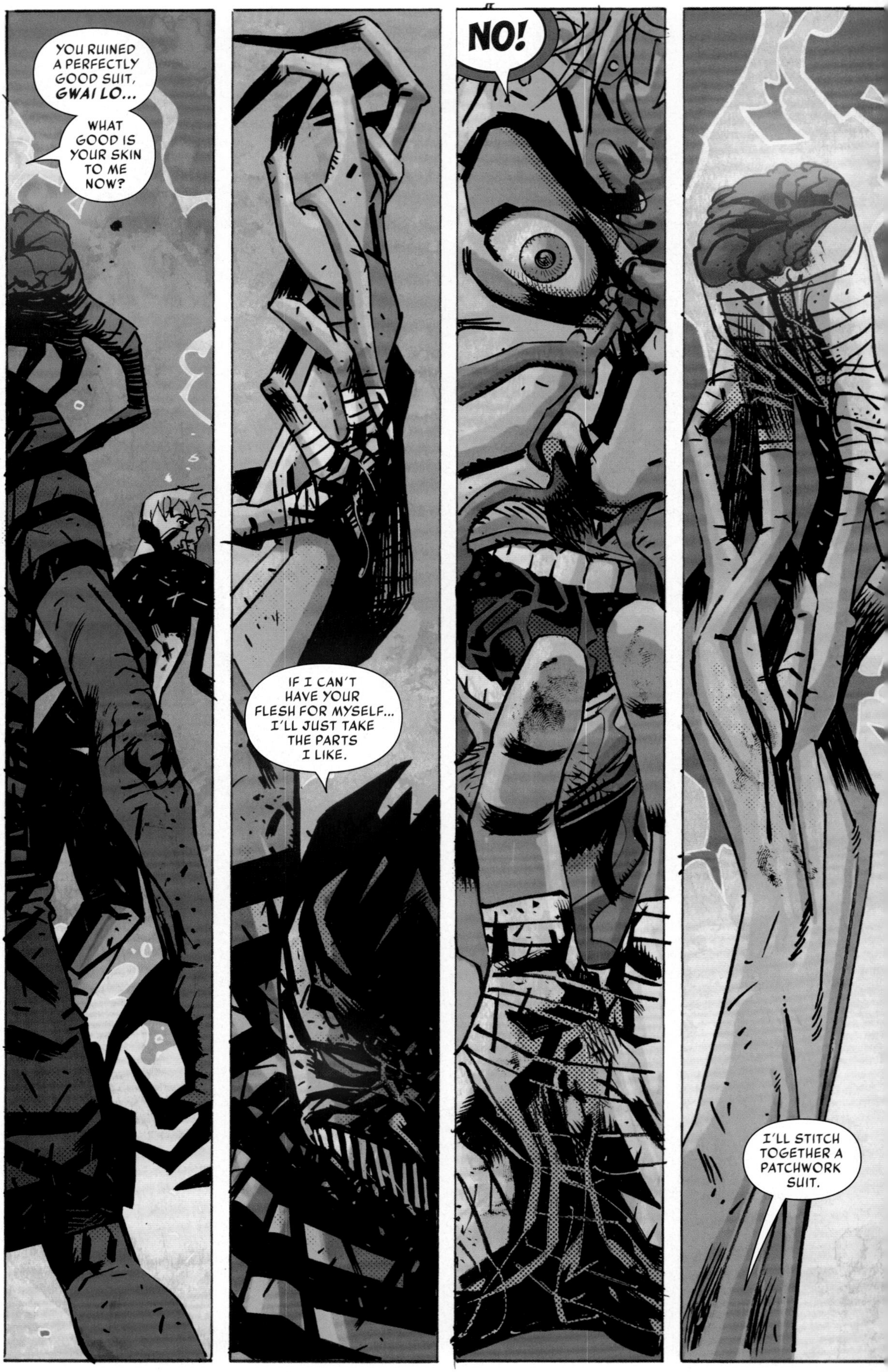
YOU RUINED A PERFECTLY GOOD SUIT, GWAI LO...
WHAT GOOD IS YOUR SKIN TO ME NOW?
IF I CAN'T HAVE YOUR FLESH FOR MYSELF... I'LL JUST TAKE THE PARTS I LIKE.
NO!
I'LL STITCH TOGETHER A PATCHWORK SUIT.

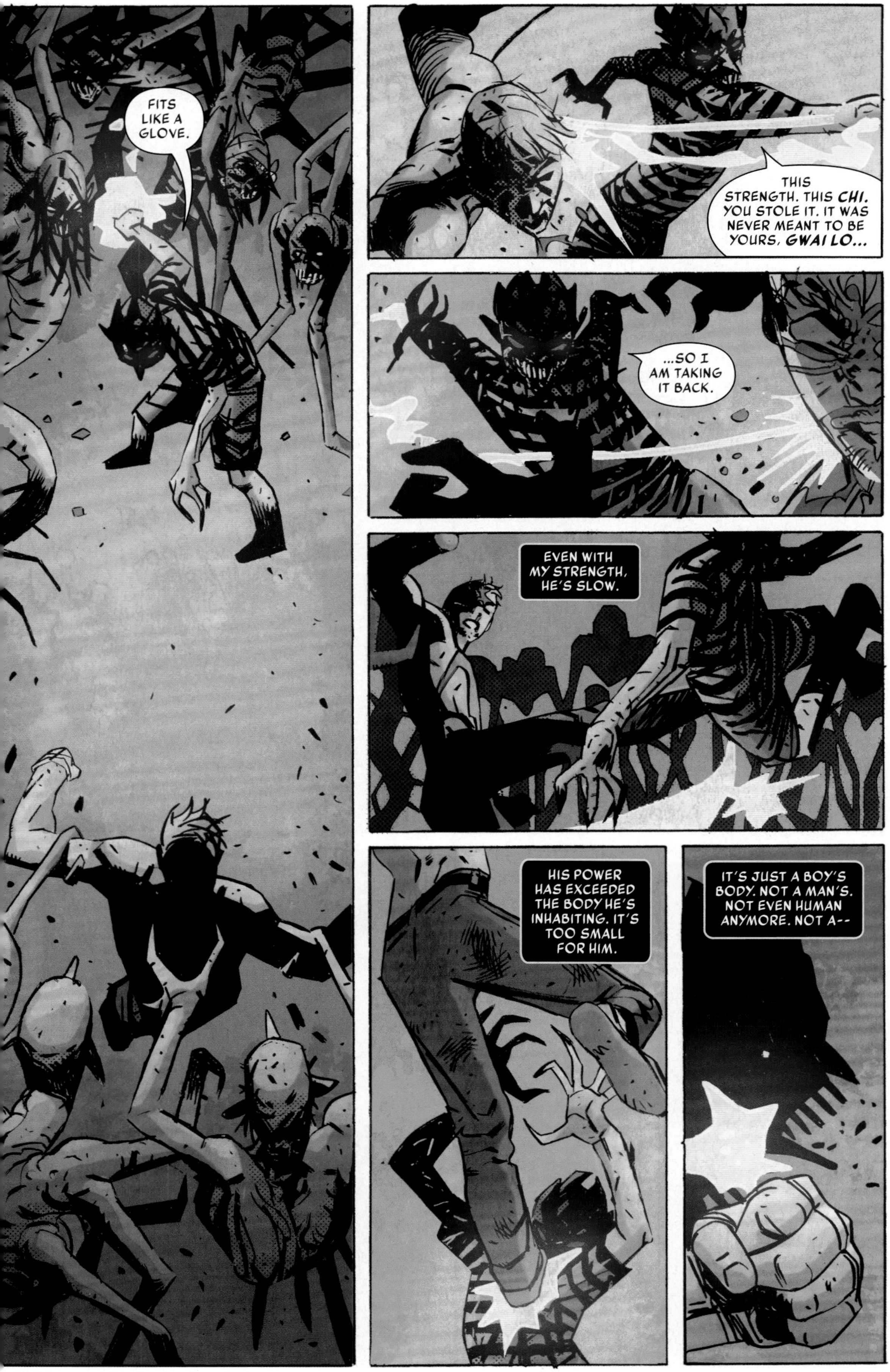
FITS LIKE A GLOVE.
THIS STRENGTH. THIS CHI. YOU STOLE IT. IT WAS NEVER MEANT TO BE YOURS, GWAI LO...
...SO I AM TAKING IT BACK.
EVEN WITH MY STRENGTH, HE'S SLOW.
HIS POWER HAS EXCEEDED THE BODY HE'S INHABITING. IT'S TOO SMALL FOR HIM.
IT'S JUST A BOY'S BODY. NOT A MAN'S. NOT EVEN HUMAN ANYMORE. NOT A--

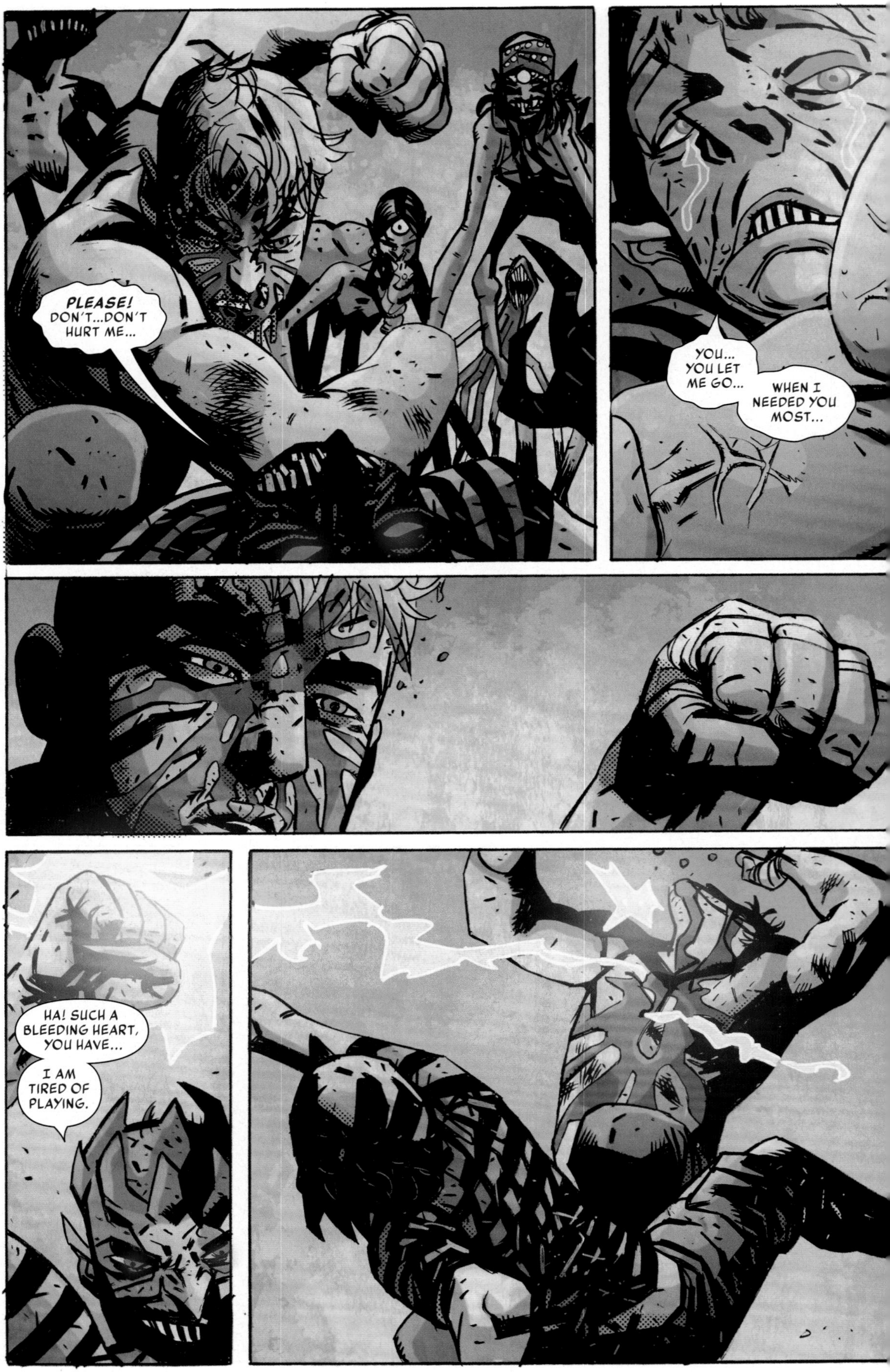
PLEASE! DON'T...DON'T HURT ME...
YOU... YOU LET ME GO...
WHEN I NEEDED YOU MOST...
HA! SUCH A BLEEDING HEART, YOU HAVE...
I AM TIRED OF PLAYING.

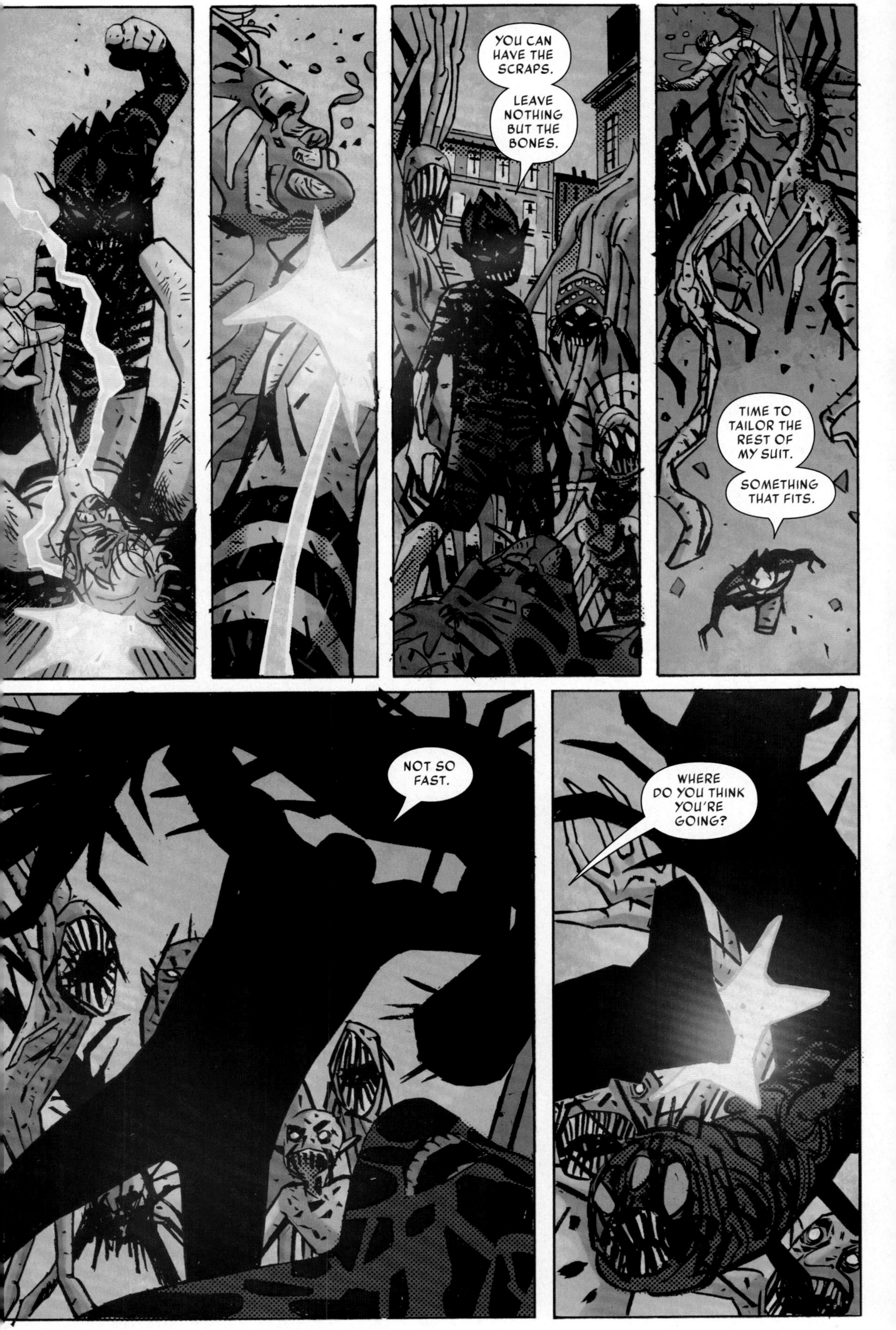
YOU CAN HAVE THE SCRAPS.
LEAVE NOTHING BUT THE BONES.
TIME TO TAILOR THE REST OF MY SUIT.
SOMETHING THAT FITS.
NOT SO FAST.
WHERE DO YOU THINK YOU'RE GOING?

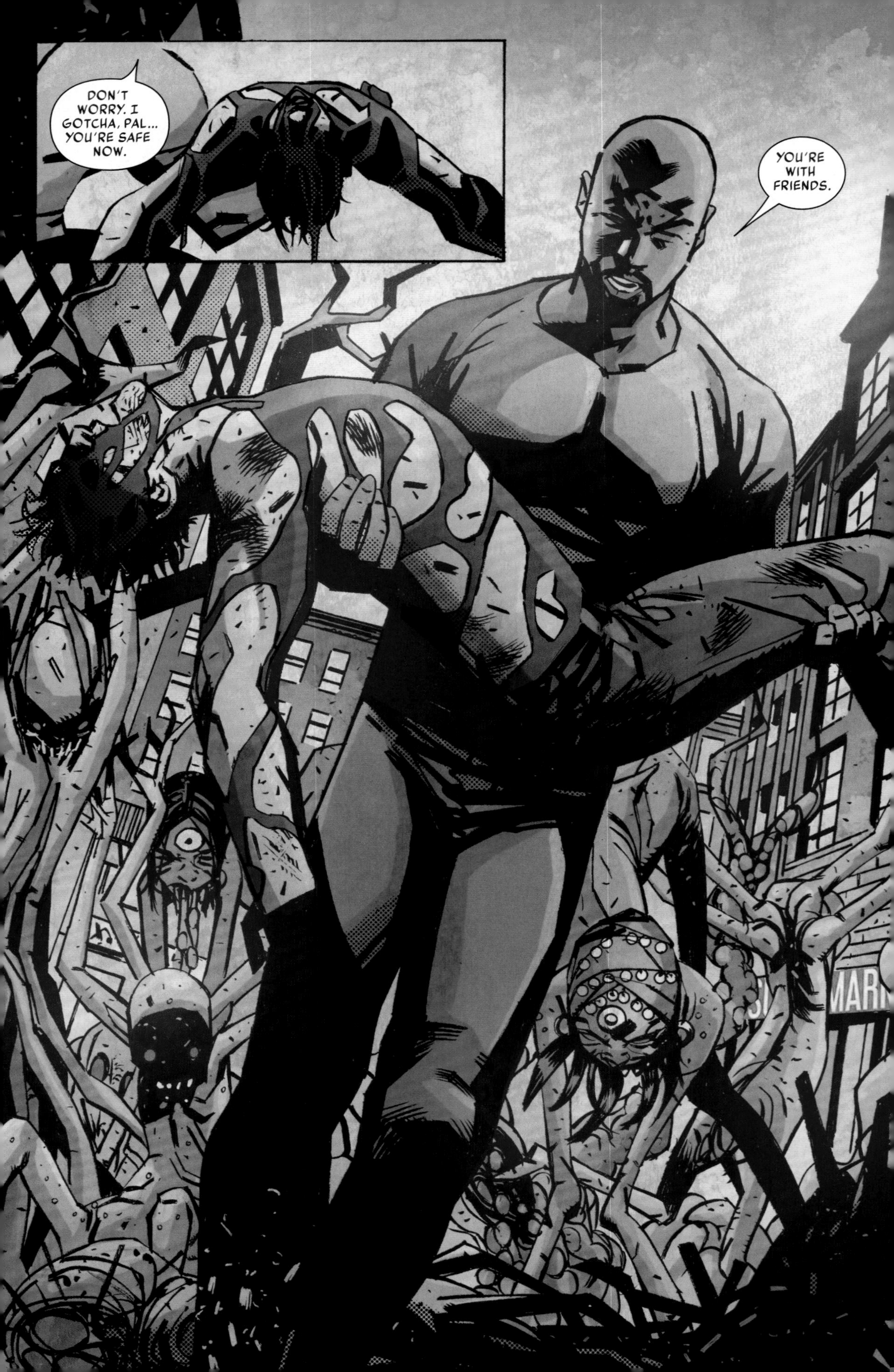

DON'T WORRY. I GOTCHA, PAL... YOU'RE SAFE NOW.
YOU'RE WITH FRIENDS.

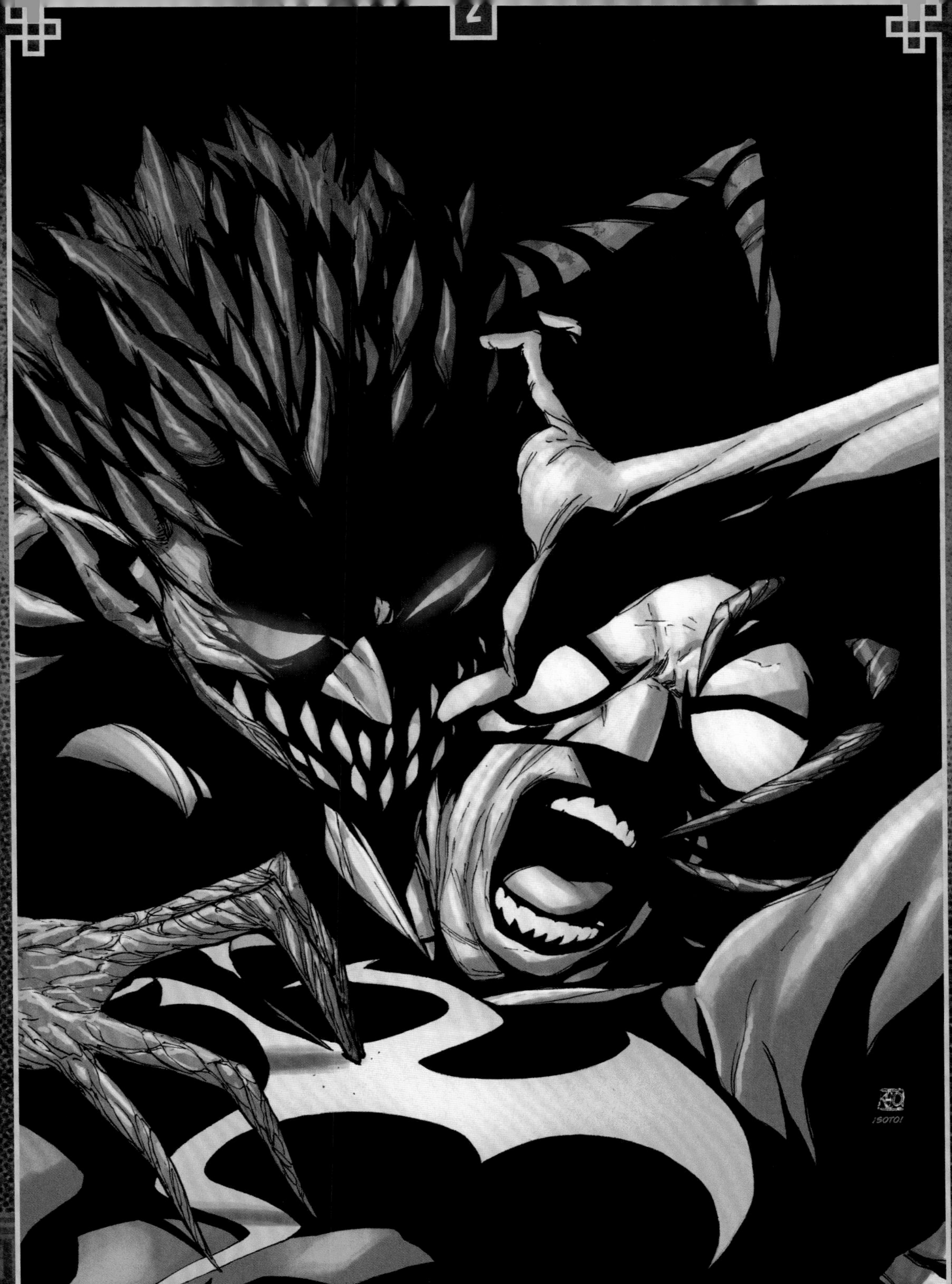
2
¡SOTO!

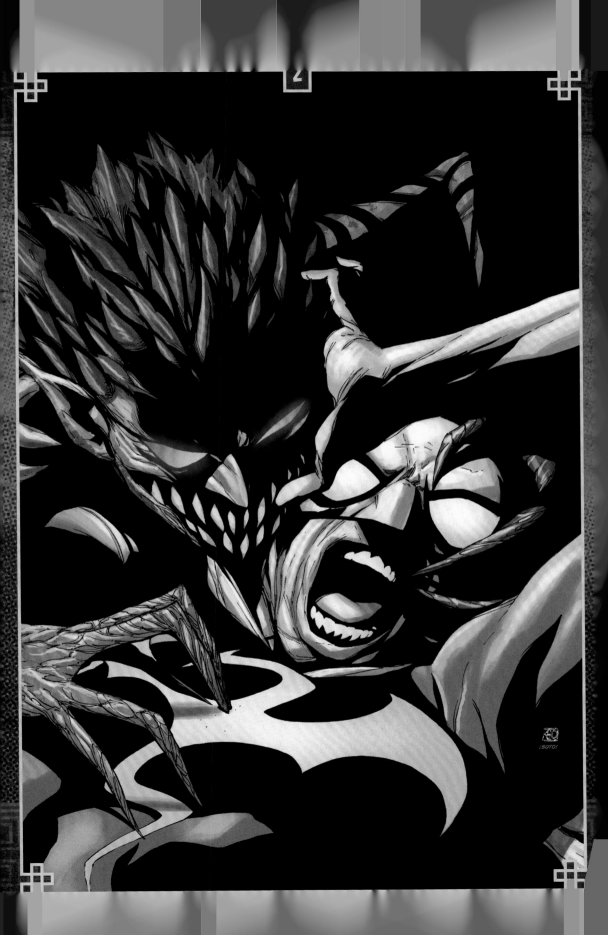

PHANTOM LIMB

CHAPTER 3

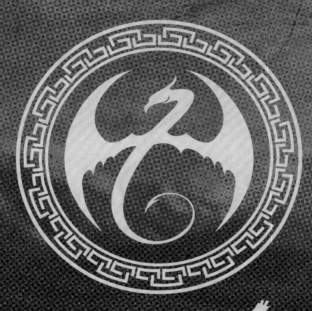

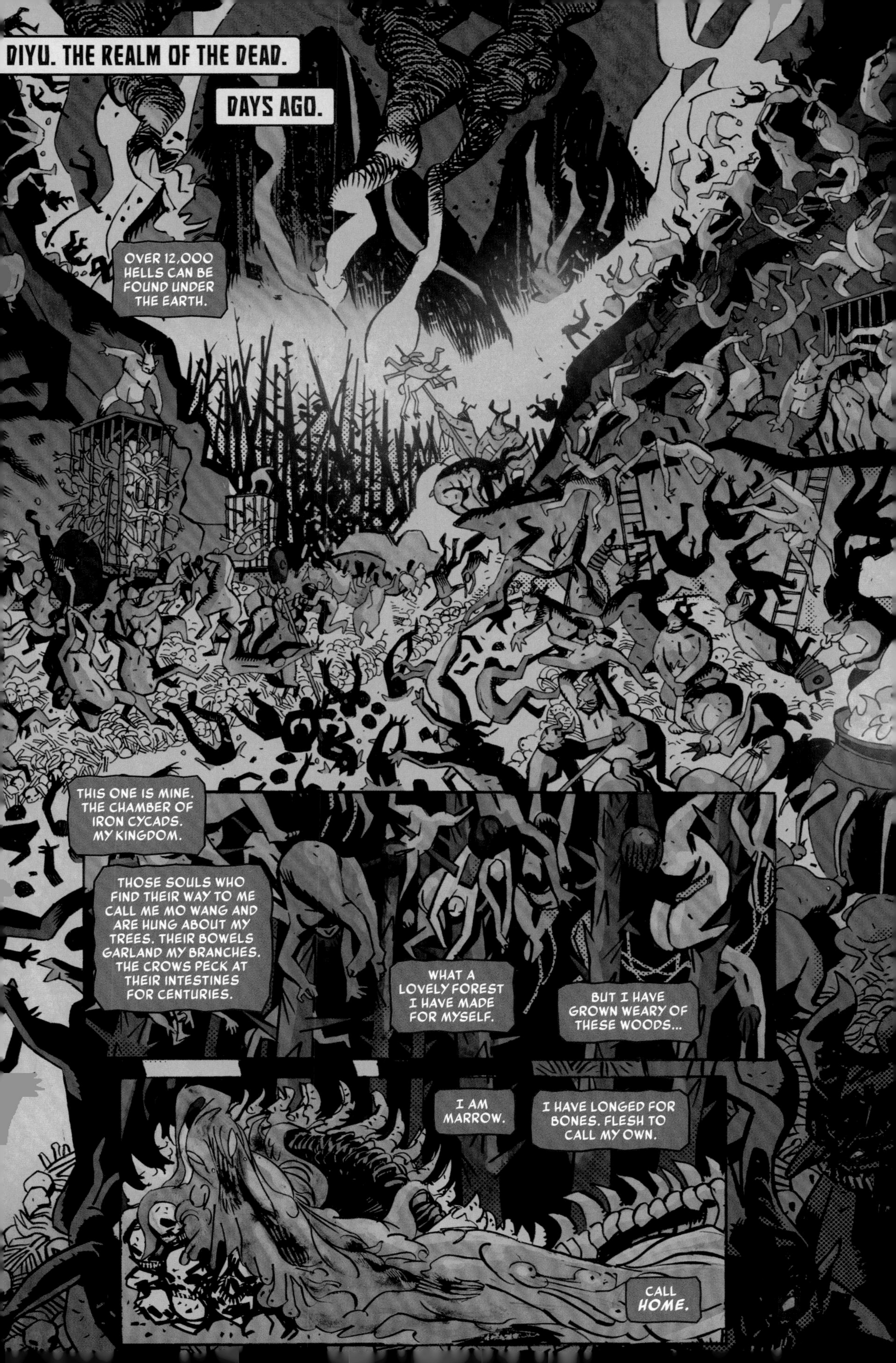

DIYU. THE REALM OF THE DEAD.
DAYS AGO.
OVER 12,000 HELLS CAN BE FOUND UNDER THE EARTH.
THIS ONE IS MINE. THE CHAMBER OF IRON CYCADS. MY KINGDOM.
THOSE SOULS WHO FIND THEIR WAY TO ME CALL ME MO WANG AND ARE HUNG ABOUT MY TREES. THEIR BOWELS GARLAND MY BRANCHES. THE CROWS PECK AT THEIR INTESTINES FOR CENTURIES.
WHAT A LOVELY FOREST I HAVE MADE FOR MYSELF.
BUT I HAVE GROWN WEARY OF THESE WOODS...
I AM MARROW.
I HAVE LONGED FOR BONES. FLESH TO CALL MY OWN.
CALL HOME.

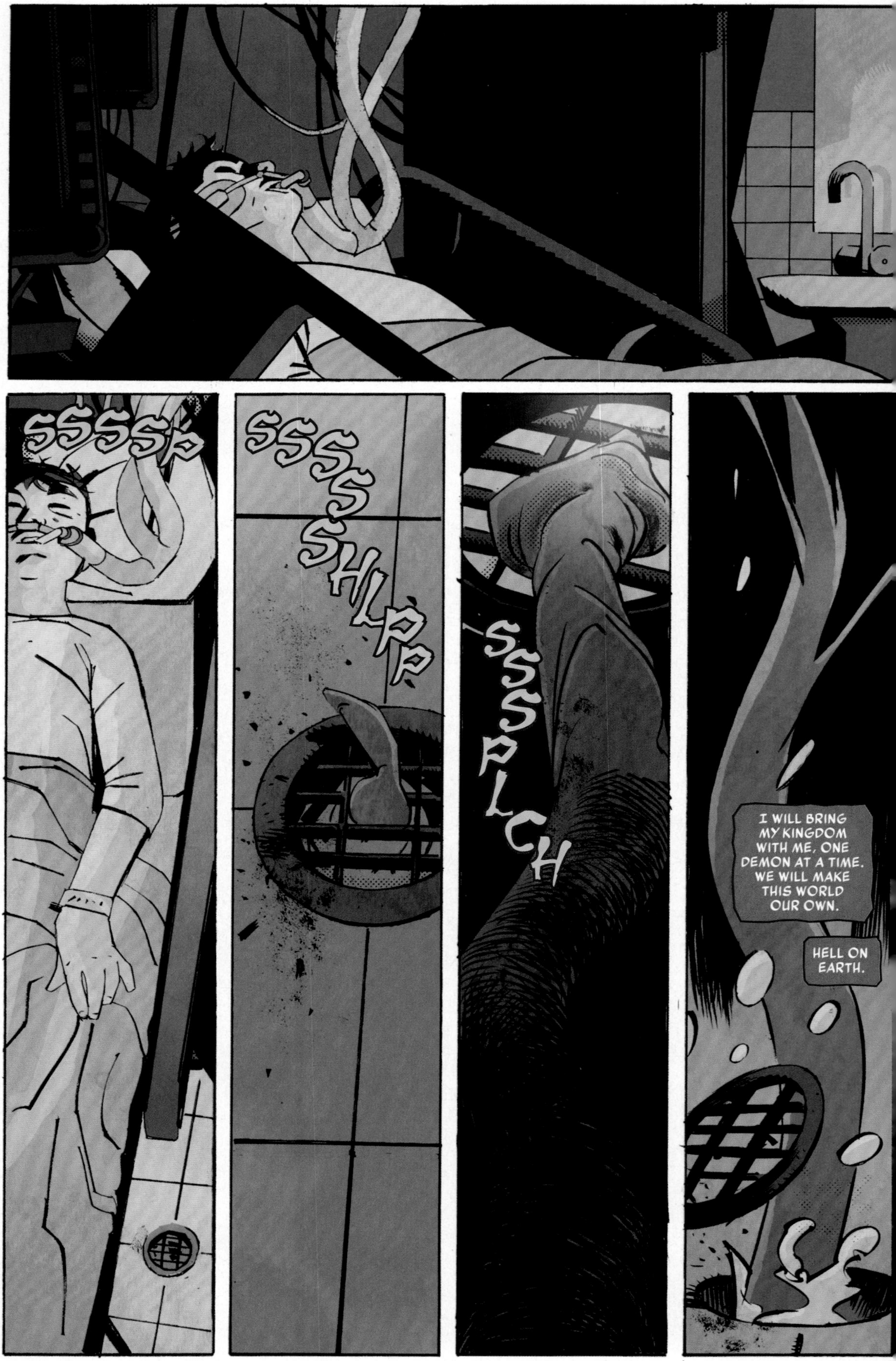
SSSSSP
SSSSSHLPPP
SSSSPLCH
I WILL BRING MY KINGDOM WITH ME. ONE DEMON AT A TIME. WE WILL MAKE THIS WORLD OUR OWN.
HELL ON EARTH.

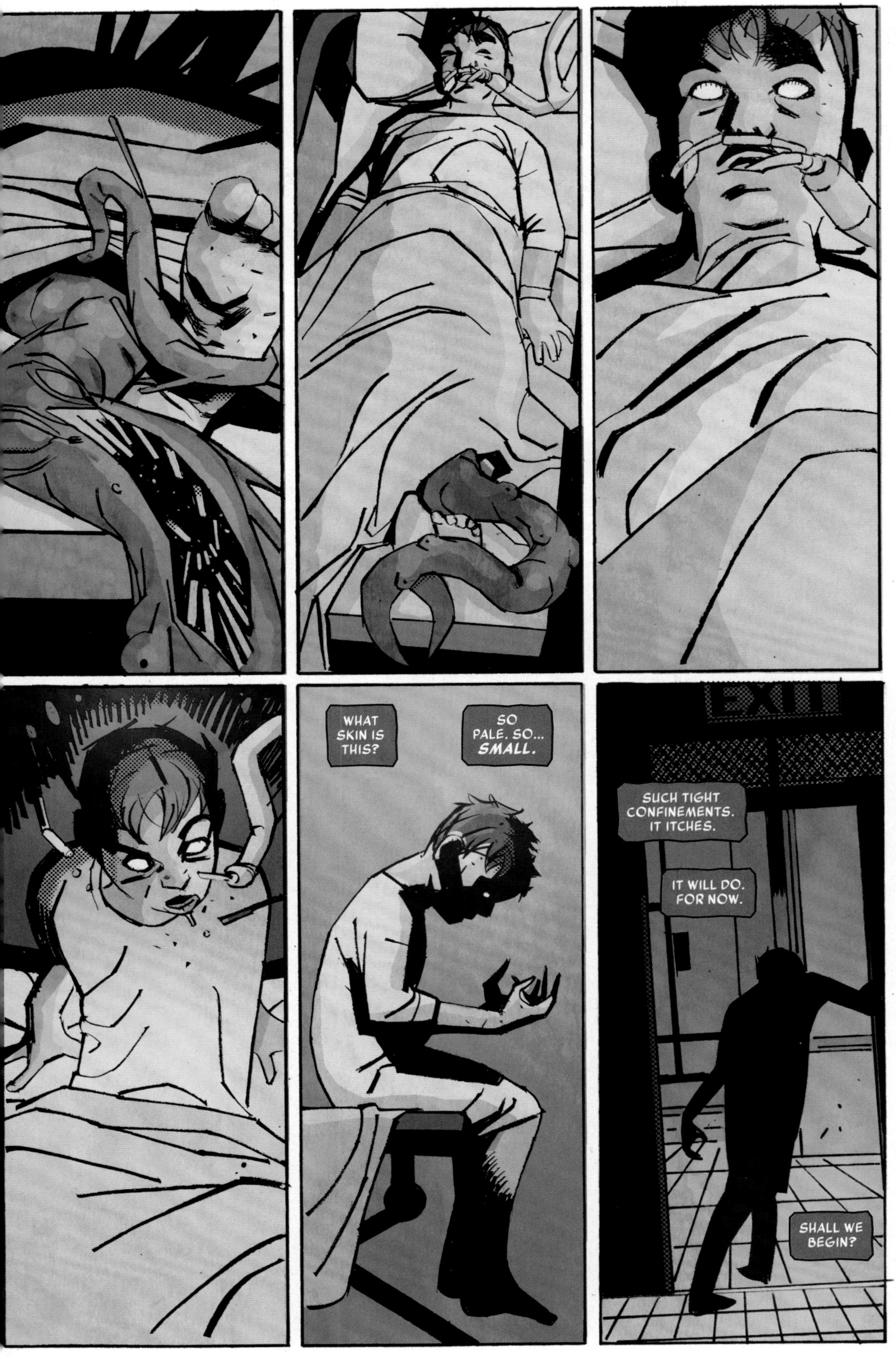

WHAT SKIN IS THIS?
SO PALE. SO... SMALL.
SUCH TIGHT CONFINEMENTS. IT ITCHES.
IT WILL DO. FOR NOW.
SHALL WE BEGIN?

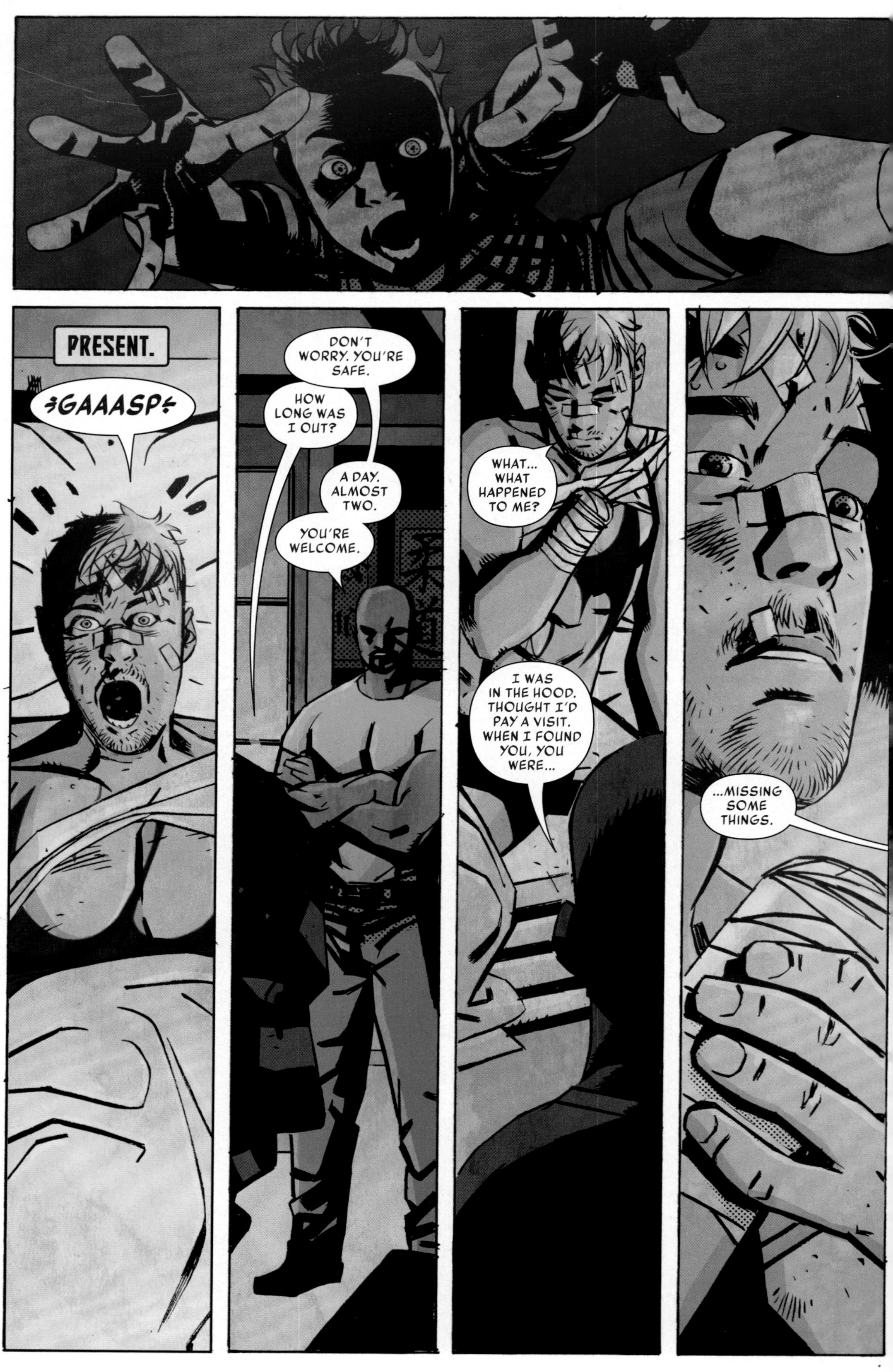
PRESENT.
GAAASP
DON'T WORRY. YOU'RE SAFE.
HOW LONG WAS I OUT?
A DAY. ALMOST TWO.
YOU'RE WELCOME.
WHAT... WHAT HAPPENED TO ME?
I WAS IN THE HOOD. THOUGHT I'D PAY A VISIT. WHEN I FOUND YOU, YOU WERE...
...MISSING SOME THINGS.

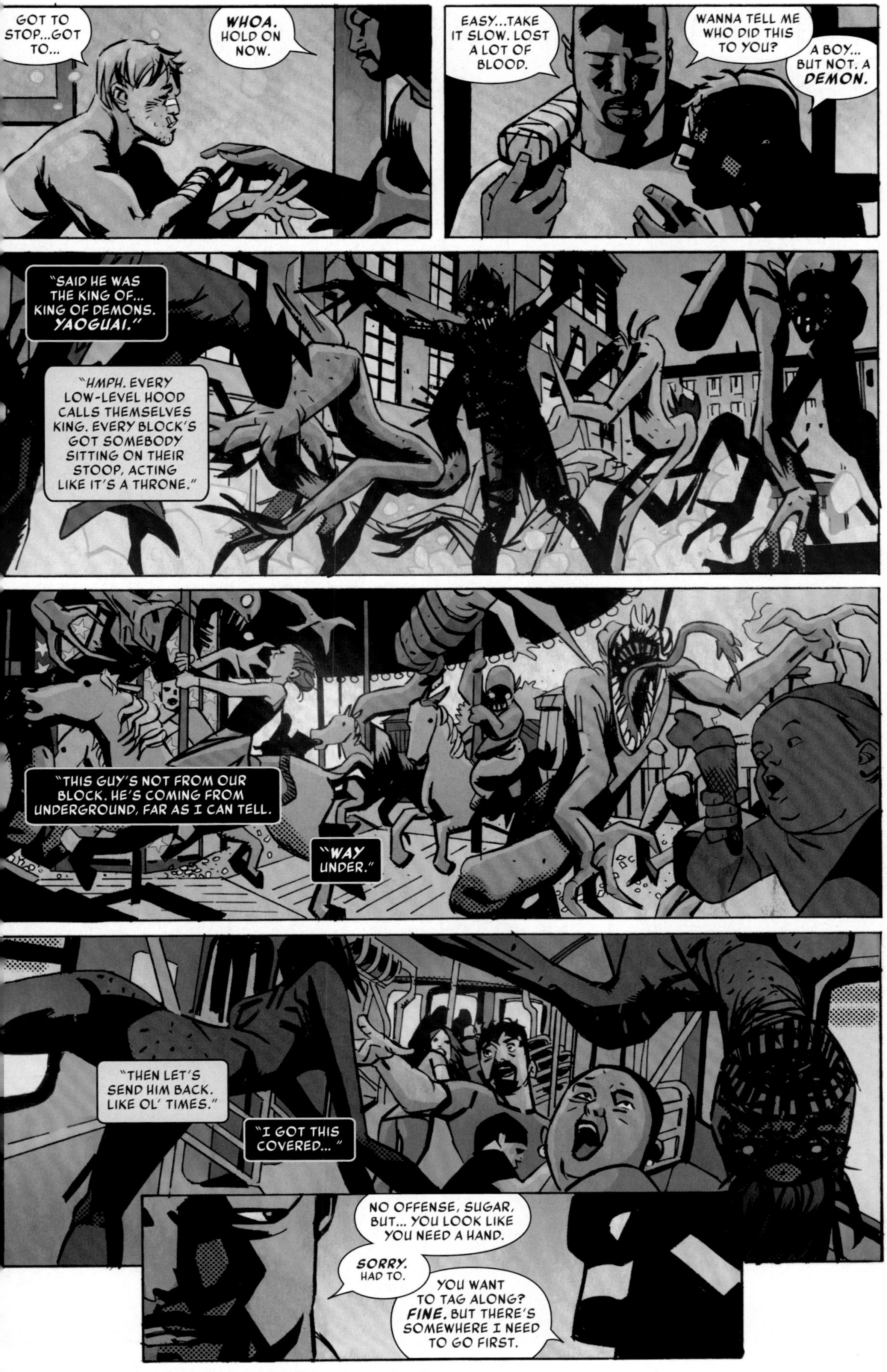
GOT TO STOP...GOT TO...
WHOA. HOLD ON NOW.
EASY...TAKE IT SLOW. LOST A LOT OF BLOOD.
WANNA TELL ME WHO DID THIS TO YOU?
A BOY... BUT NOT. A DEMON.
"SAID HE WAS THE KING OF... KING OF DEMONS. YAOGUAI."
"HMPH. EVERY LOW-LEVEL HOOD CALLS THEMSELVES KING. EVERY BLOCK'S GOT SOMEBODY SITTING ON THEIR STOOP, ACTING LIKE IT'S A THRONE."
"THIS GUY'S NOT FROM OUR BLOCK. HE'S COMING FROM UNDERGROUND, FAR AS I CAN TELL.
"WAY UNDER."
"THEN LET'S SEND HIM BACK. LIKE OL' TIMES."
"I GOT THIS COVERED..."
NO OFFENSE, SUGAR, BUT... YOU LOOK LIKE YOU NEED A HAND.
SORRY. HAD TO.
YOU WANT TO TAG ALONG? FINE. BUT THERE'S SOMEWHERE I NEED TO GO FIRST.

CROWN HEIGHTS.

"SOMEONE I NEED TO SEE."

SHE REFUSED TO LEAVE HER SON'S SIDE IN THE HOSPITAL. KEPT WAITING AND WAITING FOR HIM TO WAKE. SECURITY HAD TO DRAG HER OUT...

YOU.

CAN WE COME IN, MA'AM?

YOU SMELL THAT?

AFRAID SO. CRACK OPEN A WINDOW, MAN... NEED SOME FRESH AIR UP IN HERE.

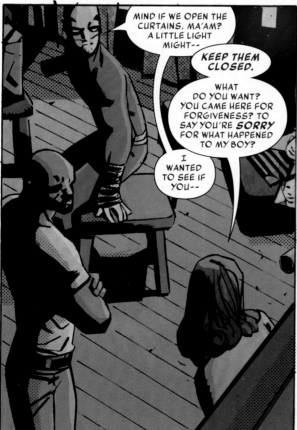

MIND IF WE OPEN THE CURTAINS, MA'AM? A LITTLE LIGHT MIGHT--

KEEP THEM CLOSED.

WHAT DO YOU WANT? YOU CAME HERE FOR FORGIVENESS? TO SAY YOU'RE SORRY FOR WHAT HAPPENED TO MY BOY?

I WANTED TO SEE IF YOU--

I WON'T. I WON'T FORGIVE YOU. NOT AFTER...

...WHAT HAS HAPPENED TO MY SON.

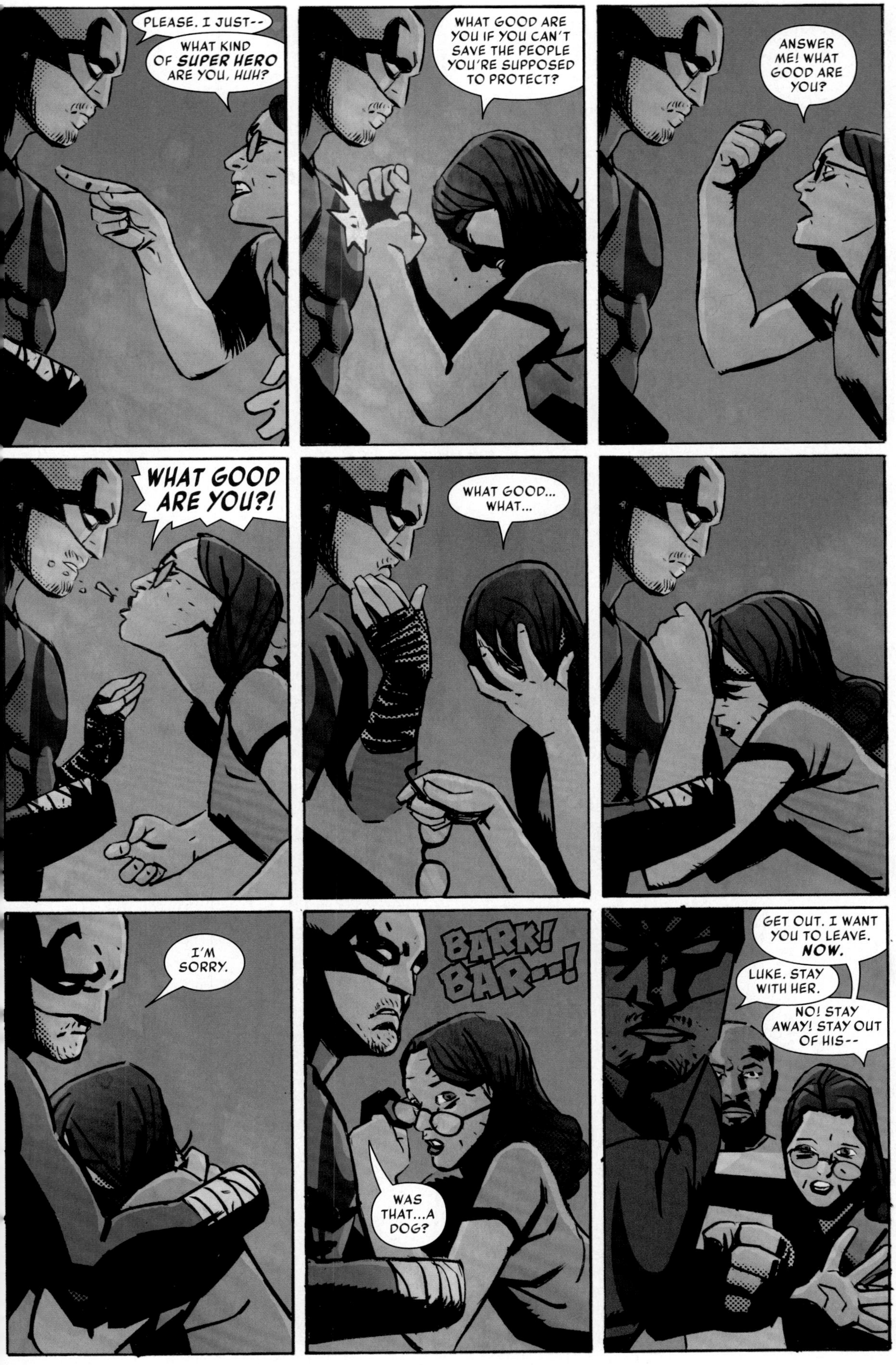
PLEASE. I JUST--
WHAT KIND OF SUPER HERO ARE YOU, HUH?
WHAT GOOD ARE YOU IF YOU CAN'T SAVE THE PEOPLE YOU'RE SUPPOSED TO PROTECT?
ANSWER ME! WHAT GOOD ARE YOU?
WHAT GOOD ARE YOU?!
WHAT GOOD... WHAT...
I'M SORRY.
BARK! BAR--!
WAS THAT...A DOG?
GET OUT. I WANT YOU TO LEAVE. NOW.
LUKE. STAY WITH HER.
NO! STAY AWAY! STAY OUT OF HIS--

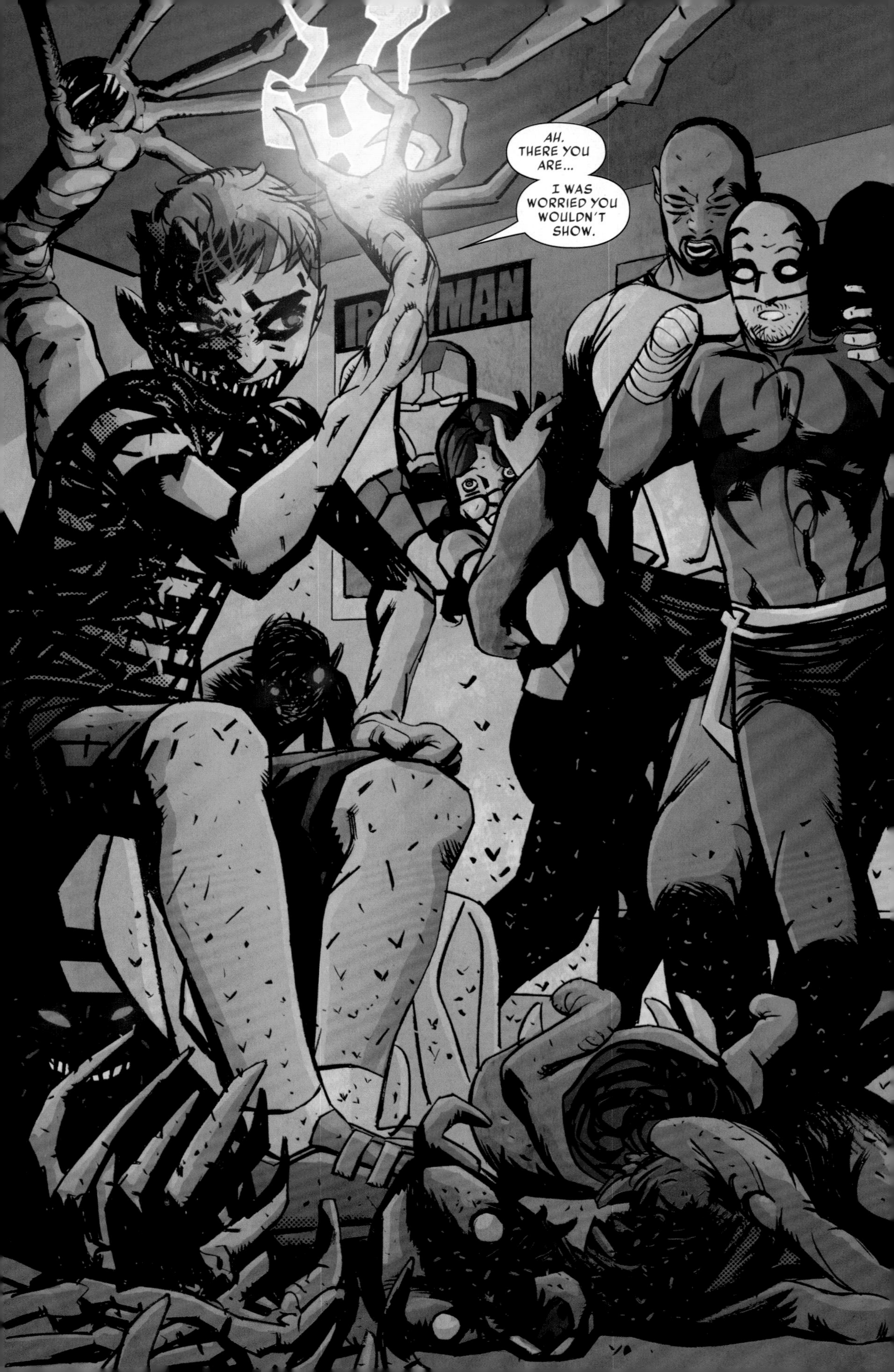

AH. THERE YOU ARE...
I WAS WORRIED YOU WOULDN'T SHOW.

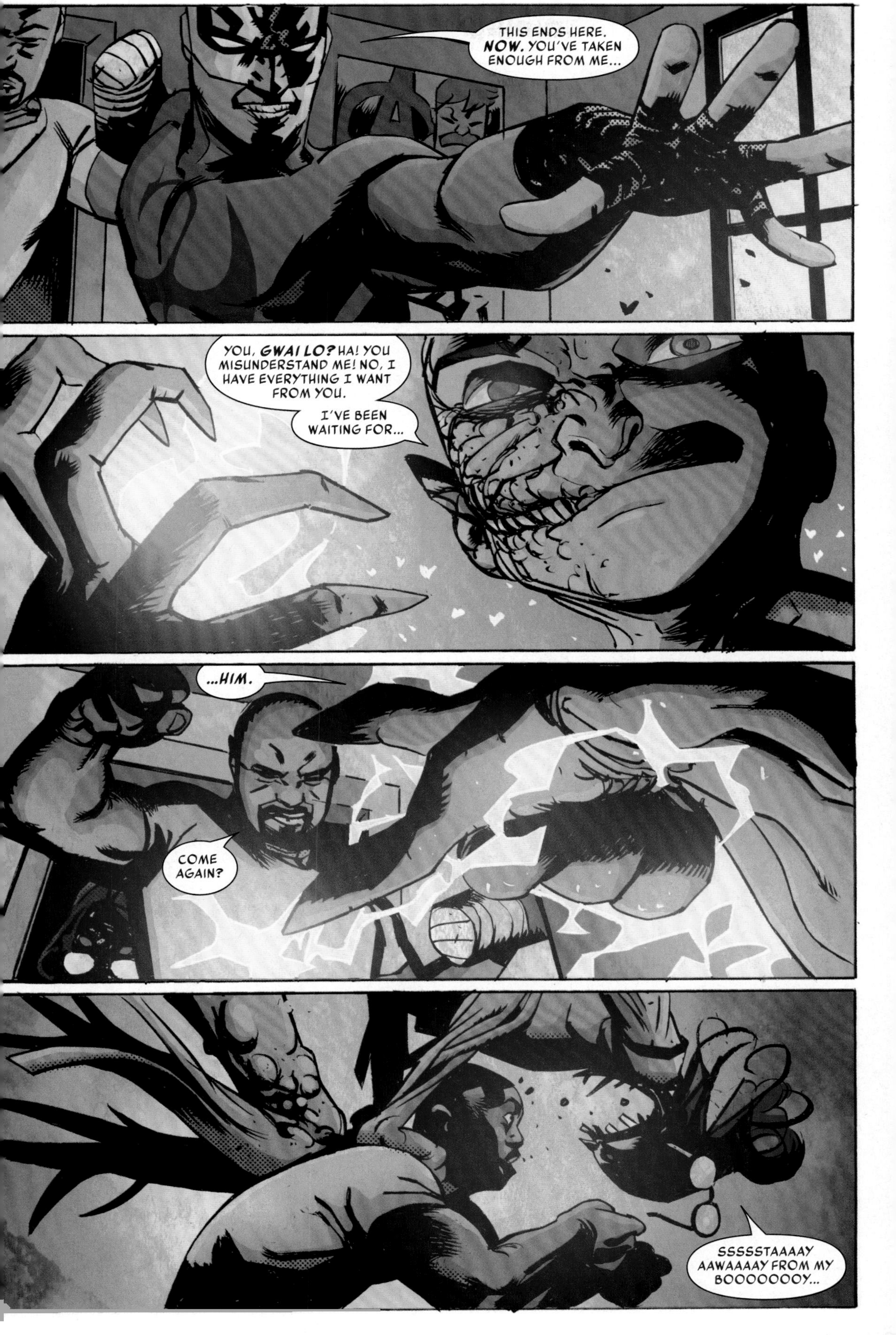
THIS ENDS HERE. NOW. YOU'VE TAKEN ENOUGH FROM ME...
YOU, GWAI LO? HA! YOU MISUNDERSTAND ME! NO, I HAVE EVERYTHING I WANT FROM YOU.
I'VE BEEN WAITING FOR...
...HIM.
COME AGAIN?
SSSSSTAAAAY AAWAAAAY FROM MY BOOOOOOOY...

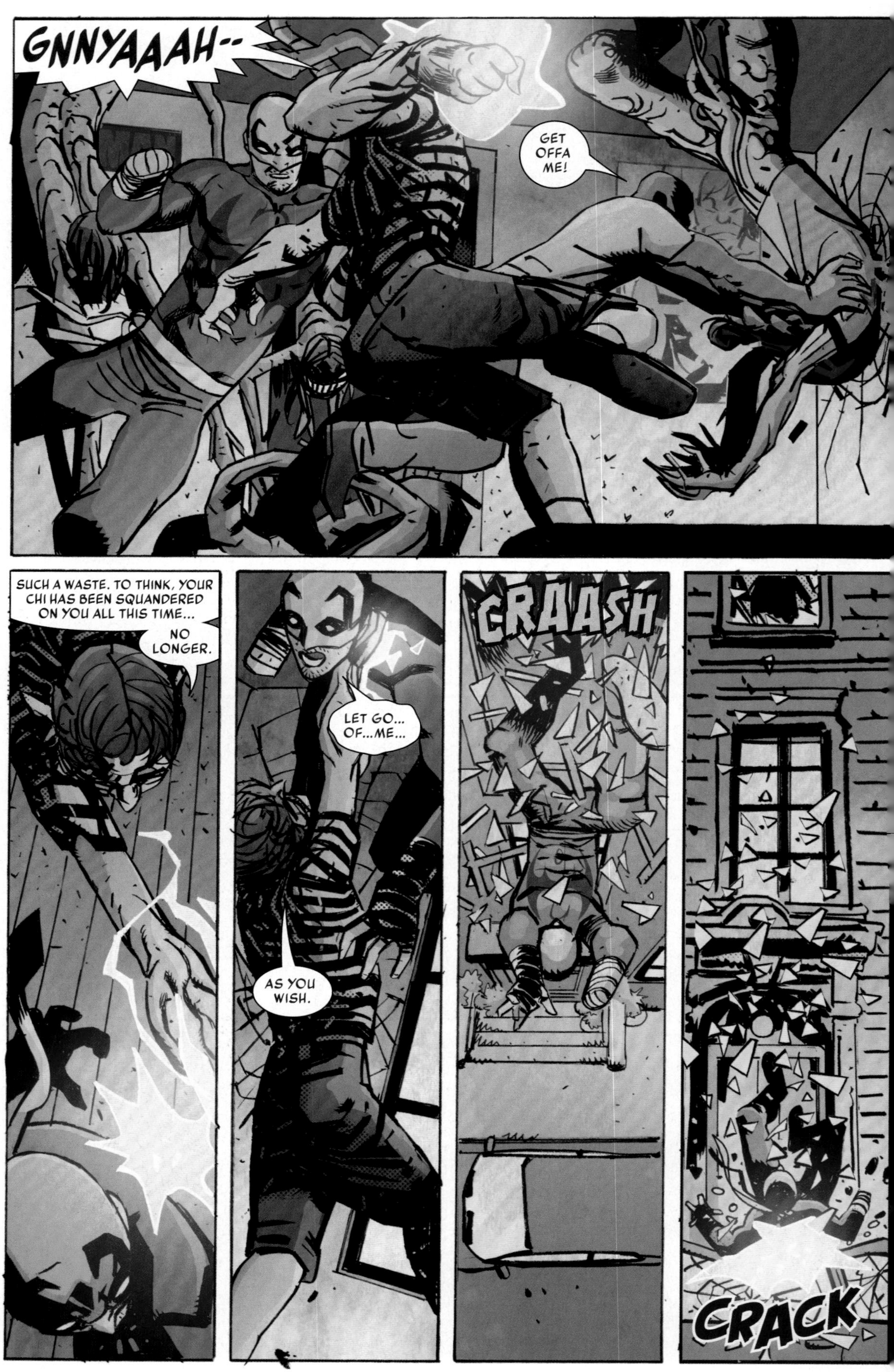
GNNYAAAH--
GET OFFA ME!
SUCH A WASTE. TO THINK, YOUR CHI HAS BEEN SQUANDERED ON YOU ALL THIS TIME...
NO LONGER.
LET GO... OF...ME...
AS YOU WISH.
CRAASH
CRACK

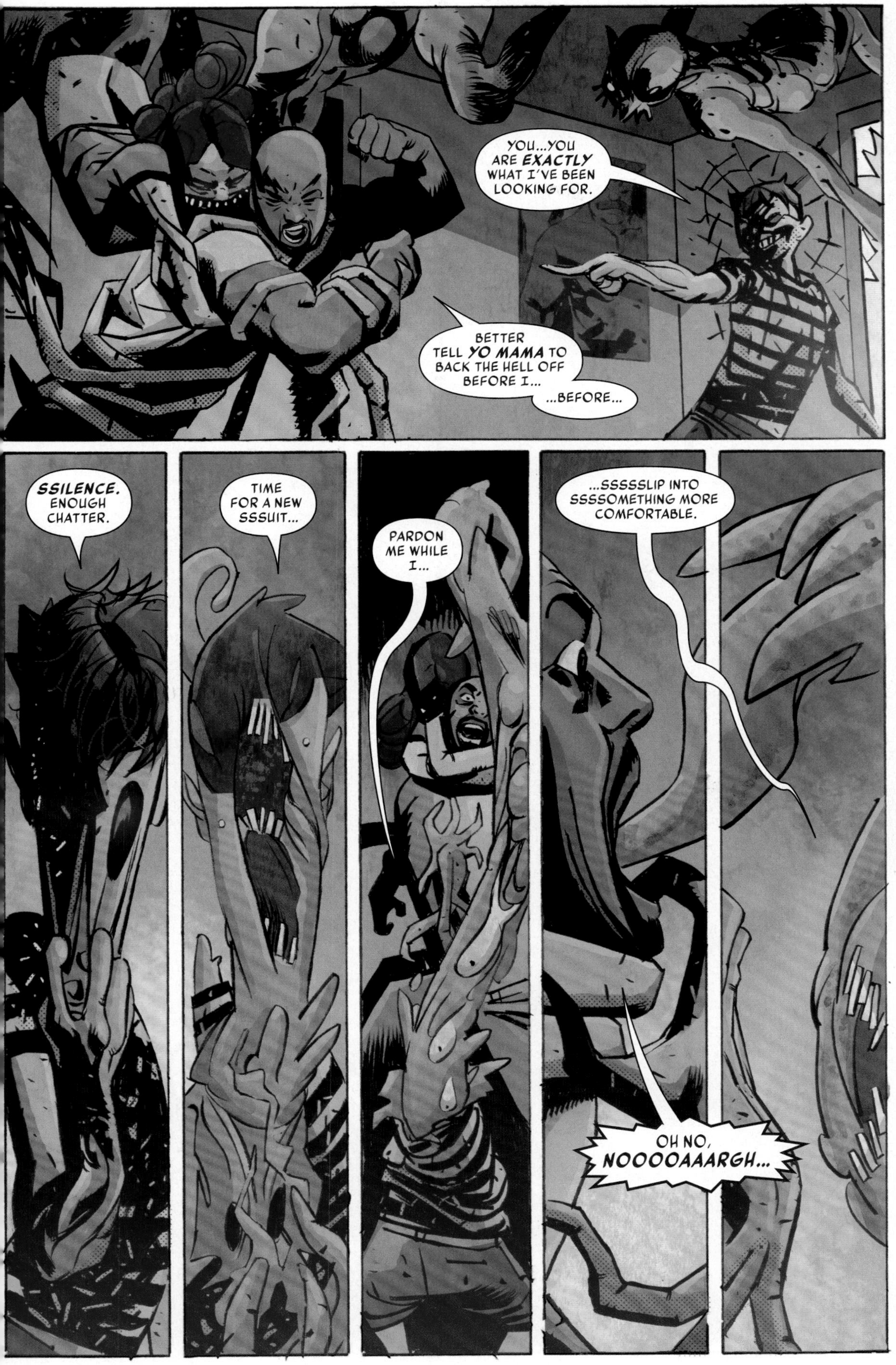
YOU...YOU ARE EXACTLY WHAT I'VE BEEN LOOKING FOR.
BETTER TELL YO MAMA TO BACK THE HELL OFF BEFORE I...
...BEFORE...
SSILENCE. ENOUGH CHATTER.
TIME FOR A NEW SSSUIT...
PARDON ME WHILE I...
...SSSSSLIP INTO SSSSOMETHING MORE COMFORTABLE.
OH NO, NOOOOAAARGH...

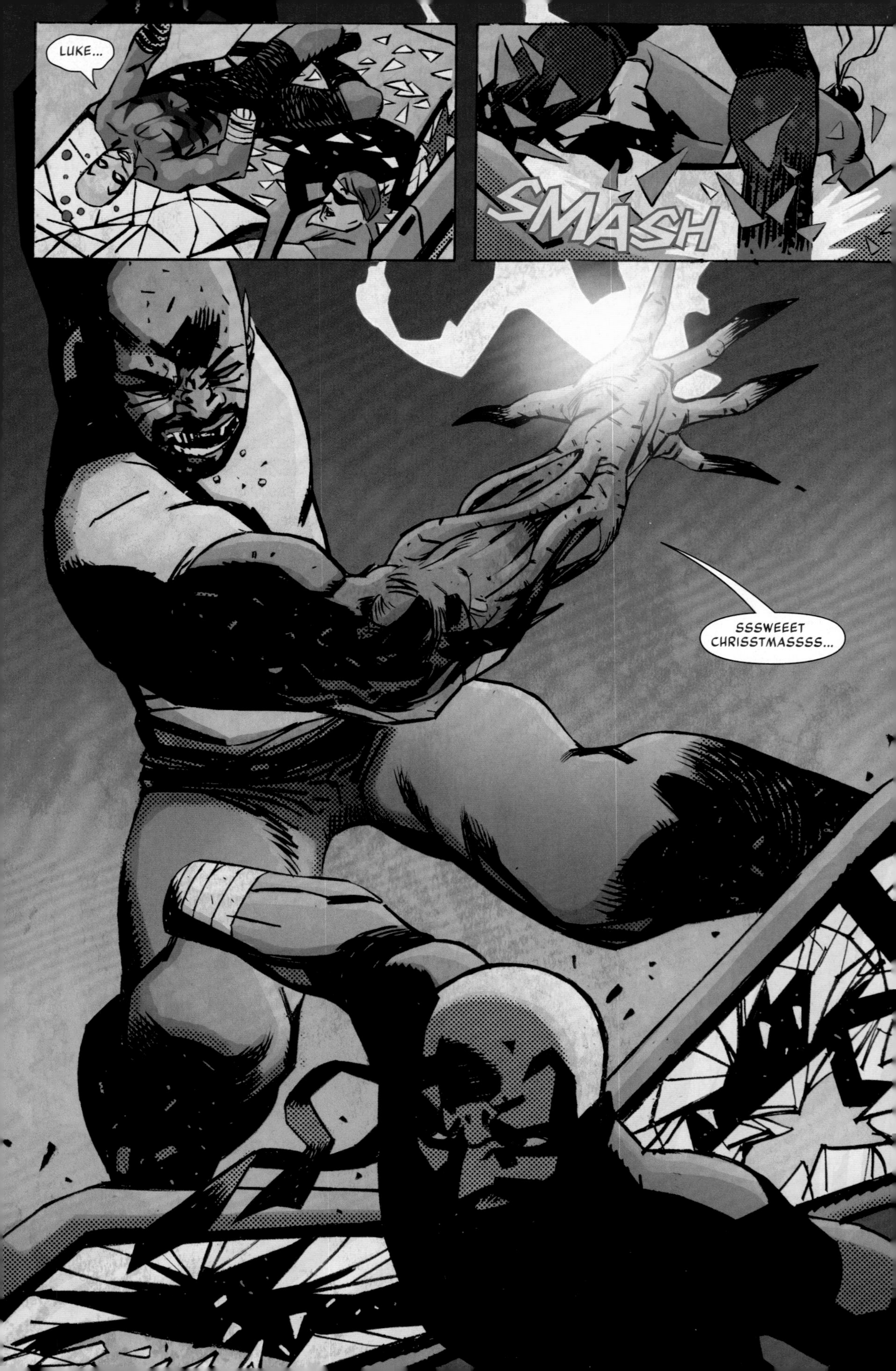
LUKE...
SMASH
SSSWEEET CHRISSTMASSSS...

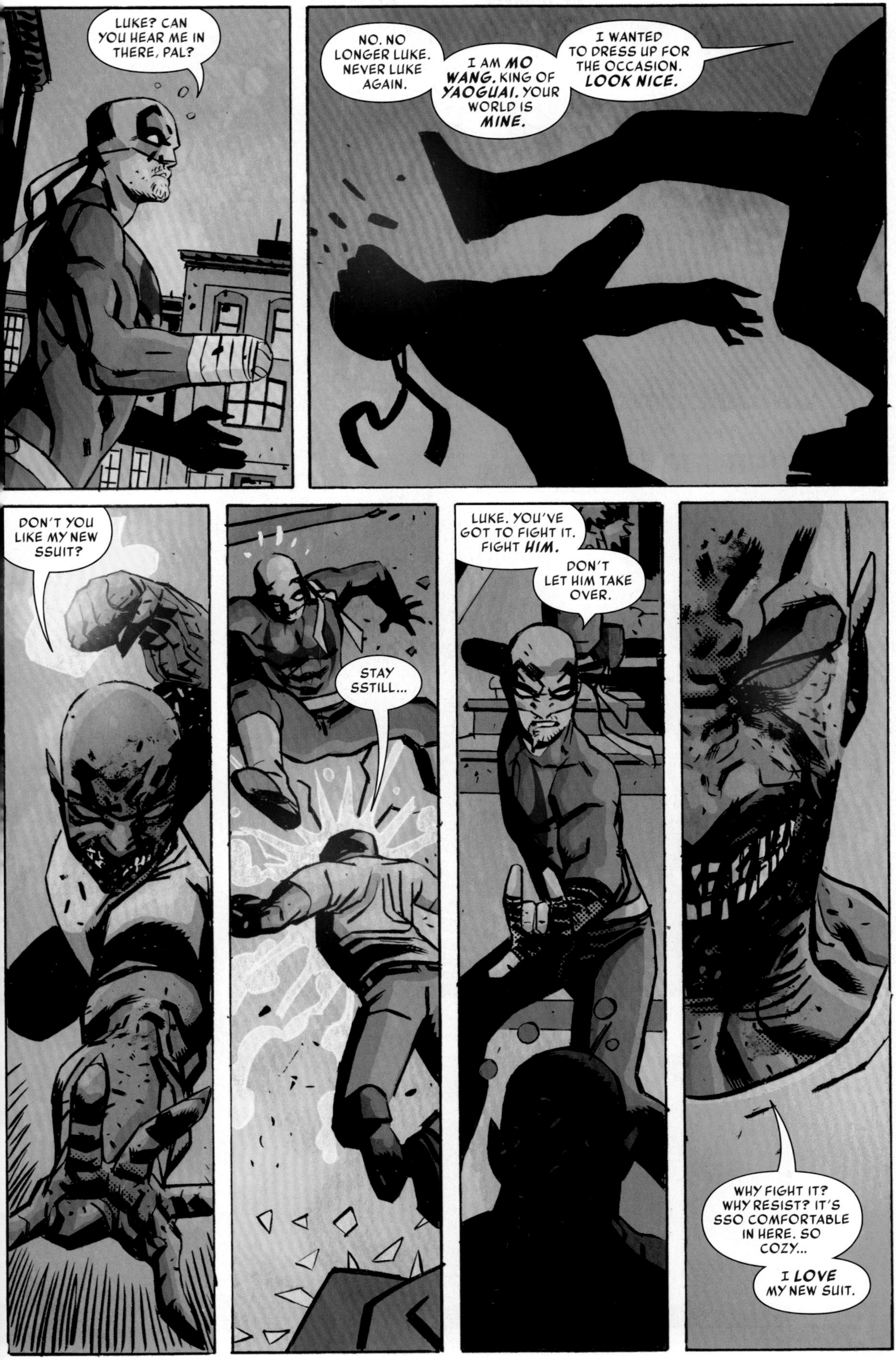
LUKE? CAN YOU HEAR ME IN THERE, PAL?
NO. NO LONGER LUKE. NEVER LUKE AGAIN.
I AM MO WANG. KING OF YAOGUAI. YOUR WORLD IS MINE.
I WANTED TO DRESS UP FOR THE OCCASION. LOOK NICE.
DON'T YOU LIKE MY NEW SSUIT?
STAY SSTILL...
LUKE. YOU'VE GOT TO FIGHT IT. FIGHT HIM.
DON'T LET HIM TAKE OVER.
WHY FIGHT IT? WHY RESIST? IT'S SSO COMFORTABLE IN HERE. SO COZY...
I LOVE MY NEW SUIT.

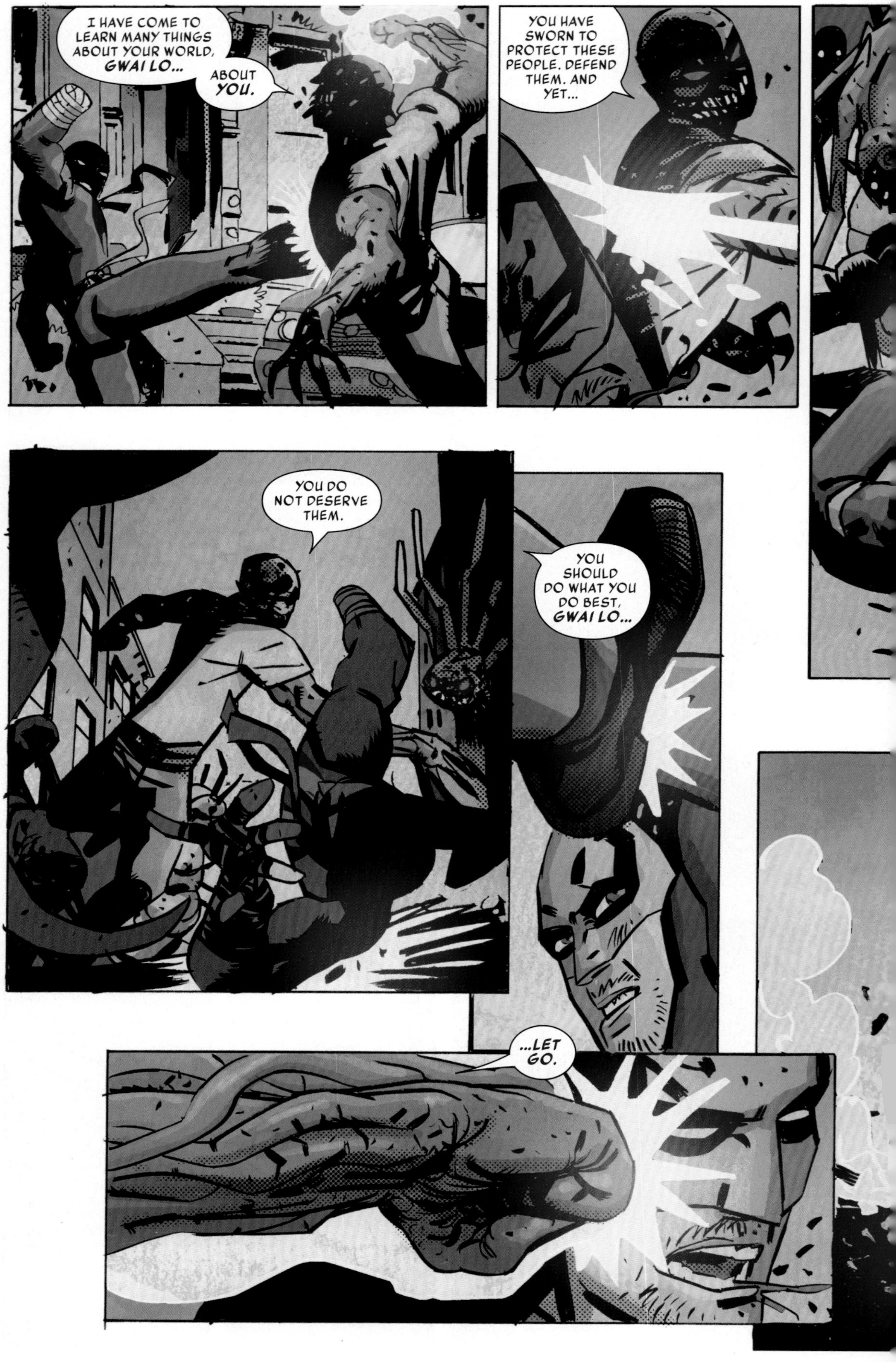
I HAVE COME TO LEARN MANY THINGS ABOUT YOUR WORLD, GWAI LO...
ABOUT YOU.
YOU HAVE SWORN TO PROTECT THESE PEOPLE. DEFEND THEM. AND YET...
YOU DO NOT DESERVE THEM.
YOU SHOULD DO WHAT YOU DO BEST, GWAI LO...
...LET GO.

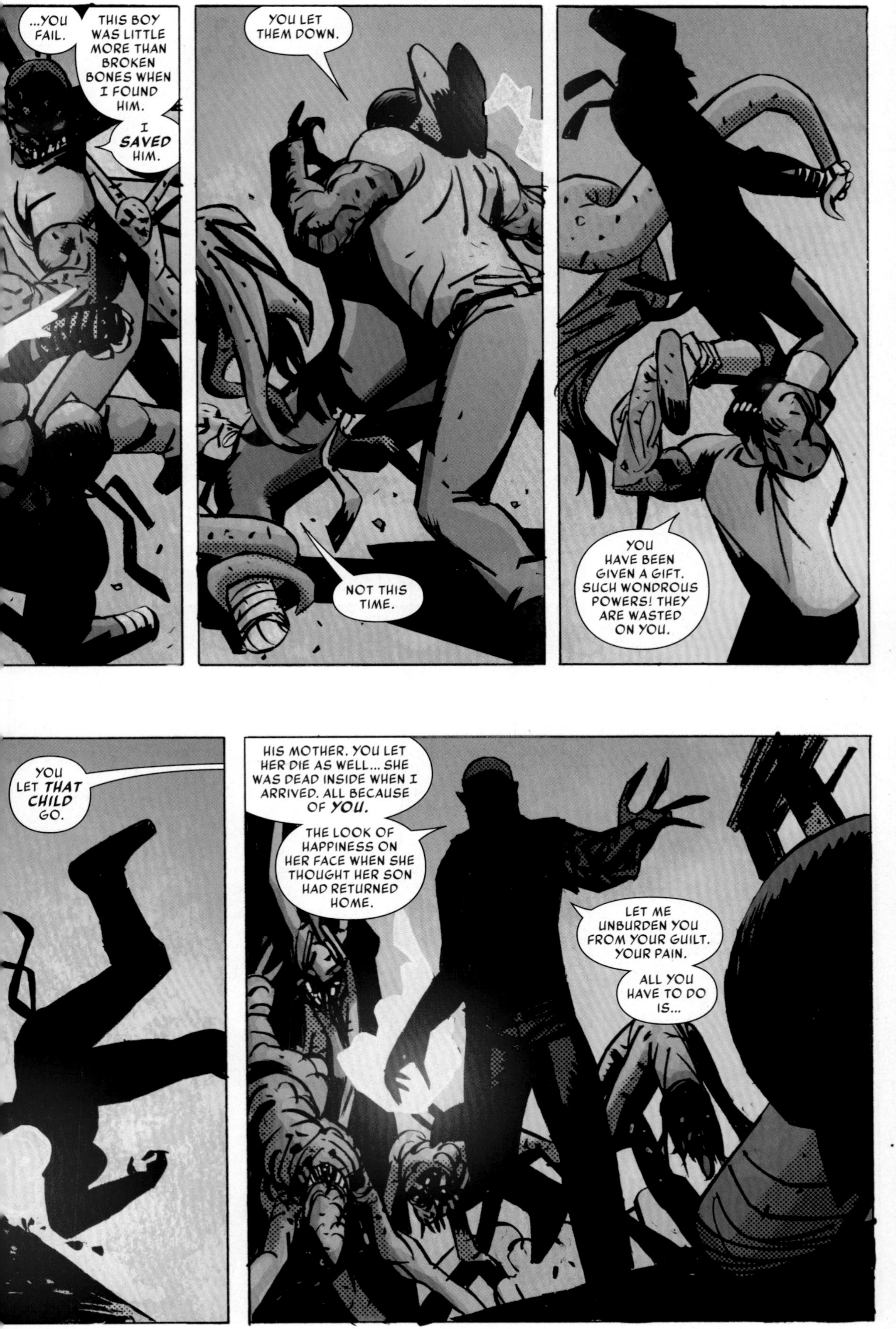
...YOU FAIL.
THIS BOY WAS LITTLE MORE THAN BROKEN BONES WHEN I FOUND HIM.
I SAVED HIM.
YOU LET THEM DOWN.
NOT THIS TIME.
YOU HAVE BEEN GIVEN A GIFT. SUCH WONDROUS POWERS! THEY ARE WASTED ON YOU.
YOU LET THAT CHILD GO.
HIS MOTHER. YOU LET HER DIE AS WELL... SHE WAS DEAD INSIDE WHEN I ARRIVED. ALL BECAUSE OF YOU.
THE LOOK OF HAPPINESS ON HER FACE WHEN SHE THOUGHT HER SON HAD RETURNED HOME.
LET ME UNBURDEN YOU FROM YOUR GUILT. YOUR PAIN.
ALL YOU HAVE TO DO IS...

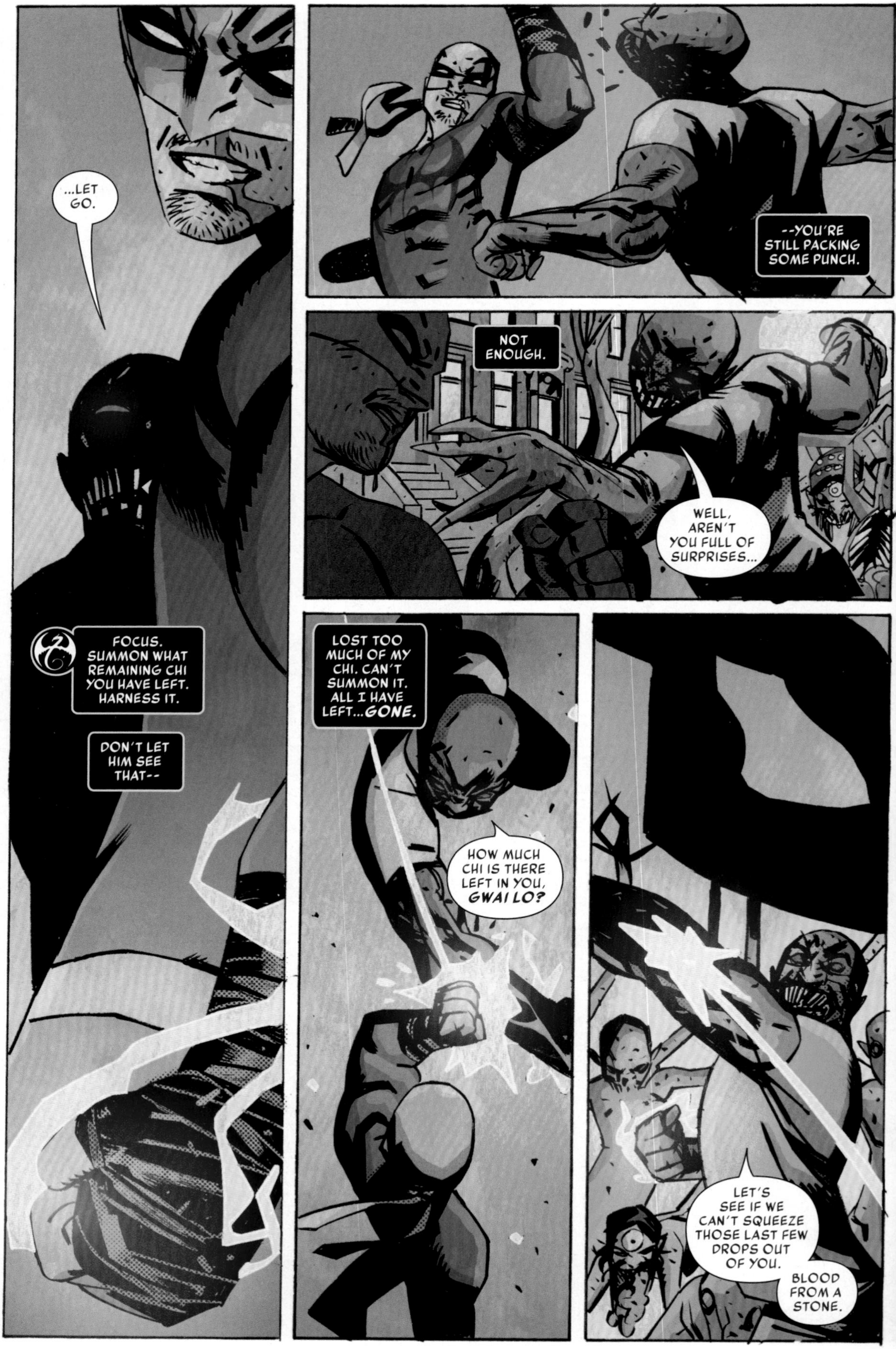
...LET GO.
--YOU'RE STILL PACKING SOME PUNCH.
NOT ENOUGH.
WELL, AREN'T YOU FULL OF SURPRISES...
FOCUS. SUMMON WHAT REMAINING CHI YOU HAVE LEFT. HARNESS IT.
DON'T LET HIM SEE THAT--
LOST TOO MUCH OF MY CHI. CAN'T SUMMON IT. ALL I HAVE LEFT...*GONE.*
HOW MUCH CHI IS THERE LEFT IN YOU, *GWAI LO?*
LET'S SEE IF WE CAN'T SQUEEZE THOSE LAST FEW DROPS OUT OF YOU.
BLOOD FROM A STONE.

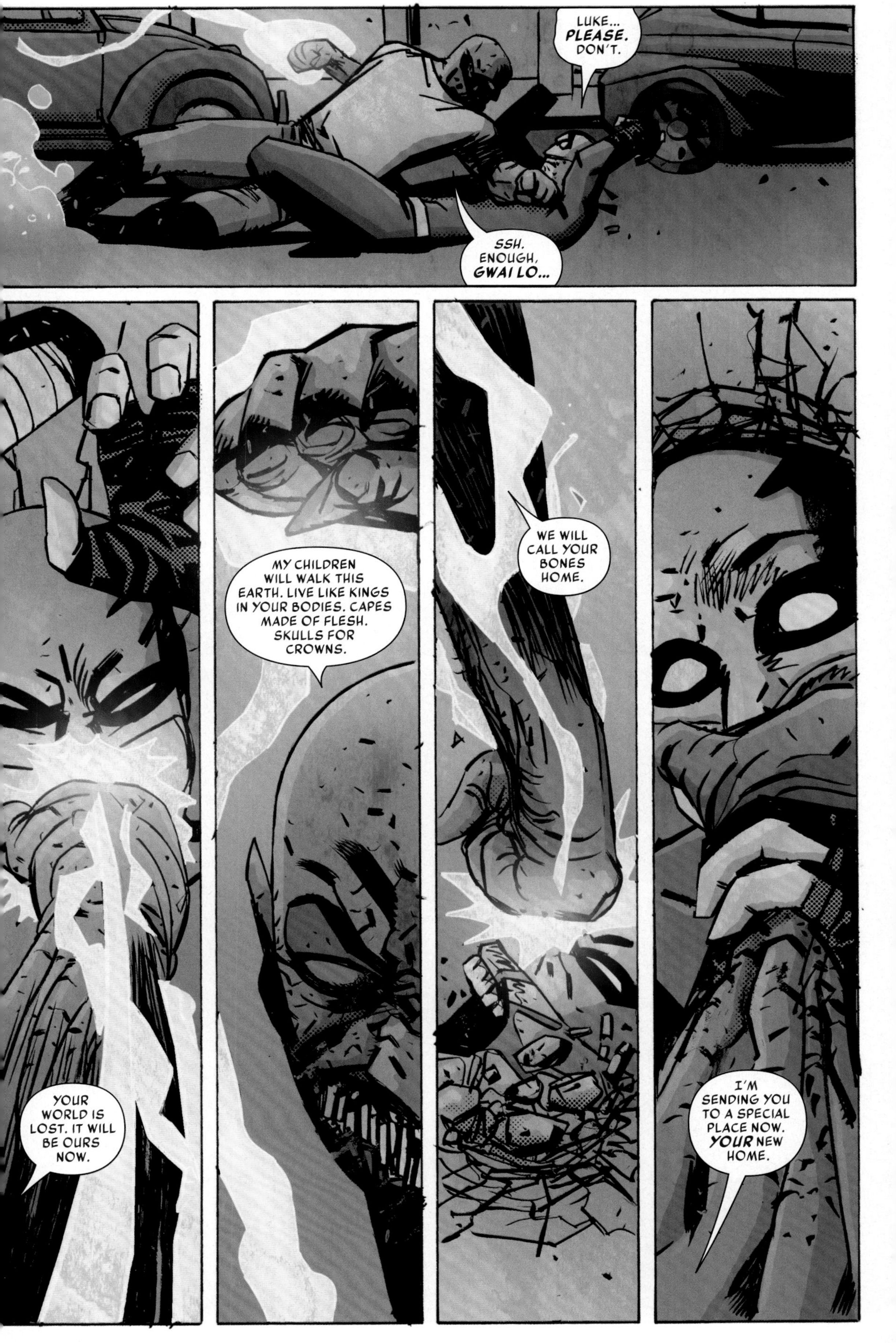
LUKE... PLEASE. DON'T.
SSH. ENOUGH, GWAI LO...
YOUR WORLD IS LOST. IT WILL BE OURS NOW.
MY CHILDREN WILL WALK THIS EARTH. LIVE LIKE KINGS IN YOUR BODIES. CAPES MADE OF FLESH. SKULLS FOR CROWNS.
WE WILL CALL YOUR BONES HOME.
I'M SENDING YOU TO A SPECIAL PLACE NOW. YOUR NEW HOME.

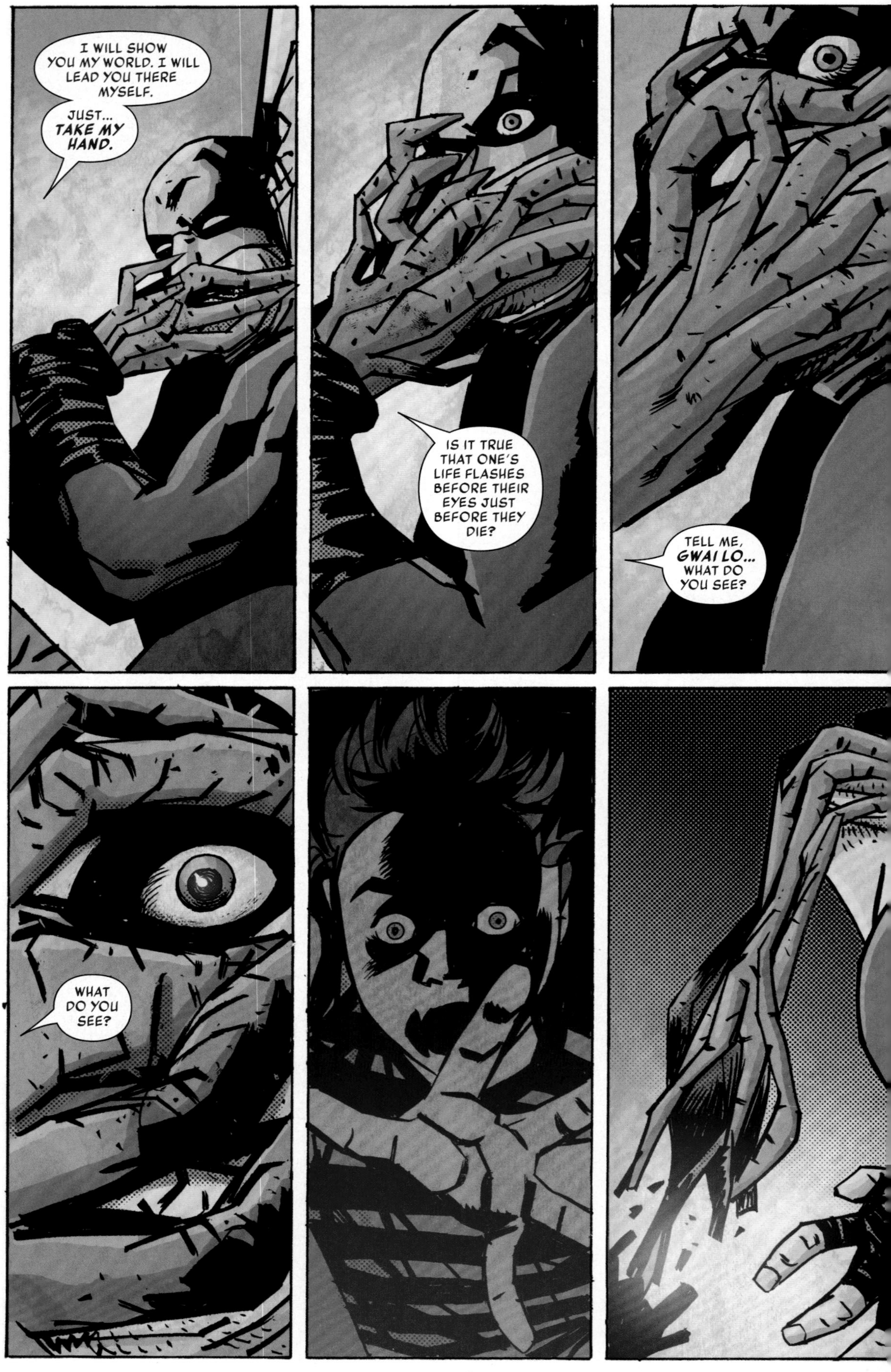

I WILL SHOW YOU MY WORLD. I WILL LEAD YOU THERE MYSELF.
JUST... TAKE MY HAND.
IS IT TRUE THAT ONE'S LIFE FLASHES BEFORE THEIR EYES JUST BEFORE THEY DIE?
TELL ME, GWAI LO... WHAT DO YOU SEE?
WHAT DO YOU SEE?

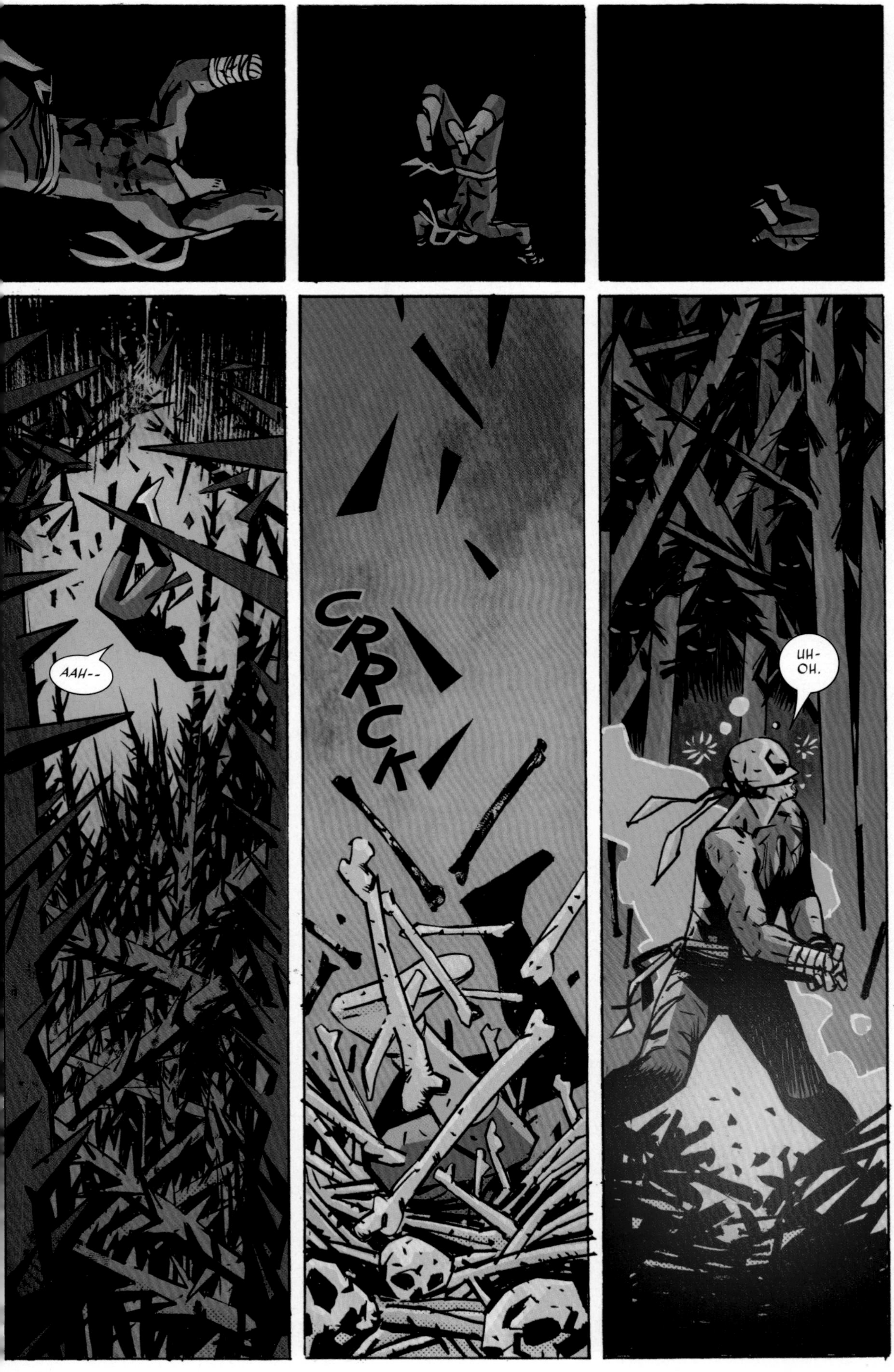
AAH--
CRRCK
UH-
OH.

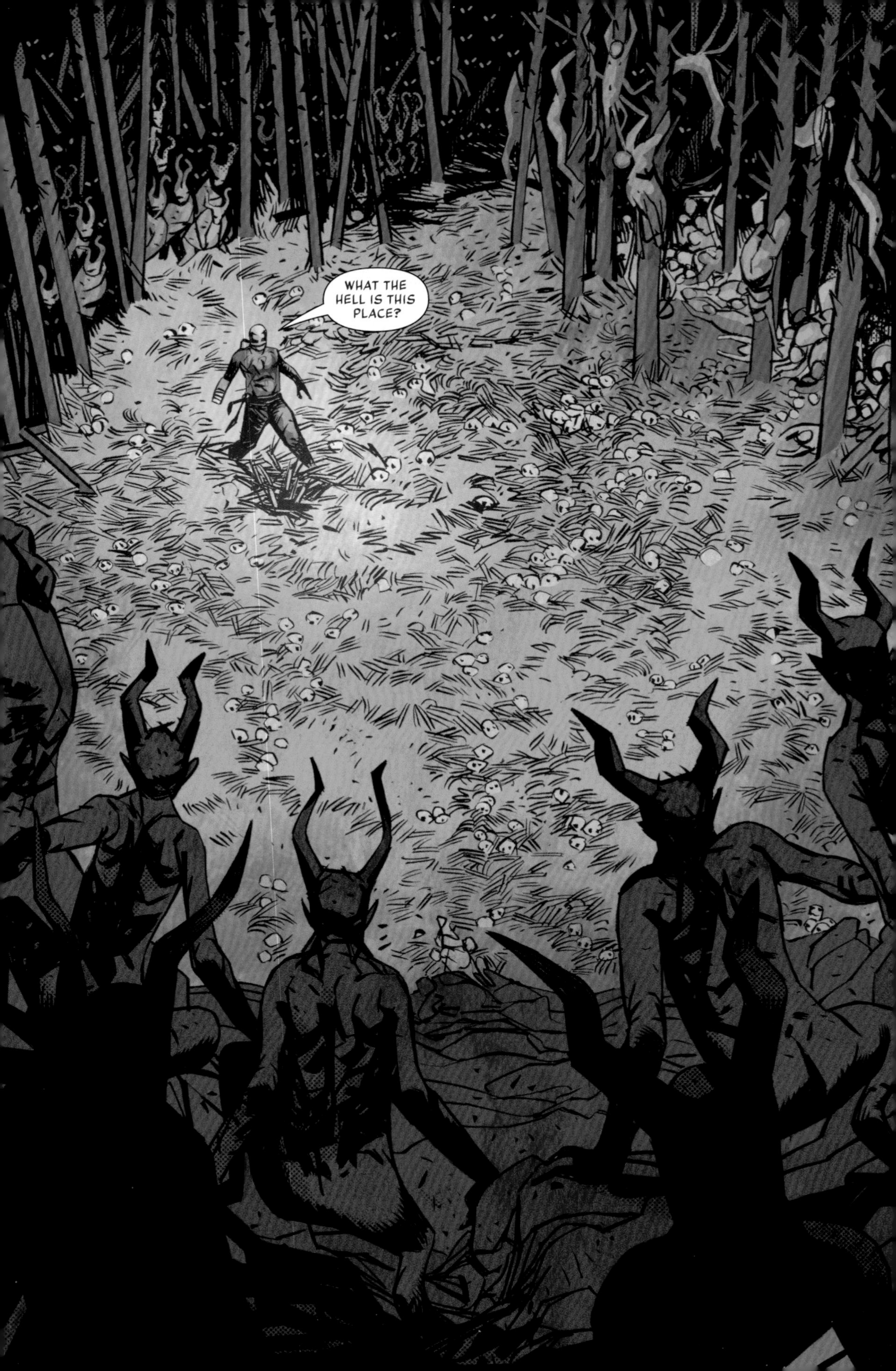
WHAT THE HELL IS THIS PLACE?

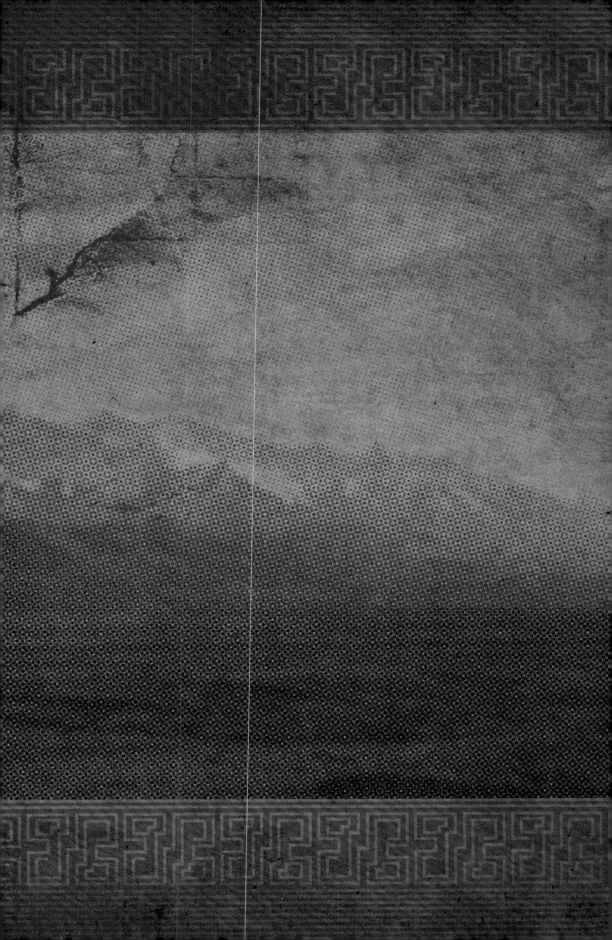

PHANTOM LIMB

CHAPTER 4

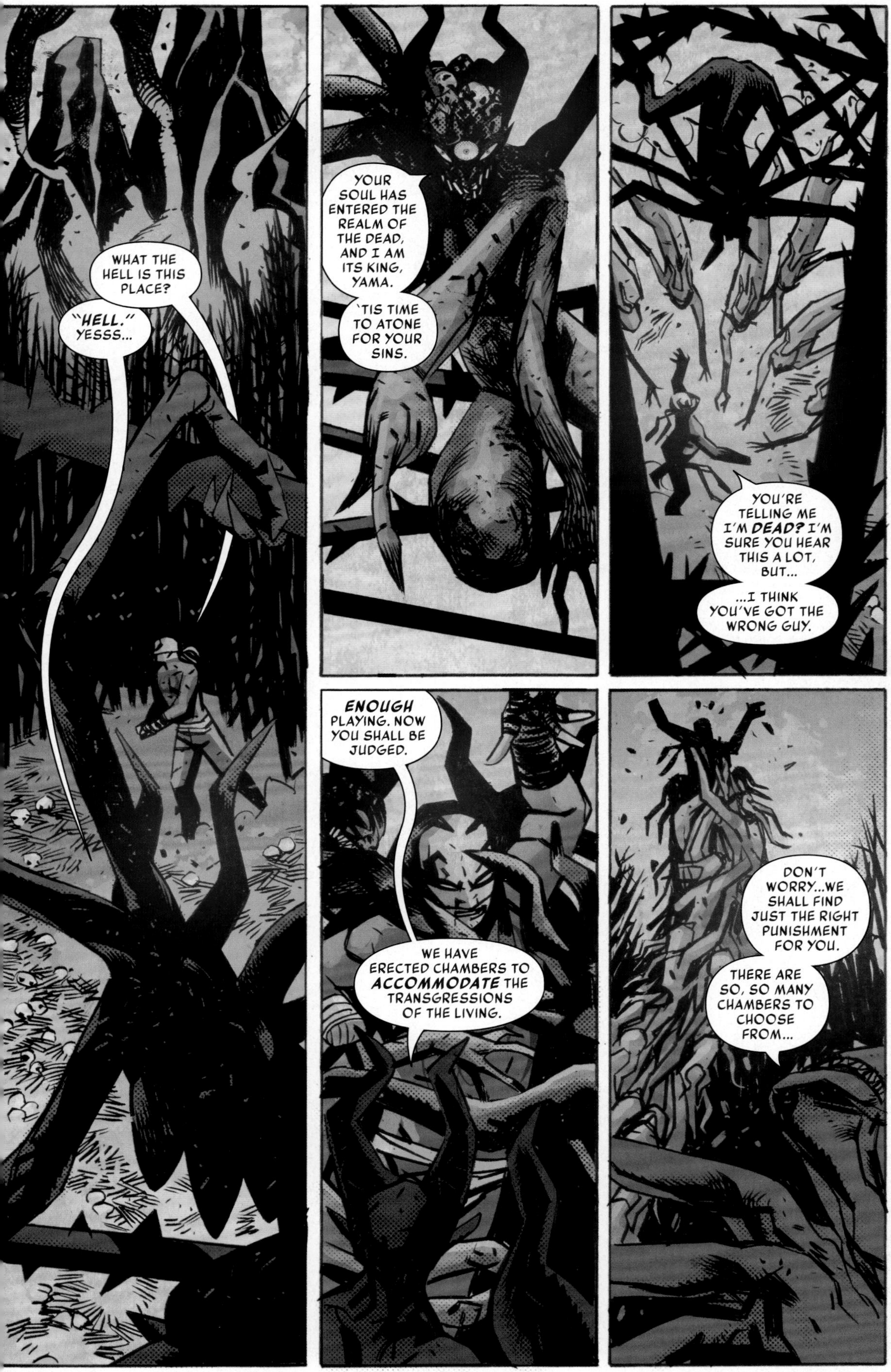
WHAT THE HELL IS THIS PLACE?
"HELL." YESSS...
YOUR SOUL HAS ENTERED THE REALM OF THE DEAD, AND I AM ITS KING, YAMA.
'TIS TIME TO ATONE FOR YOUR SINS.
YOU'RE TELLING ME I'M DEAD? I'M SURE YOU HEAR THIS A LOT, BUT...
...I THINK YOU'VE GOT THE WRONG GUY.
ENOUGH PLAYING. NOW YOU SHALL BE JUDGED.
WE HAVE ERECTED CHAMBERS TO ACCOMMODATE THE TRANSGRESSIONS OF THE LIVING.
DON'T WORRY...WE SHALL FIND JUST THE RIGHT PUNISHMENT FOR YOU.
THERE ARE SO, SO MANY CHAMBERS TO CHOOSE FROM...

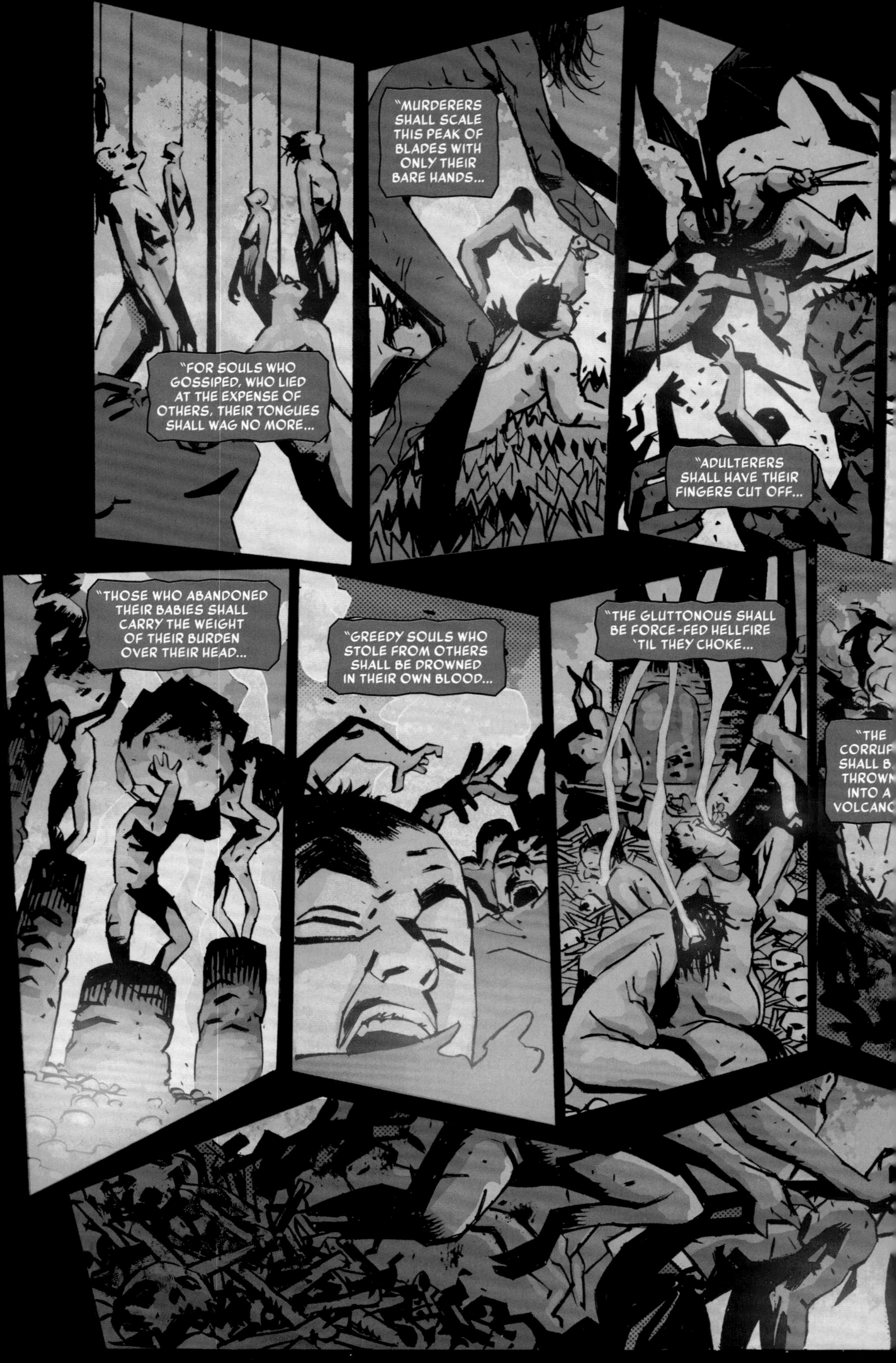
"FOR SOULS WHO GOSSIPED, WHO LIED AT THE EXPENSE OF OTHERS, THEIR TONGUES SHALL WAG NO MORE...
"MURDERERS SHALL SCALE THIS PEAK OF BLADES WITH ONLY THEIR BARE HANDS...
"ADULTERERS SHALL HAVE THEIR FINGERS CUT OFF...
"THOSE WHO ABANDONED THEIR BABIES SHALL CARRY THE WEIGHT OF THEIR BURDEN OVER THEIR HEAD...
"GREEDY SOULS WHO STOLE FROM OTHERS SHALL BE DROWNED IN THEIR OWN BLOOD...
"THE GLUTTONOUS SHALL BE FORCE-FED HELLFIRE 'TIL THEY CHOKE...
"THE CORRUP SHALL B THROWN INTO A VOLCANC

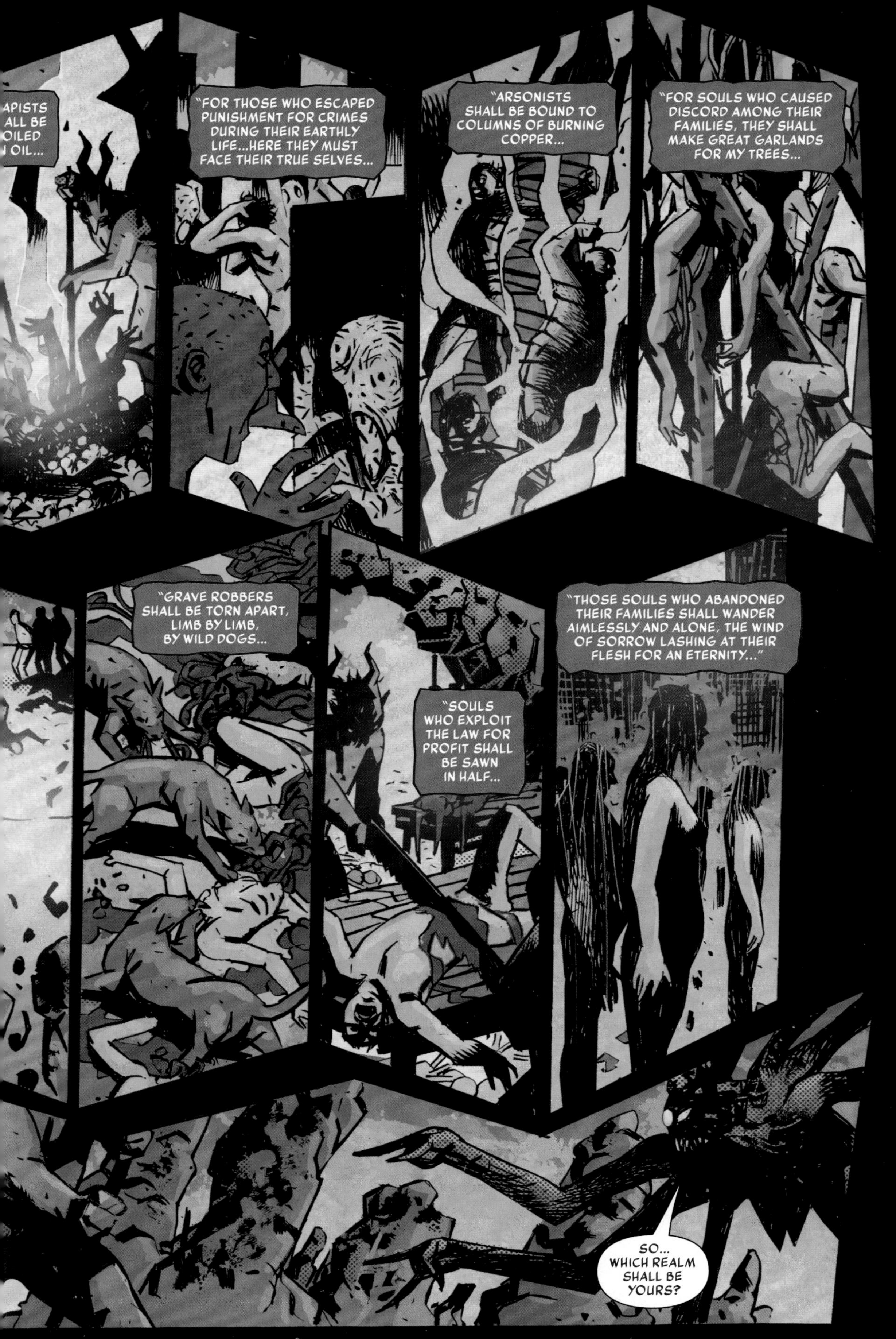

APISTS ALL BE OILED N OIL...
"FOR THOSE WHO ESCAPED PUNISHMENT FOR CRIMES DURING THEIR EARTHLY LIFE...HERE THEY MUST FACE THEIR TRUE SELVES...
"ARSONISTS SHALL BE BOUND TO COLUMNS OF BURNING COPPER...
"FOR SOULS WHO CAUSED DISCORD AMONG THEIR FAMILIES, THEY SHALL MAKE GREAT GARLANDS FOR MY TREES...
"GRAVE ROBBERS SHALL BE TORN APART, LIMB BY LIMB, BY WILD DOGS...
"SOULS WHO EXPLOIT THE LAW FOR PROFIT SHALL BE SAWN IN HALF...
"THOSE SOULS WHO ABANDONED THEIR FAMILIES SHALL WANDER AIMLESSLY AND ALONE, THE WIND OF SORROW LASHING AT THEIR FLESH FOR AN ETERNITY..."
SO... WHICH REALM SHALL BE YOURS?

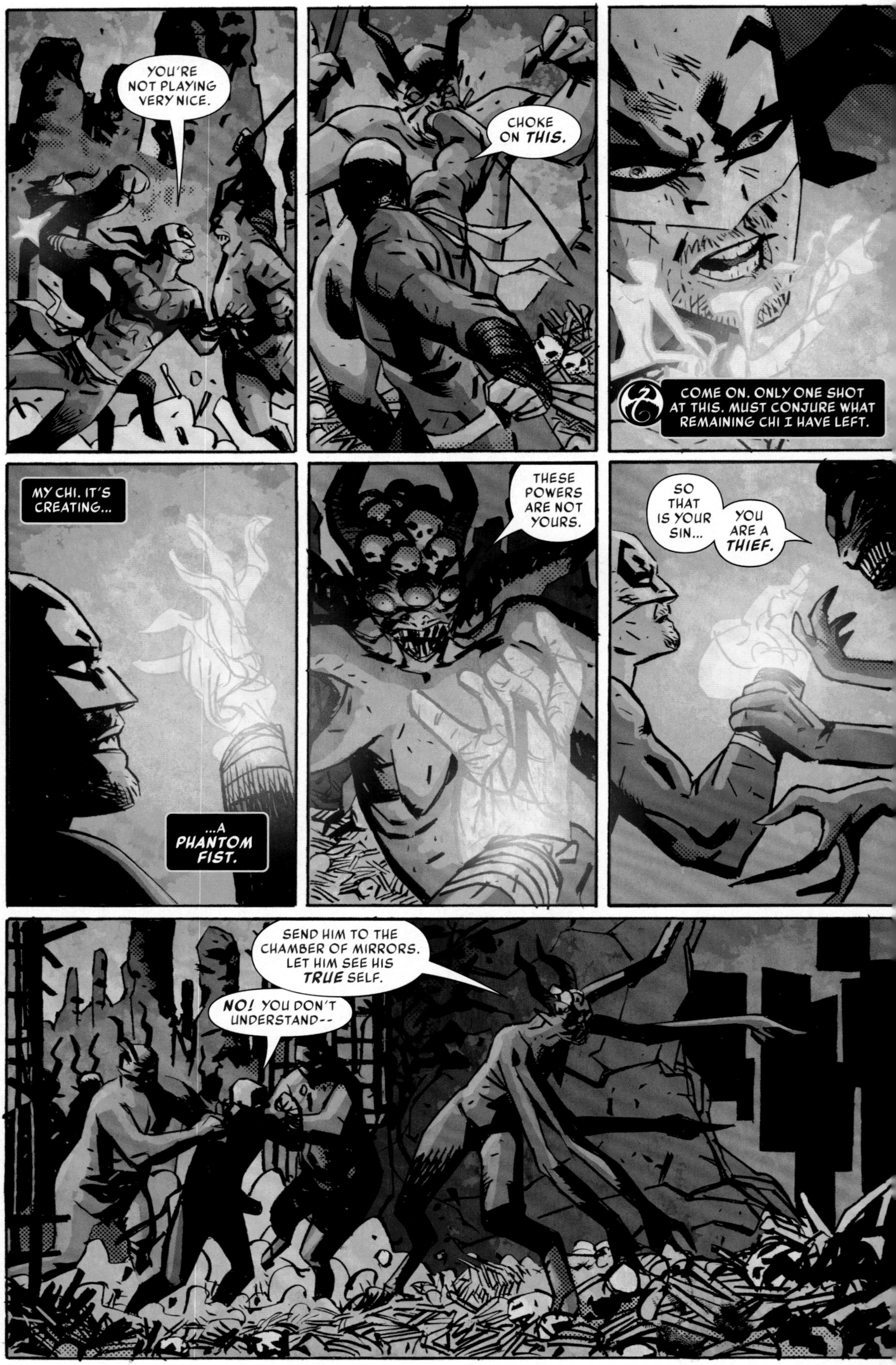
YOU'RE NOT PLAYING VERY NICE.
CHOKE ON THIS.
COME ON. ONLY ONE SHOT AT THIS. MUST CONJURE WHAT REMAINING CHI I HAVE LEFT.
MY CHI. IT'S CREATING...
...A PHANTOM FIST.
THESE POWERS ARE NOT YOURS.
SO THAT IS YOUR SIN...
YOU ARE A THIEF.
SEND HIM TO THE CHAMBER OF MIRRORS. LET HIM SEE HIS TRUE SELF.
NO! YOU DON'T UNDERSTAND--

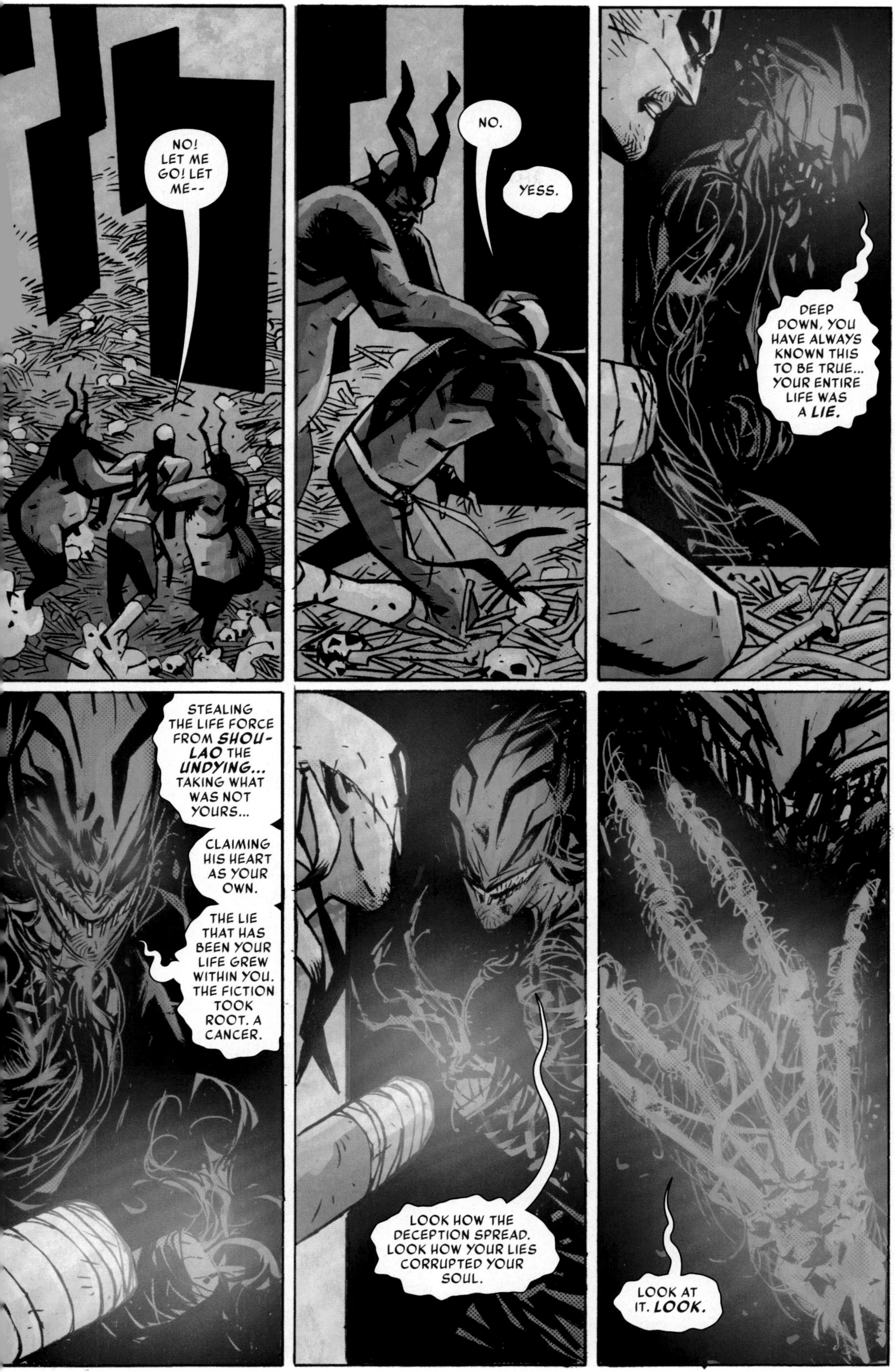
NO! LET ME GO! LET ME--
NO.
YESS.
DEEP DOWN, YOU HAVE ALWAYS KNOWN THIS TO BE TRUE... YOUR ENTIRE LIFE WAS A LIE.
STEALING THE LIFE FORCE FROM SHOU-LAO THE UNDYING... TAKING WHAT WAS NOT YOURS...
CLAIMING HIS HEART AS YOUR OWN.
THE LIE THAT HAS BEEN YOUR LIFE GREW WITHIN YOU. THE FICTION TOOK ROOT. A CANCER.
LOOK HOW THE DECEPTION SPREAD. LOOK HOW YOUR LIES CORRUPTED YOUR SOUL.
LOOK AT IT. LOOK.

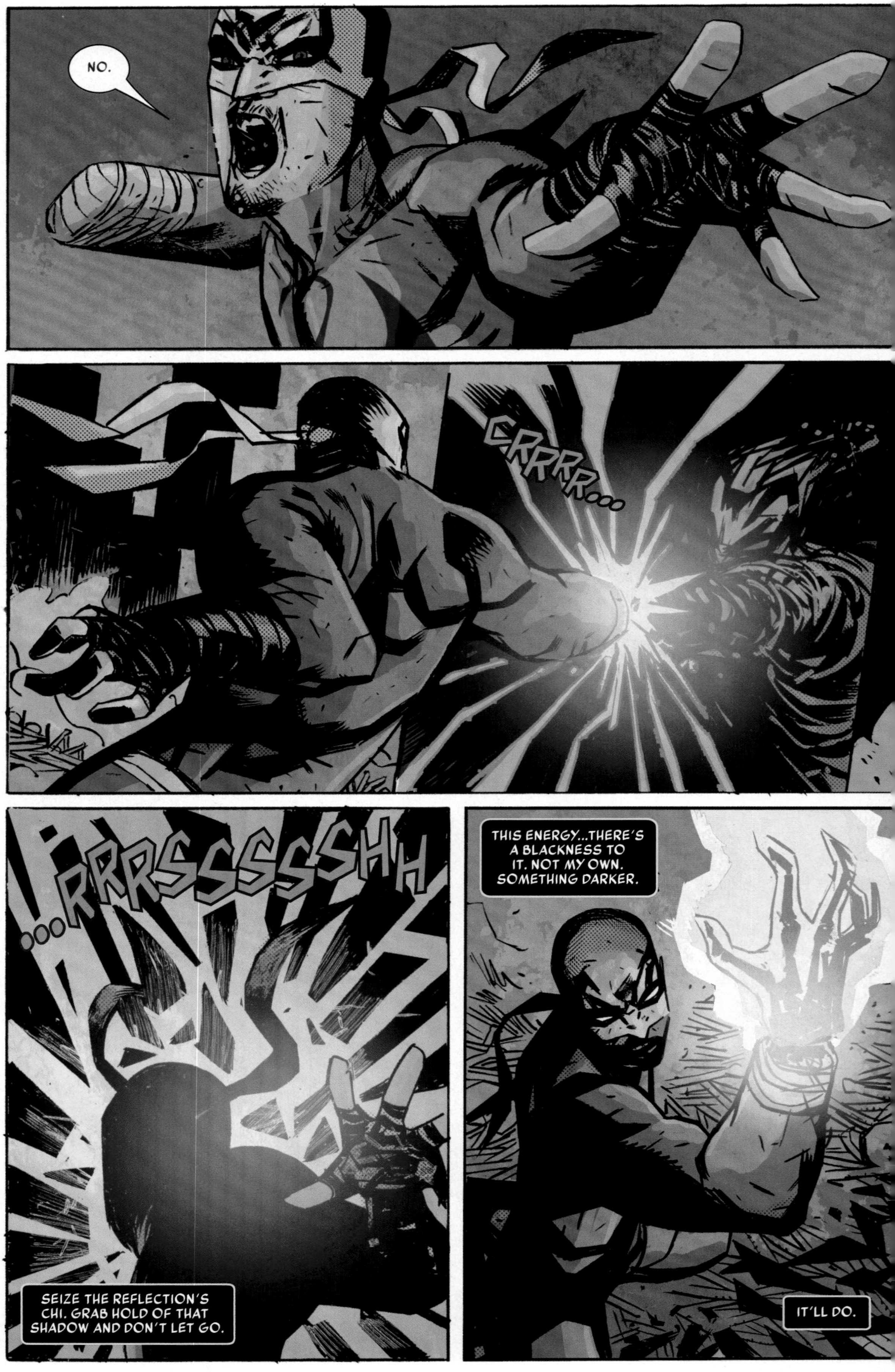

NO.
CRRRR...
...RRRSSSSSHH
SEIZE THE REFLECTION'S CHI. GRAB HOLD OF THAT SHADOW AND DON'T LET GO.
THIS ENERGY...THERE'S A BLACKNESS TO IT. NOT MY OWN. SOMETHING DARKER.
IT'LL DO.

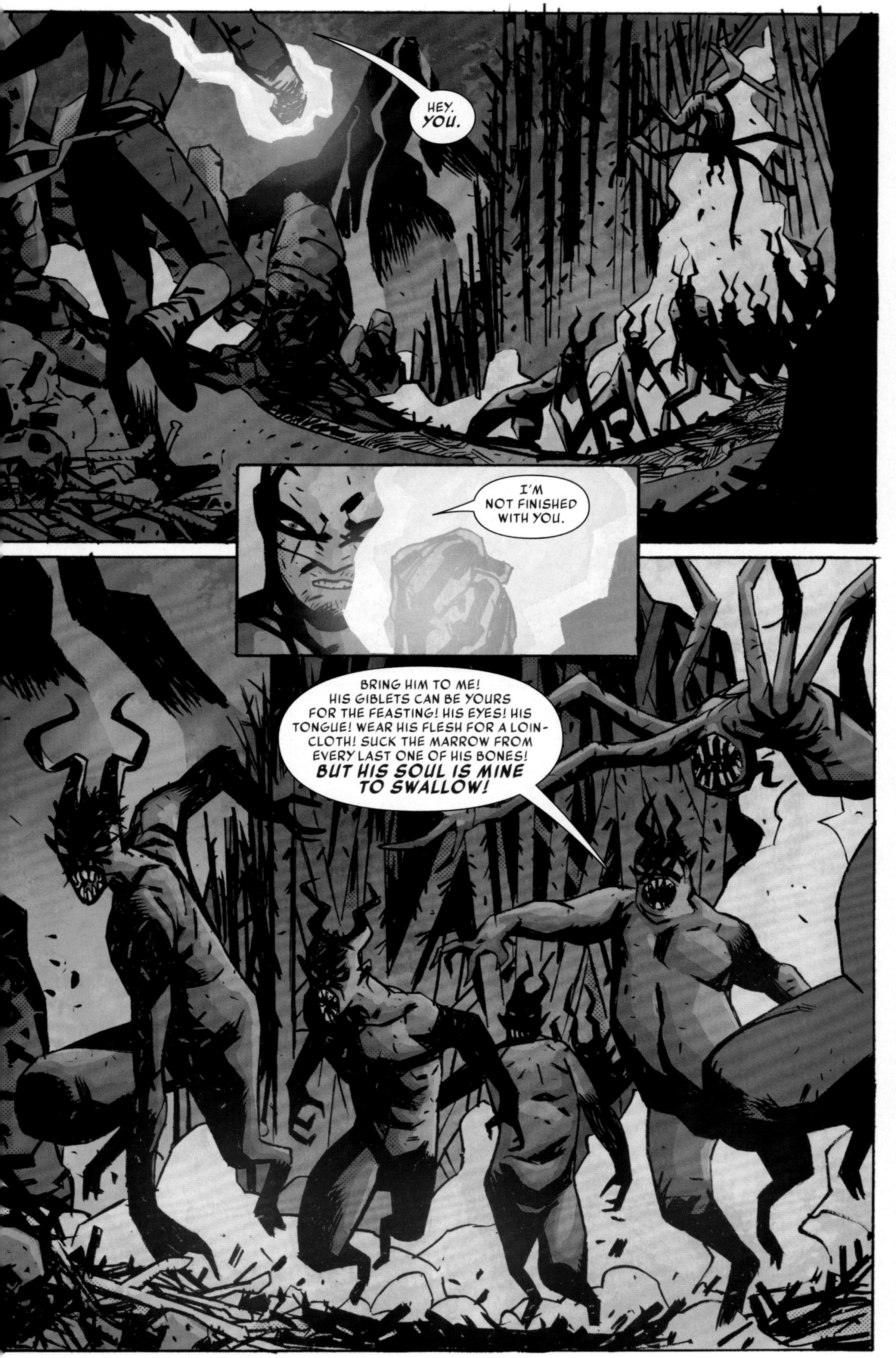
HEY. YOU.
I'M NOT FINISHED WITH YOU.
BRING HIM TO ME! HIS GIBLETS CAN BE YOURS FOR THE FEASTING! HIS EYES! HIS TONGUE! WEAR HIS FLESH FOR A LOIN-CLOTH! SUCK THE MARROW FROM EVERY LAST ONE OF HIS BONES! BUT HIS SOUL IS MINE TO SWALLOW!

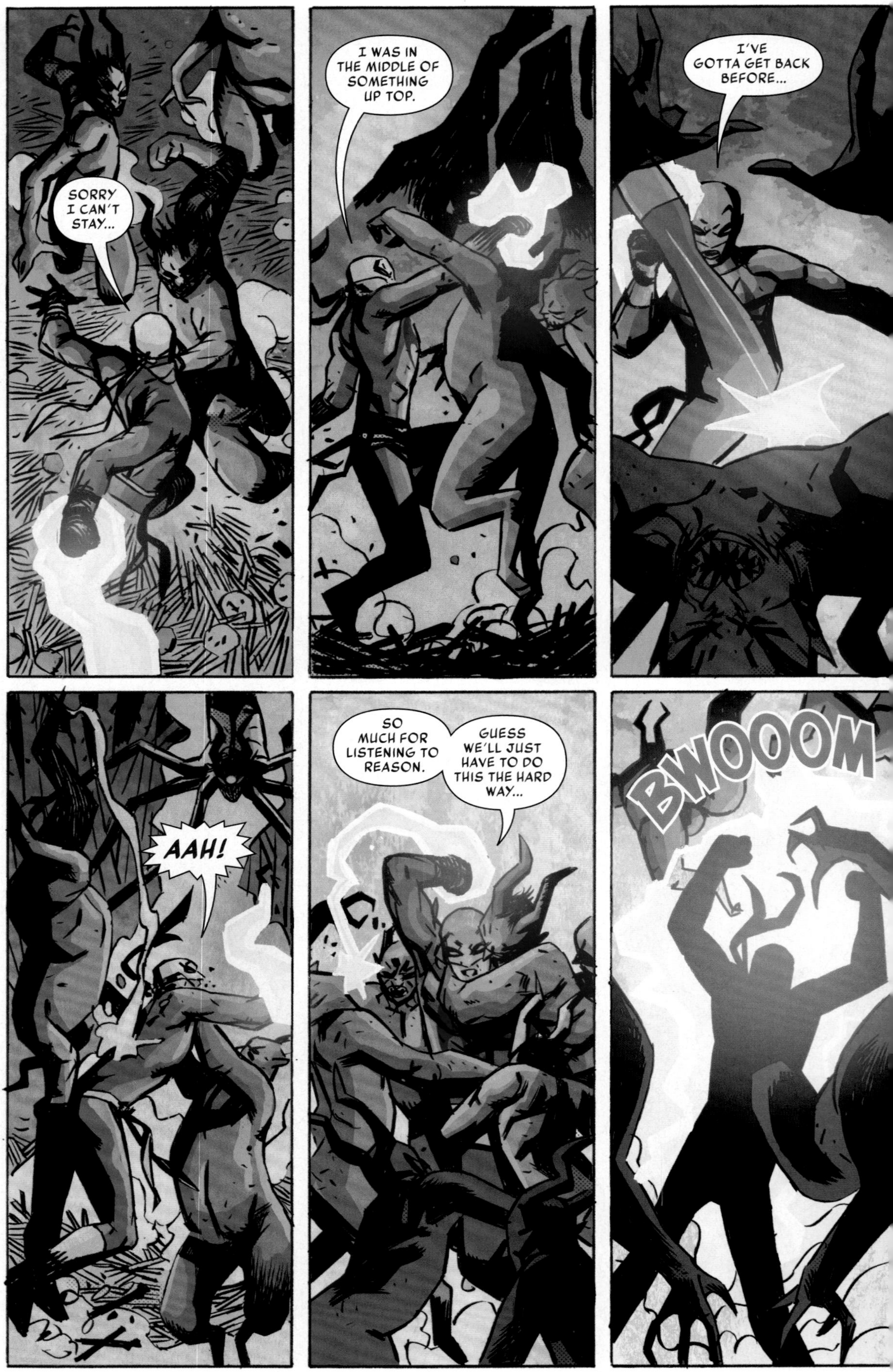
SORRY I CAN'T STAY...
I WAS IN THE MIDDLE OF SOMETHING UP TOP.
I'VE GOTTA GET BACK BEFORE...
AAH!
SO MUCH FOR LISTENING TO REASON.
GUESS WE'LL JUST HAVE TO DO THIS THE HARD WAY...
BWOOOM

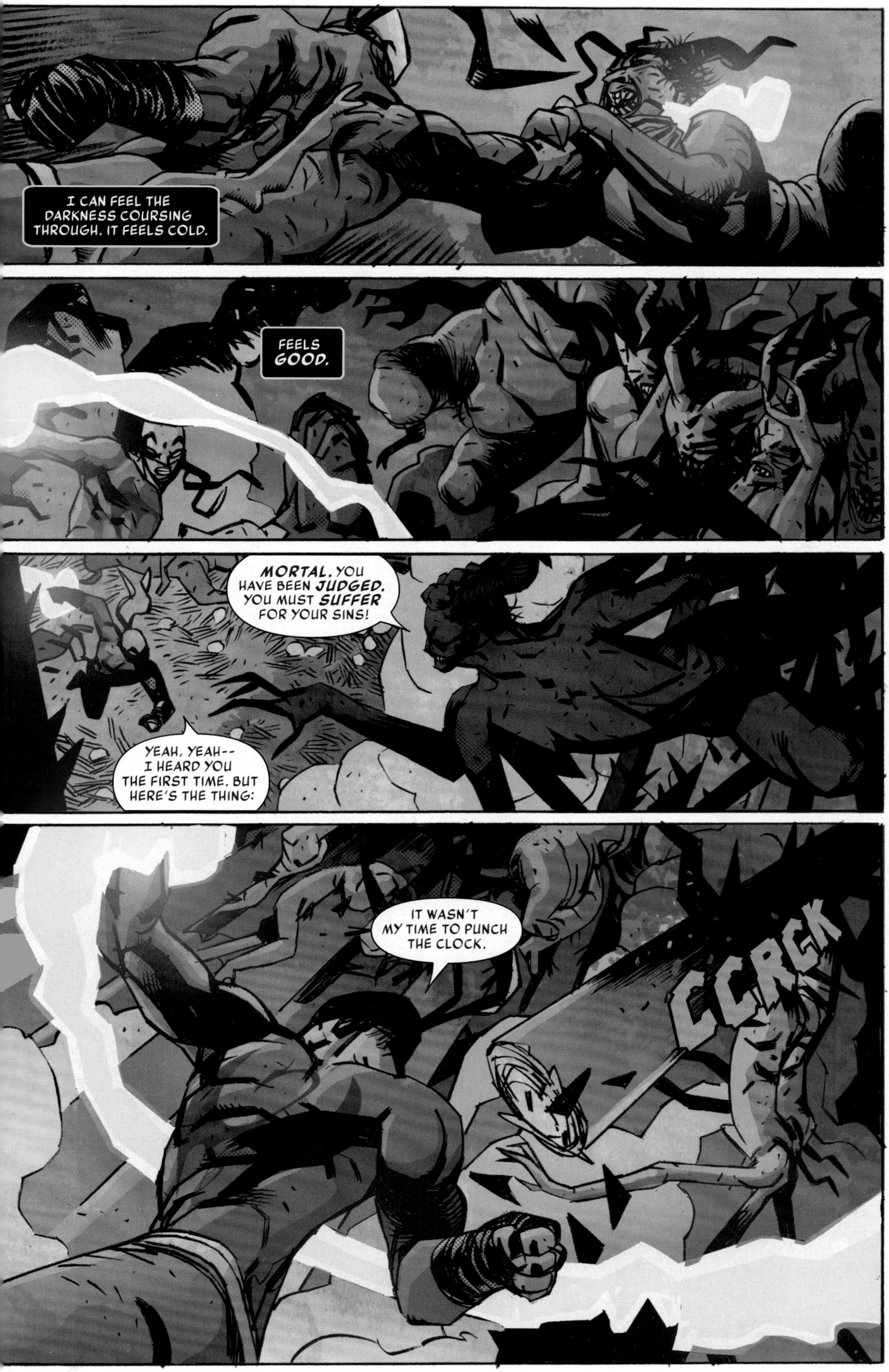
I CAN FEEL THE DARKNESS COURSING THROUGH. IT FEELS COLD.
FEELS *GOOD.*
MORTAL. YOU HAVE BEEN *JUDGED.* YOU MUST *SUFFER* FOR YOUR SINS!
YEAH, YEAH-- I HEARD YOU THE FIRST TIME. BUT HERE'S THE THING:
IT WASN'T MY TIME TO PUNCH THE CLOCK.
CCRGK

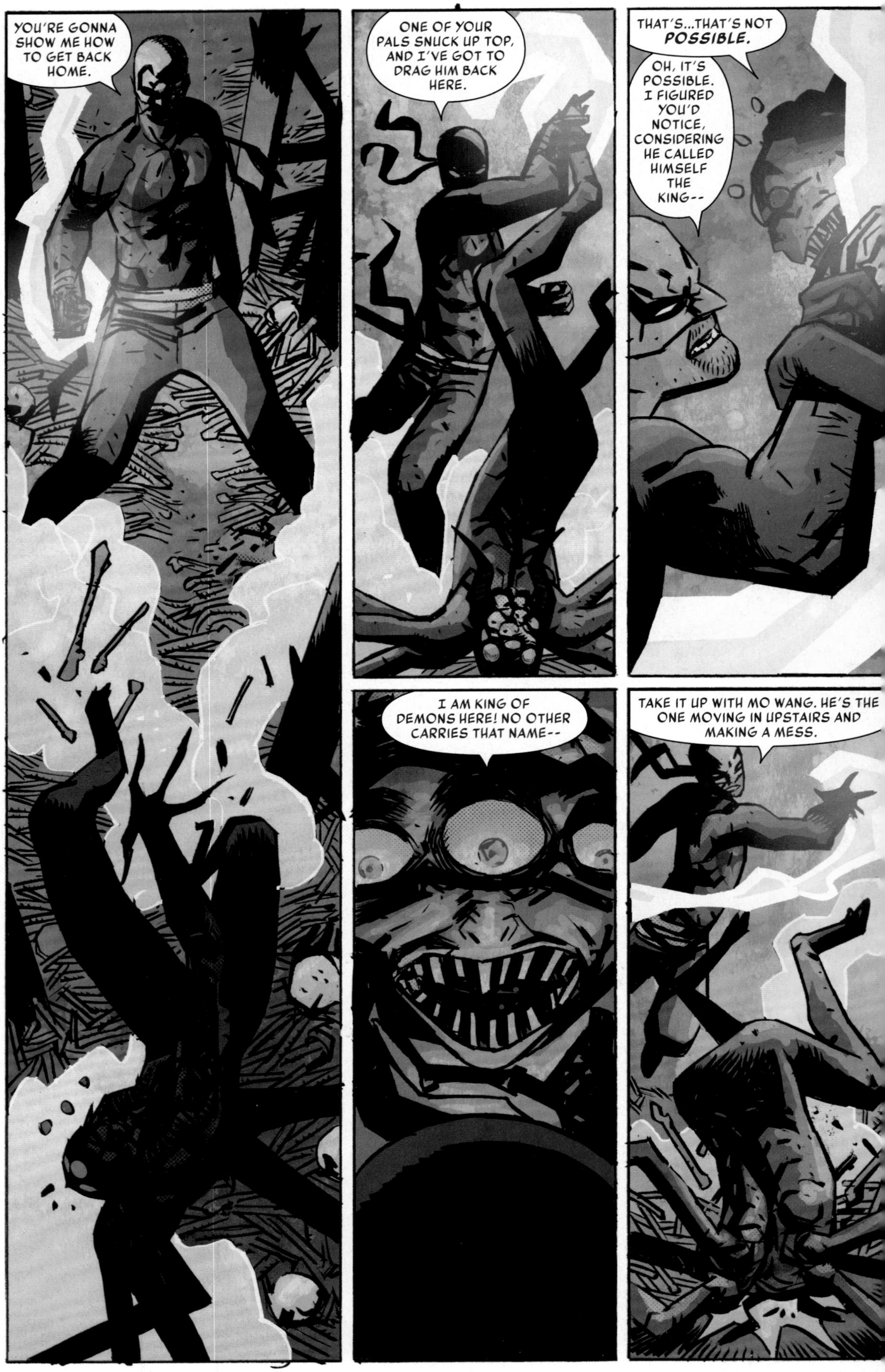
YOU'RE GONNA SHOW ME HOW TO GET BACK HOME.
ONE OF YOUR PALS SNUCK UP TOP, AND I'VE GOT TO DRAG HIM BACK HERE.
THAT'S...THAT'S NOT POSSIBLE.
OH, IT'S POSSIBLE. I FIGURED YOU'D NOTICE, CONSIDERING HE CALLED HIMSELF THE KING--
I AM KING OF DEMONS HERE! NO OTHER CARRIES THAT NAME--
TAKE IT UP WITH MO WANG. HE'S THE ONE MOVING IN UPSTAIRS AND MAKING A MESS.

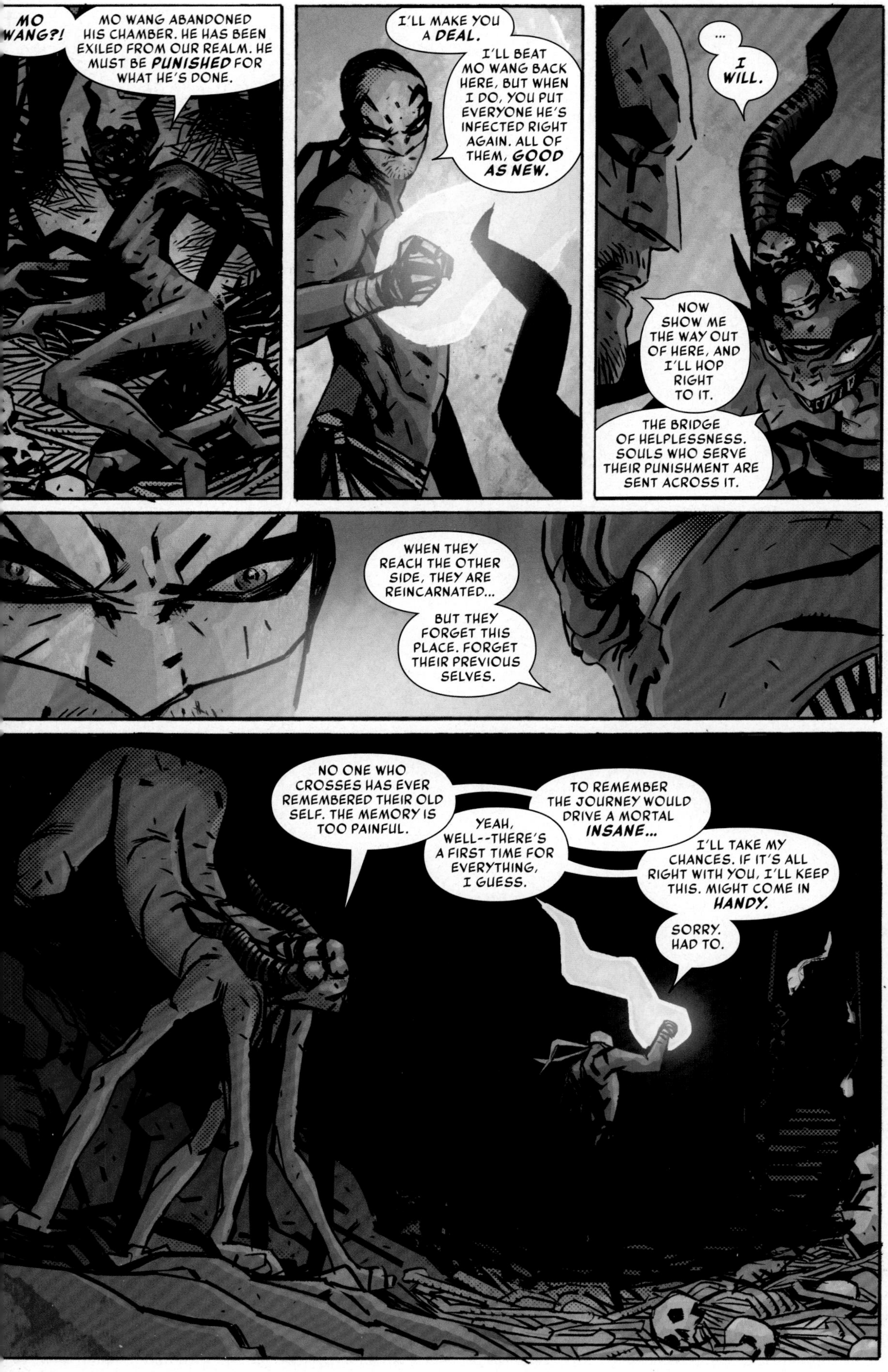
MO WANG?!
MO WANG ABANDONED HIS CHAMBER. HE HAS BEEN EXILED FROM OUR REALM. HE MUST BE PUNISHED FOR WHAT HE'S DONE.
I'LL MAKE YOU A DEAL.
I'LL BEAT MO WANG BACK HERE, BUT WHEN I DO, YOU PUT EVERYONE HE'S INFECTED RIGHT AGAIN. ALL OF THEM, GOOD AS NEW.
...
I WILL.
NOW SHOW ME THE WAY OUT OF HERE, AND I'LL HOP RIGHT TO IT.
THE BRIDGE OF HELPLESSNESS. SOULS WHO SERVE THEIR PUNISHMENT ARE SENT ACROSS IT.
WHEN THEY REACH THE OTHER SIDE, THEY ARE REINCARNATED...
BUT THEY FORGET THIS PLACE. FORGET THEIR PREVIOUS SELVES.
NO ONE WHO CROSSES HAS EVER REMEMBERED THEIR OLD SELF. THE MEMORY IS TOO PAINFUL.
TO REMEMBER THE JOURNEY WOULD DRIVE A MORTAL INSANE...
YEAH, WELL--THERE'S A FIRST TIME FOR EVERYTHING, I GUESS.
I'LL TAKE MY CHANCES. IF IT'S ALL RIGHT WITH YOU, I'LL KEEP THIS. MIGHT COME IN HANDY.
SORRY. HAD TO.

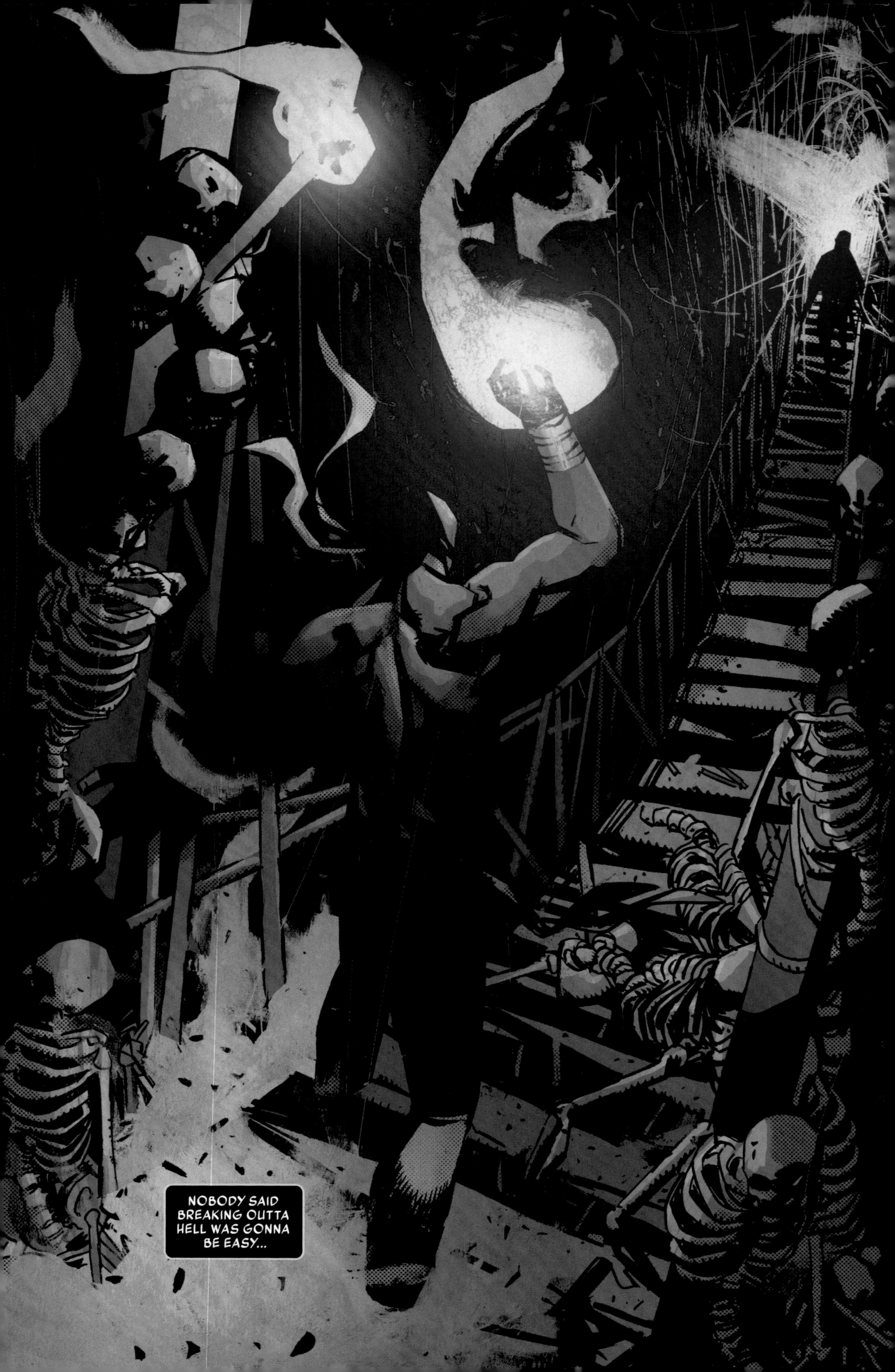
NOBODY SAID
BREAKING OUTTA
HELL WAS GONNA
BE EASY...

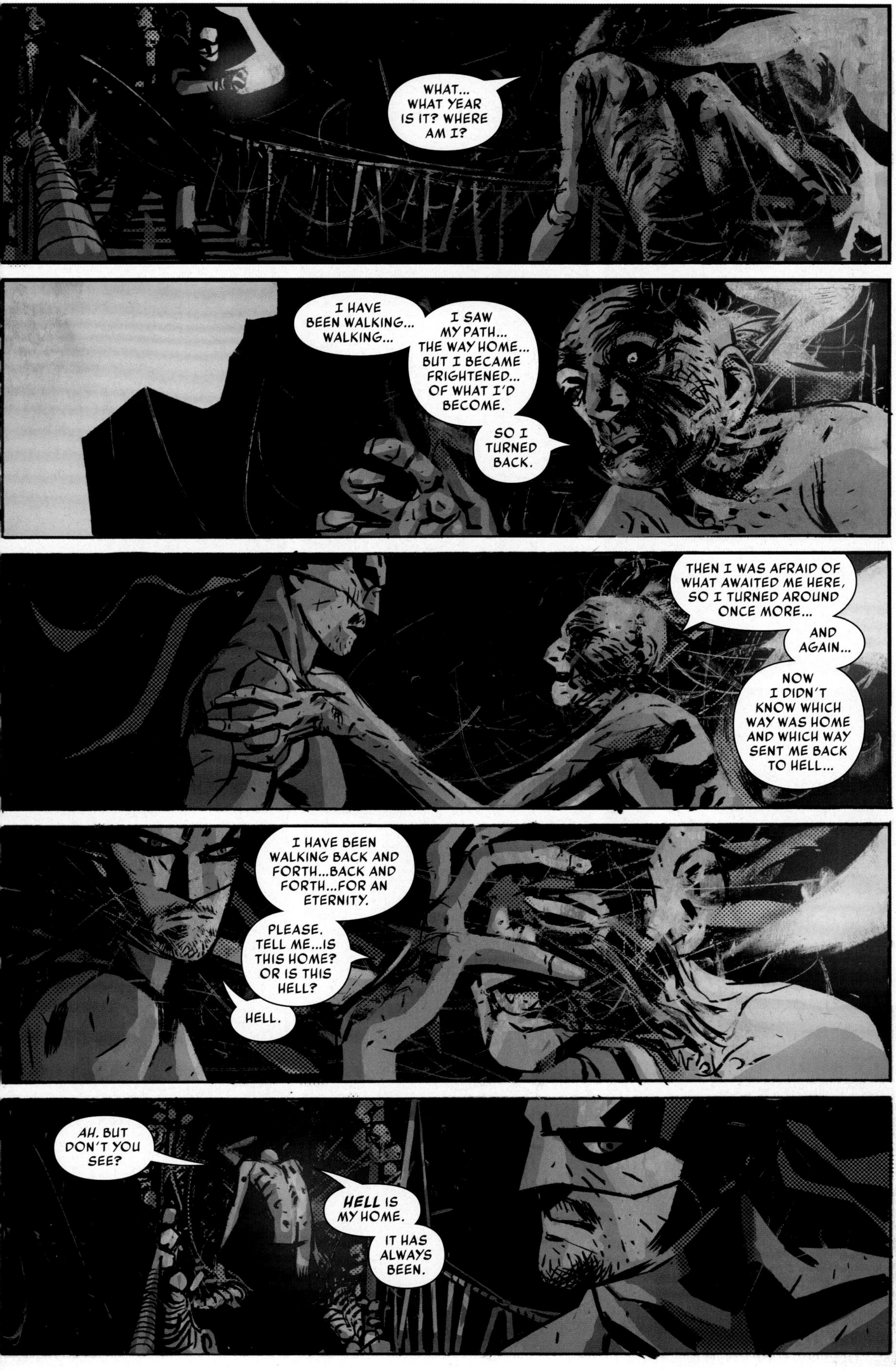
WHAT... WHAT YEAR IS IT? WHERE AM I?
I HAVE BEEN WALKING... WALKING...
I SAW MY PATH... THE WAY HOME... BUT I BECAME FRIGHTENED... OF WHAT I'D BECOME.
SO I TURNED BACK.
THEN I WAS AFRAID OF WHAT AWAITED ME HERE, SO I TURNED AROUND ONCE MORE...
AND AGAIN...
NOW I DIDN'T KNOW WHICH WAY WAS HOME AND WHICH WAY SENT ME BACK TO HELL...
I HAVE BEEN WALKING BACK AND FORTH...BACK AND FORTH...FOR AN ETERNITY.
PLEASE. TELL ME...IS THIS HOME? OR IS THIS HELL?
HELL.
AH. BUT DON'T YOU SEE?
HELL IS MY HOME.
IT HAS ALWAYS BEEN.

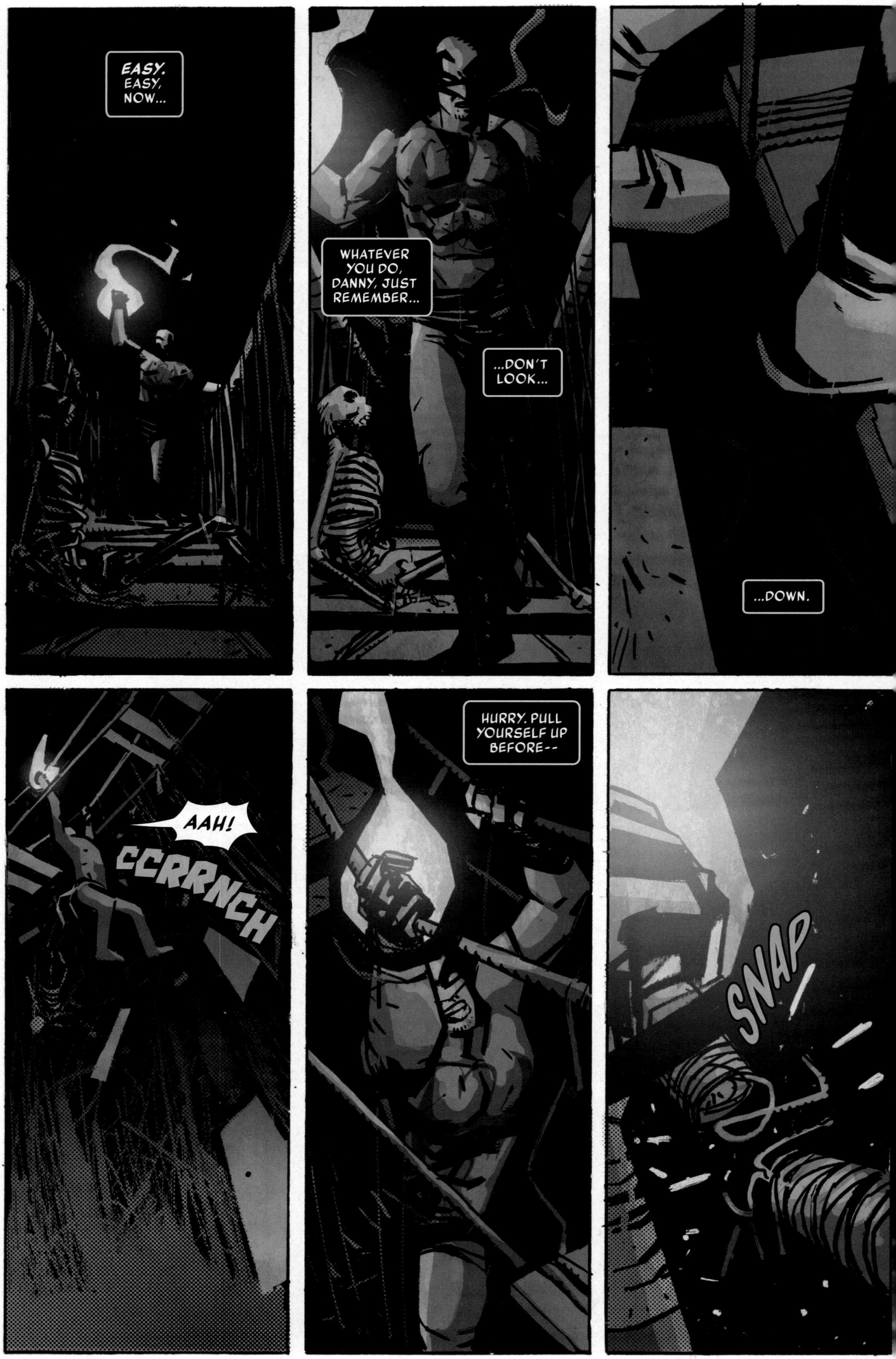
EASY. EASY, NOW...
WHATEVER YOU DO, DANNY, JUST REMEMBER...
...DON'T LOOK...
...DOWN.
AAH!
CCRRNCH
HURRY. PULL YOURSELF UP BEFORE--
SNAP

EERRR...

AAH...

ALMOST THERE. ALMOST...

CCRCK

FEELS LIKE I FALL FOR AN ETERNITY.

MAYBE I DO.

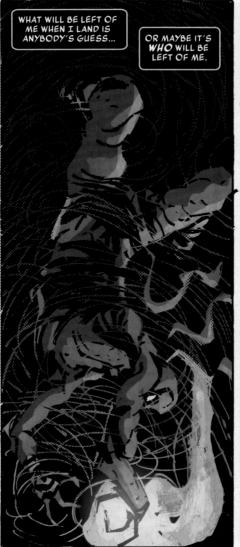

WHAT WILL BE LEFT OF ME WHEN I LAND IS ANYBODY'S GUESS...

OR MAYBE IT'S WHO WILL BE LEFT OF ME.

CAN'T TELL WHICH WAY IS UP ANYMORE. IF I'M FALLING OR FLYING. CAN'T TELL IF I...

...IF I...CAN'T TELL...IF...

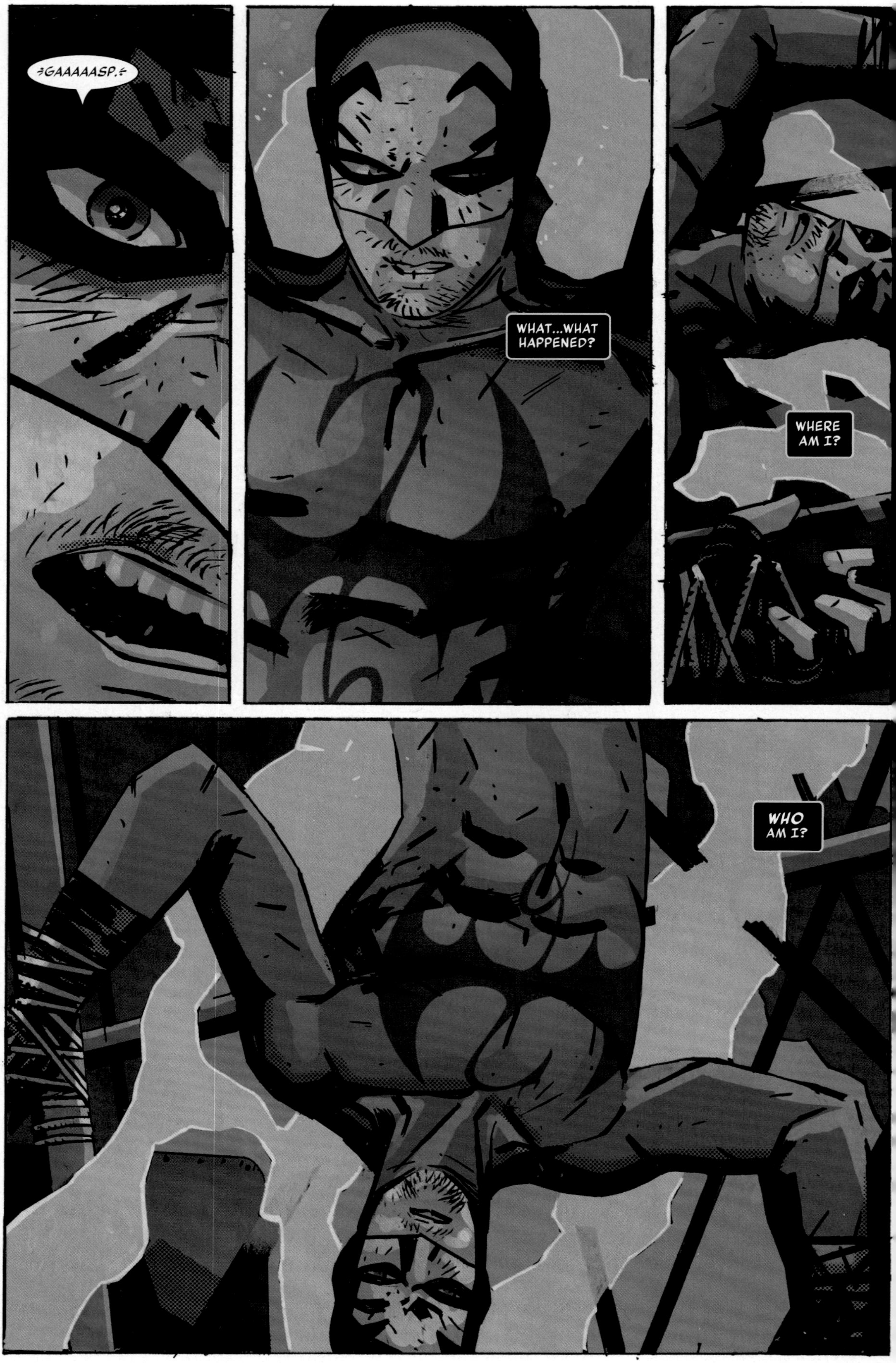

GAAAAASP.
WHAT...WHAT HAPPENED?
WHERE AM I?
WHO AM I?

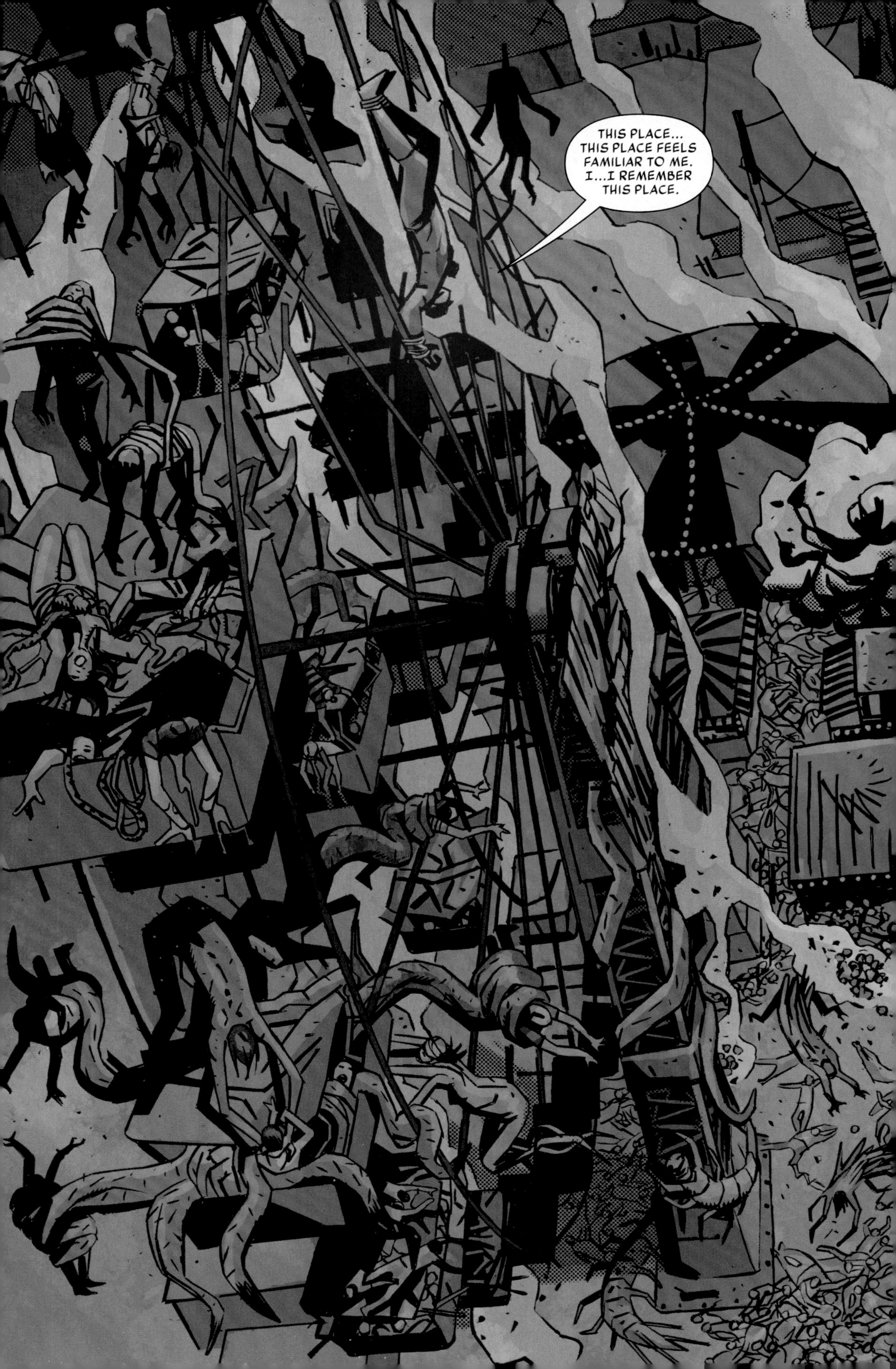
THIS PLACE...
THIS PLACE FEELS
FAMILIAR TO ME.
I...I REMEMBER
THIS PLACE.

I HOPED YOU WOULD. I PICKED IT JUST FOR YOU...

I NEEDED A THRONE.

AND YOU AND I HAD SUCH *FOND* MEMORIES OF THIS PLACE...

I GOTTA SAY...I REALLY DON'T DIG THE REDECORATING.

I SENT YOU TO HELL. HOW DID YOU GET BACK?

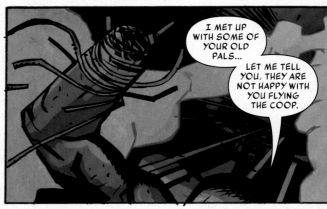

I MET UP WITH SOME OF YOUR OLD PALS...

LET ME TELL YOU, THEY ARE NOT HAPPY WITH YOU FLYING THE COOP.

FOOLS. THEY WERE CONTENT TO SPEND ETERNITY BELOW! WHILE HERE...

HERE I CAN CREATE A KINGDOM ALL FOR MYSELF.

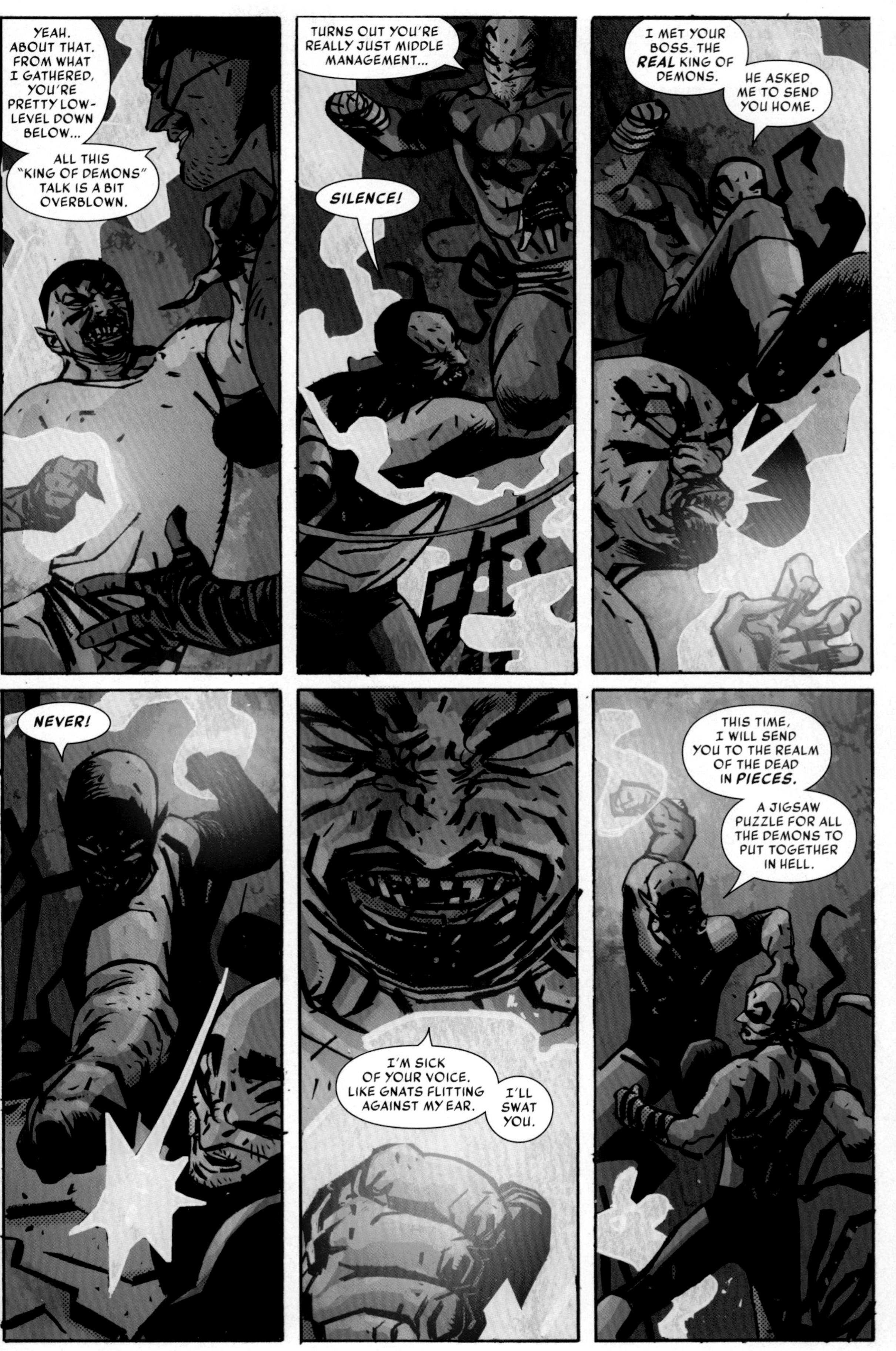
YEAH. ABOUT THAT. FROM WHAT I GATHERED, YOU'RE PRETTY LOW-LEVEL DOWN BELOW...
ALL THIS "KING OF DEMONS" TALK IS A BIT OVERBLOWN.
TURNS OUT YOU'RE REALLY JUST MIDDLE MANAGEMENT...
SILENCE!
I MET YOUR BOSS. THE REAL KING OF DEMONS.
HE ASKED ME TO SEND YOU HOME.
NEVER!
I'M SICK OF YOUR VOICE. LIKE GNATS FLITTING AGAINST MY EAR.
I'LL SWAT YOU.
THIS TIME, I WILL SEND YOU TO THE REALM OF THE DEAD IN PIECES.
A JIGSAW PUZZLE FOR ALL THE DEMONS TO PUT TOGETHER IN HELL.

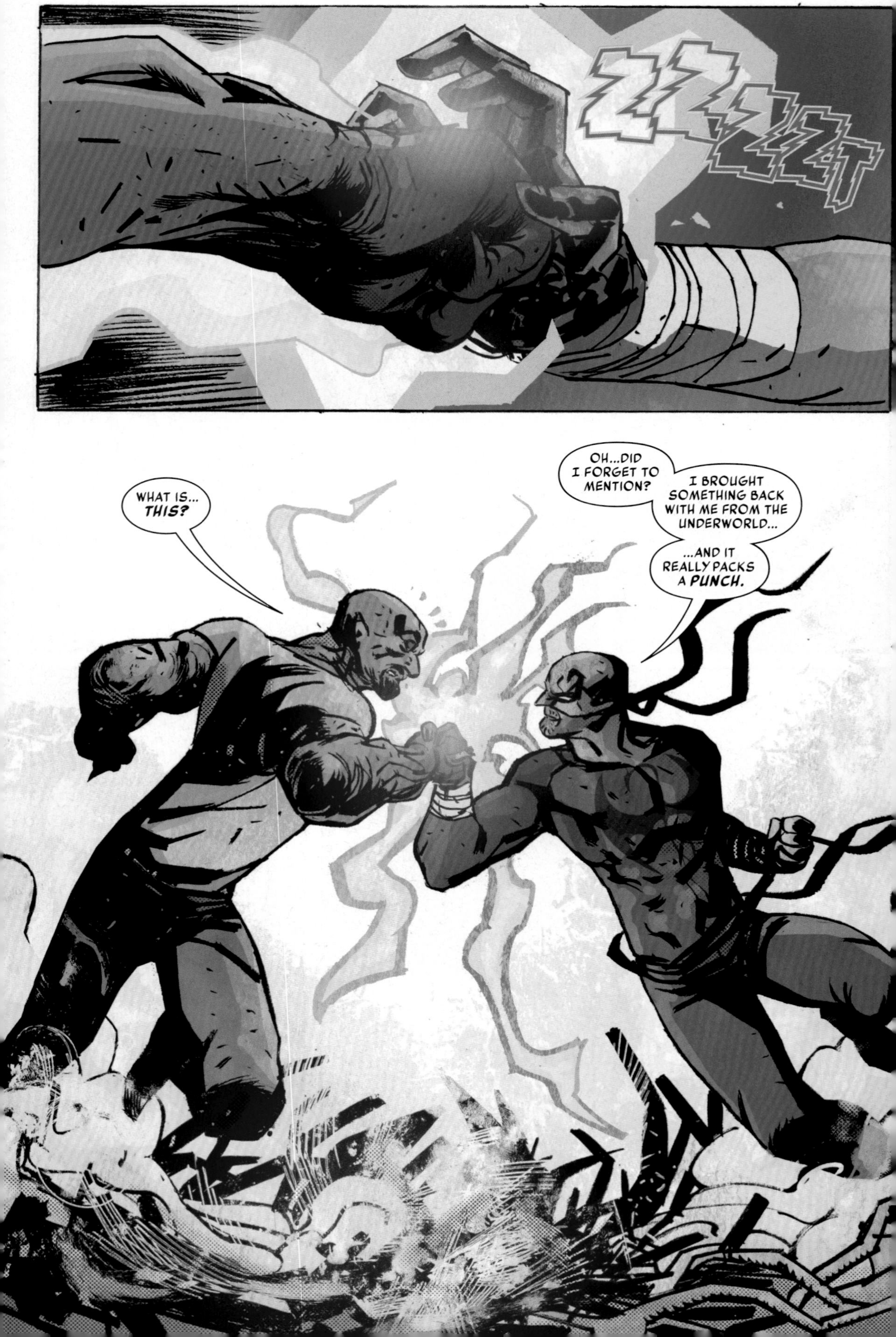
WHAT IS... THIS?
OH...DID I FORGET TO MENTION?
I BROUGHT SOMETHING BACK WITH ME FROM THE UNDERWORLD...
...AND IT REALLY PACKS A PUNCH.

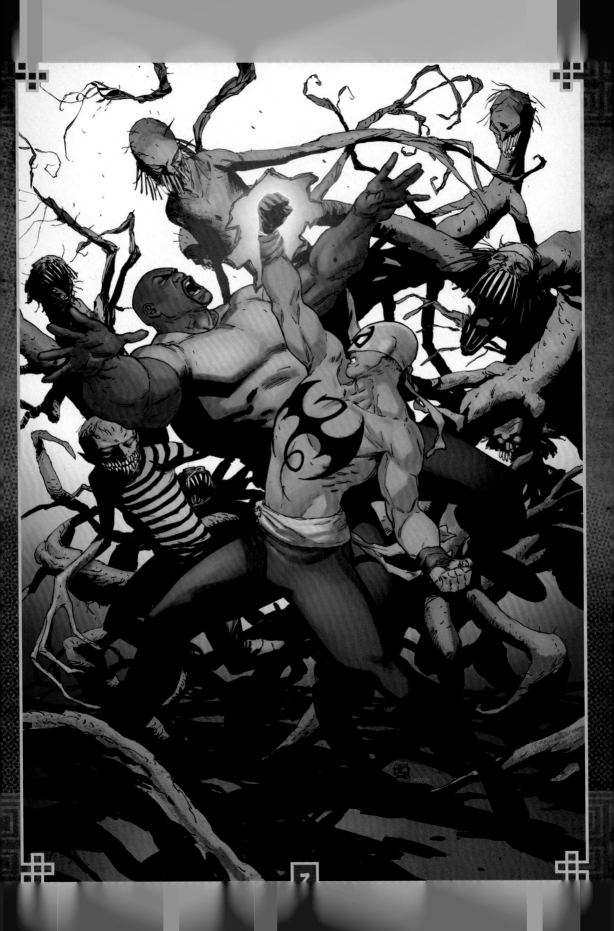

PHANTOM LIMB

CHAPTER 5

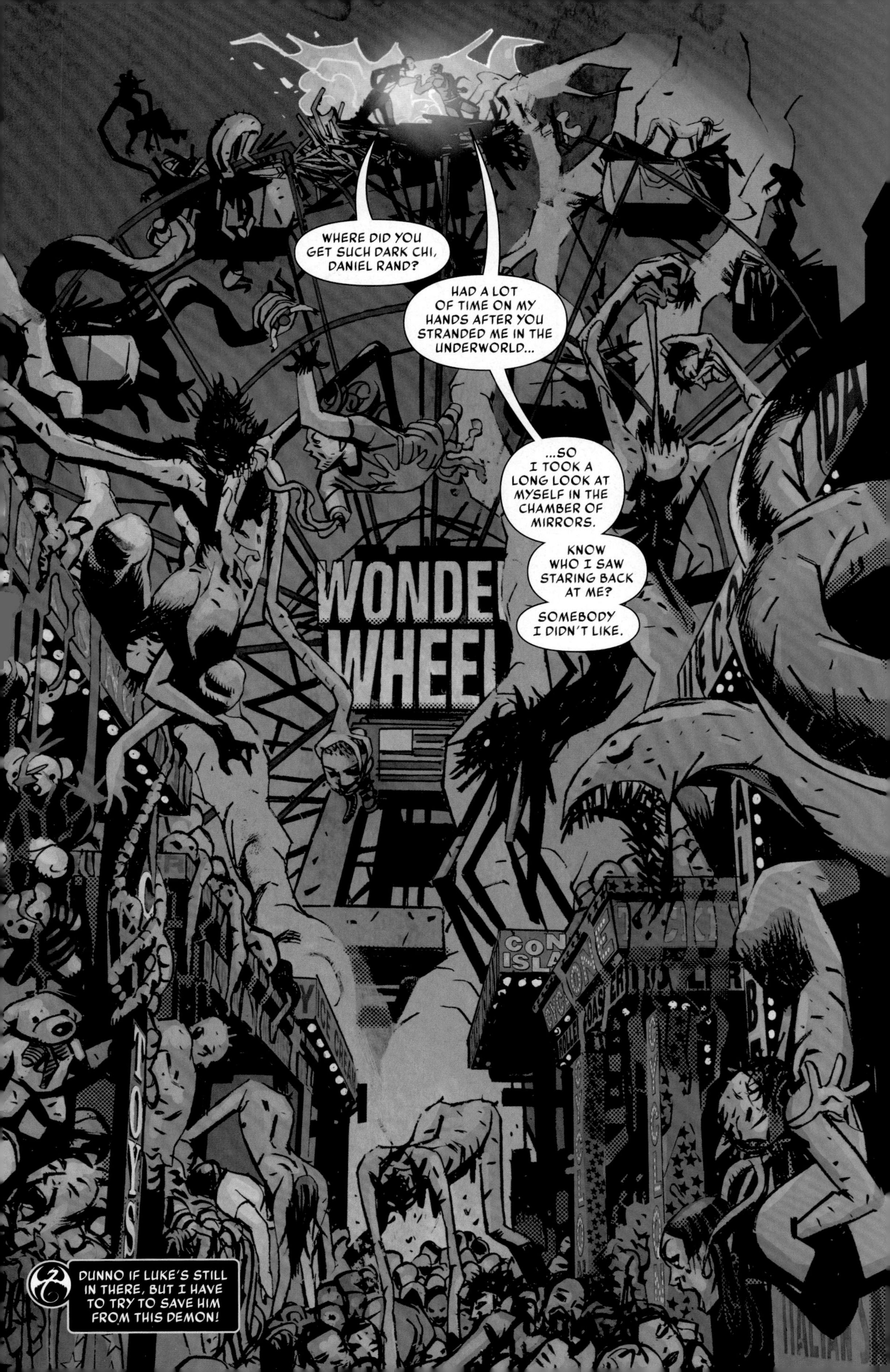
WHERE DID YOU GET SUCH DARK CHI, DANIEL RAND?
HAD A LOT OF TIME ON MY HANDS AFTER YOU STRANDED ME IN THE UNDERWORLD...
...SO I TOOK A LONG LOOK AT MYSELF IN THE CHAMBER OF MIRRORS.
KNOW WHO I SAW STARING BACK AT ME?
SOMEBODY I DIDN'T LIKE.
WONDER WHEEL
TOYS
ICE CREAM
DUNNO IF LUKE'S STILL IN THERE, BUT I HAVE TO TRY TO SAVE HIM FROM THIS DEMON!

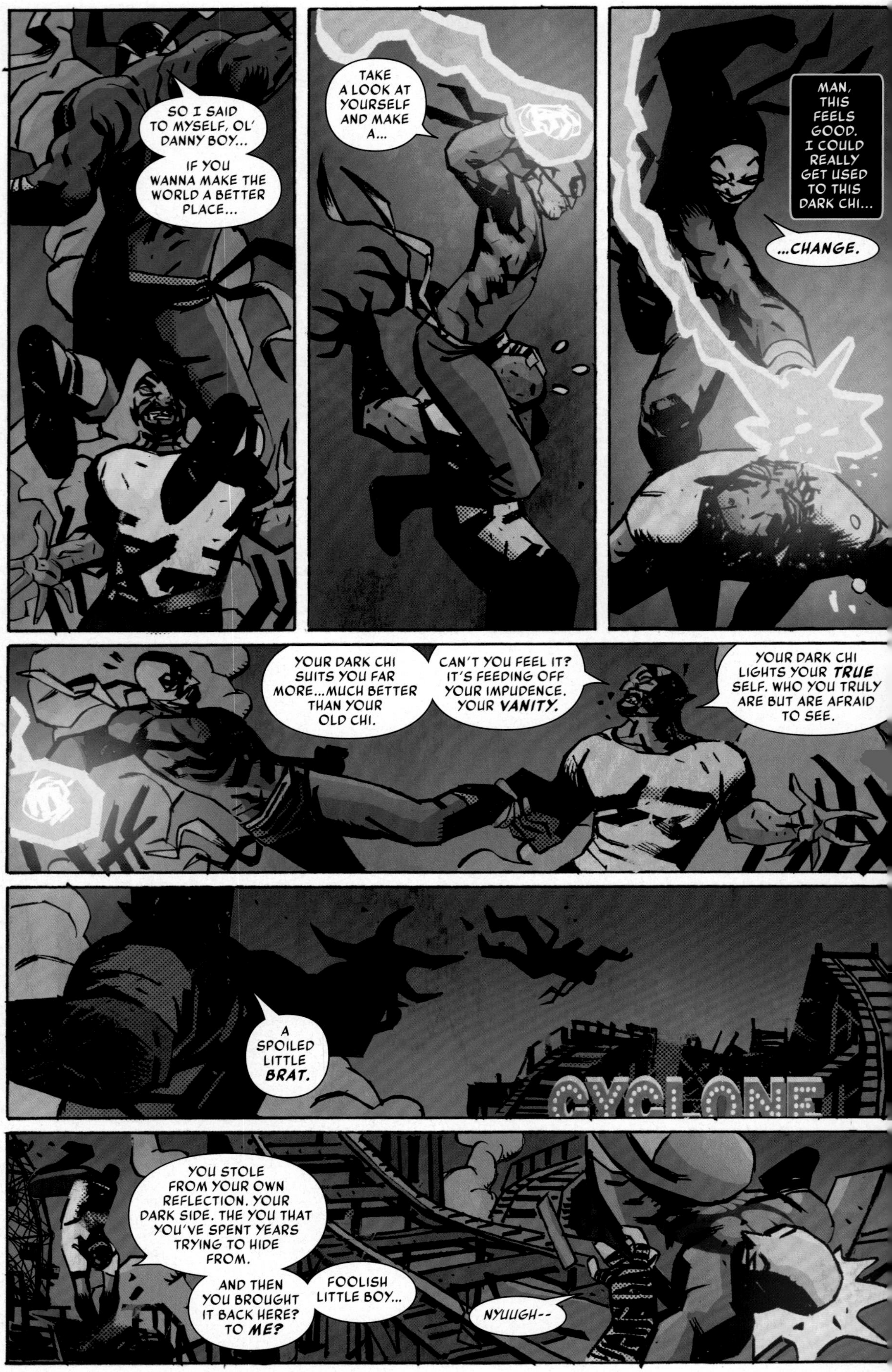
SO I SAID TO MYSELF, OL' DANNY BOY...
IF YOU WANNA MAKE THE WORLD A BETTER PLACE...
TAKE A LOOK AT YOURSELF AND MAKE A...
MAN, THIS FEELS GOOD. I COULD REALLY GET USED TO THIS DARK CHI...
...CHANGE.
YOUR DARK CHI SUITS YOU FAR MORE...MUCH BETTER THAN YOUR OLD CHI.
CAN'T YOU FEEL IT? IT'S FEEDING OFF YOUR IMPUDENCE. YOUR VANITY.
YOUR DARK CHI LIGHTS YOUR TRUE SELF. WHO YOU TRULY ARE BUT ARE AFRAID TO SEE.
A SPOILED LITTLE BRAT.
CYCLONE
YOU STOLE FROM YOUR OWN REFLECTION. YOUR DARK SIDE. THE YOU THAT YOU'VE SPENT YEARS TRYING TO HIDE FROM.
AND THEN YOU BROUGHT IT BACK HERE? TO ME?
FOOLISH LITTLE BOY...
NYUUGH--

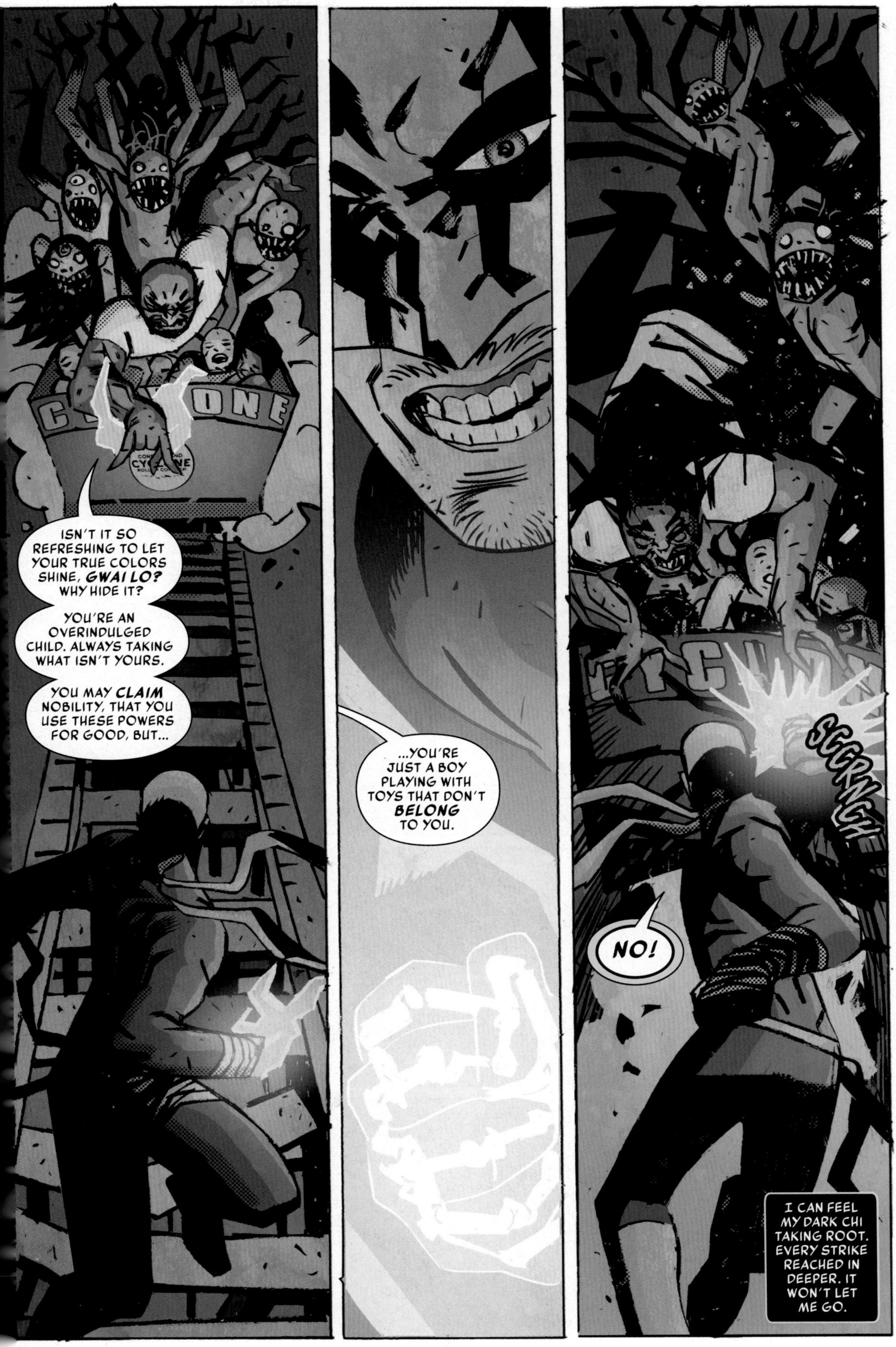
ISN'T IT SO REFRESHING TO LET YOUR TRUE COLORS SHINE, GWAI LO? WHY HIDE IT?
YOU'RE AN OVERINDULGED CHILD. ALWAYS TAKING WHAT ISN'T YOURS.
YOU MAY CLAIM NOBILITY, THAT YOU USE THESE POWERS FOR GOOD, BUT...
...YOU'RE JUST A BOY PLAYING WITH TOYS THAT DON'T BELONG TO YOU.
SCCRNCH
NO!
I CAN FEEL MY DARK CHI TAKING ROOT. EVERY STRIKE REACHED IN DEEPER. IT WON'T LET ME GO.

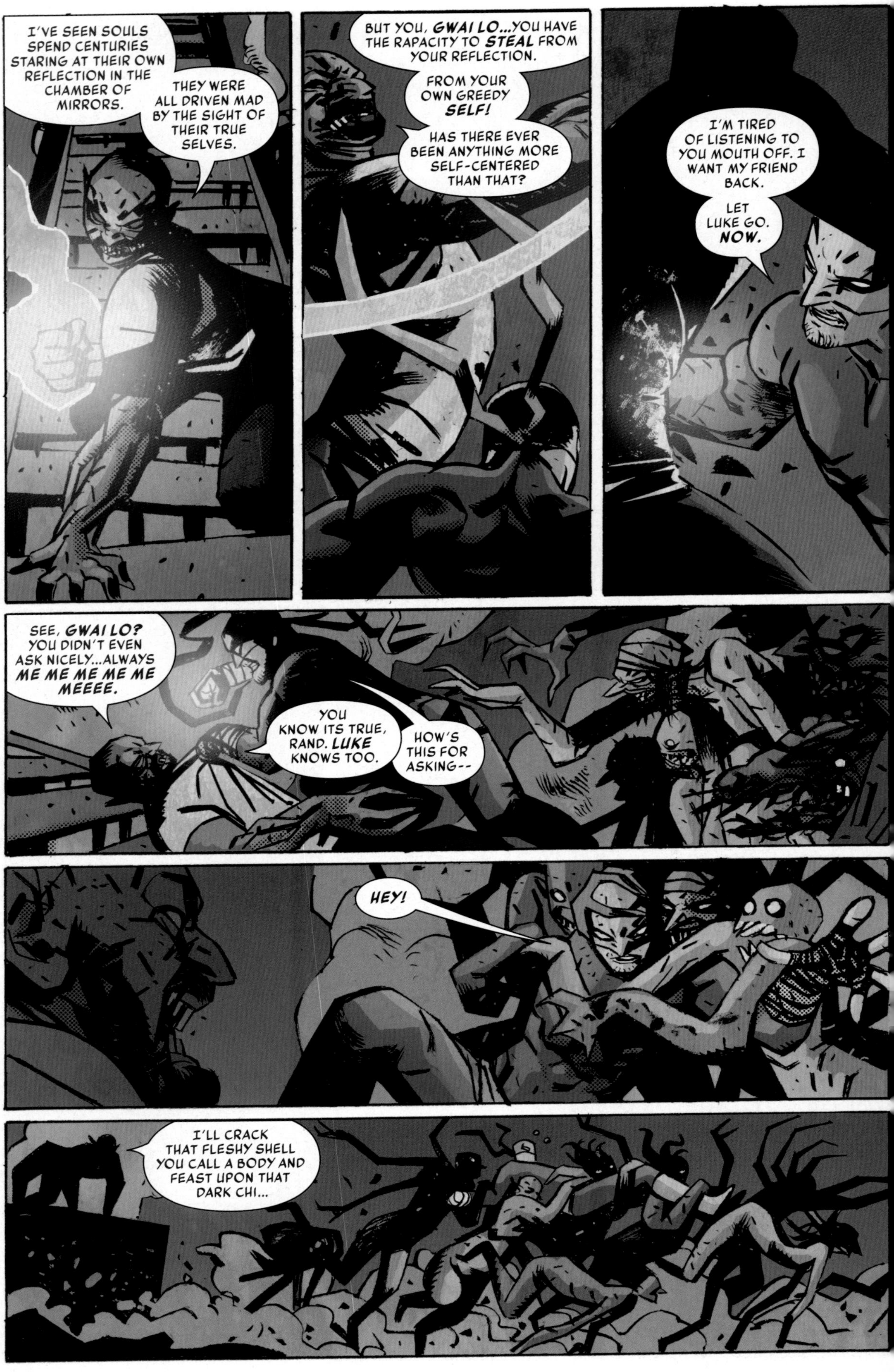
I'VE SEEN SOULS SPEND CENTURIES STARING AT THEIR OWN REFLECTION IN THE CHAMBER OF MIRRORS.
THEY WERE ALL DRIVEN MAD BY THE SIGHT OF THEIR TRUE SELVES.
BUT YOU, GWAI LO...YOU HAVE THE RAPACITY TO STEAL FROM YOUR REFLECTION.
FROM YOUR OWN GREEDY SELF!
HAS THERE EVER BEEN ANYTHING MORE SELF-CENTERED THAN THAT?
I'M TIRED OF LISTENING TO YOU MOUTH OFF. I WANT MY FRIEND BACK.
LET LUKE GO. NOW.
SEE, GWAI LO? YOU DIDN'T EVEN ASK NICELY...ALWAYS ME ME ME ME ME MEEEE.
YOU KNOW ITS TRUE, RAND. LUKE KNOWS TOO.
HOW'S THIS FOR ASKING--
HEY!
I'LL CRACK THAT FLESHY SHELL YOU CALL A BODY AND FEAST UPON THAT DARK CHI...

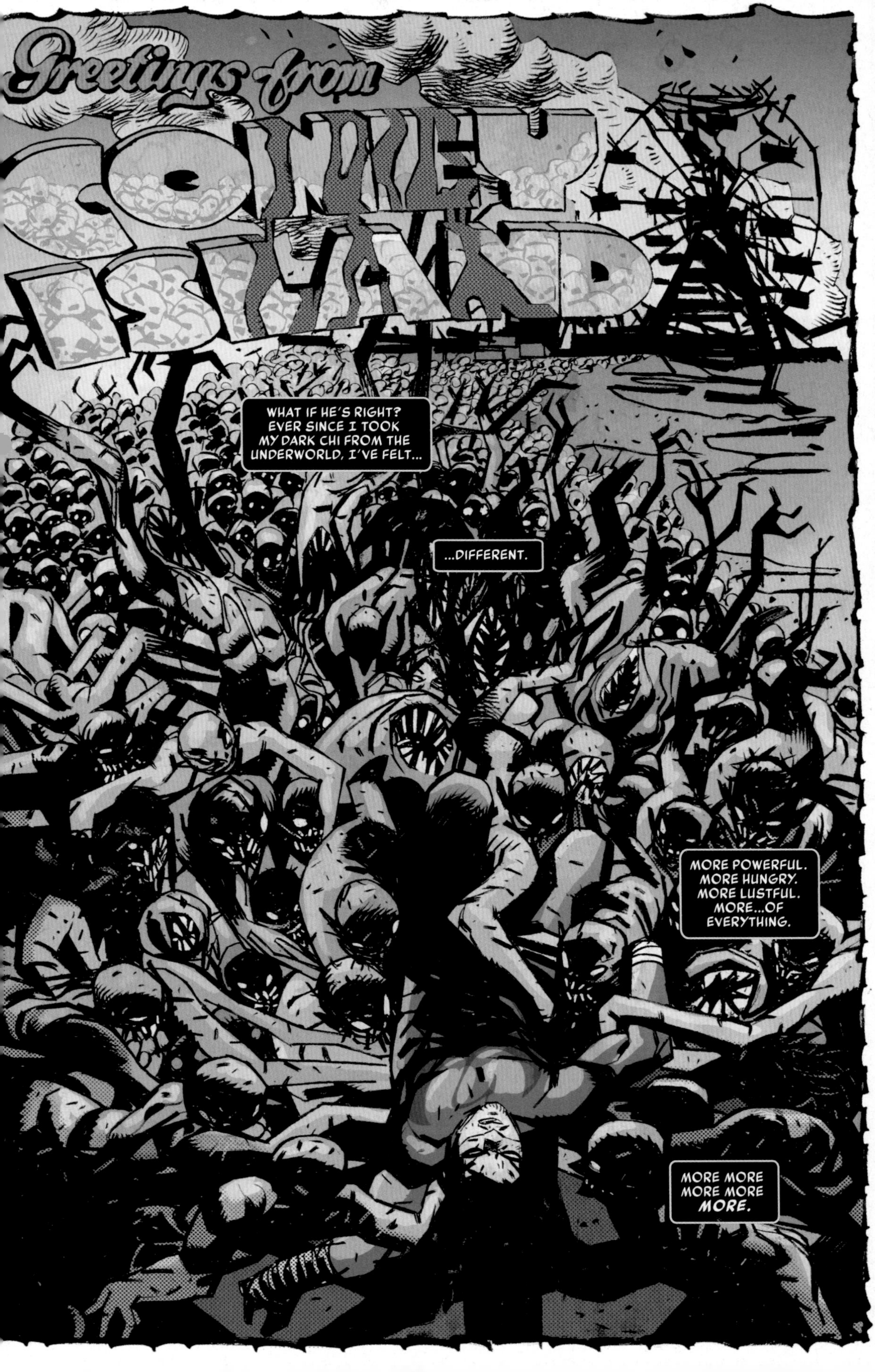
Greetings from
CONEY ISLAND
WHAT IF HE'S RIGHT? EVER SINCE I TOOK MY DARK CHI FROM THE UNDERWORLD, I'VE FELT...
...DIFFERENT.
MORE POWERFUL. MORE HUNGRY. MORE LUSTFUL. MORE...OF EVERYTHING.
MORE MORE MORE MORE *MORE.*

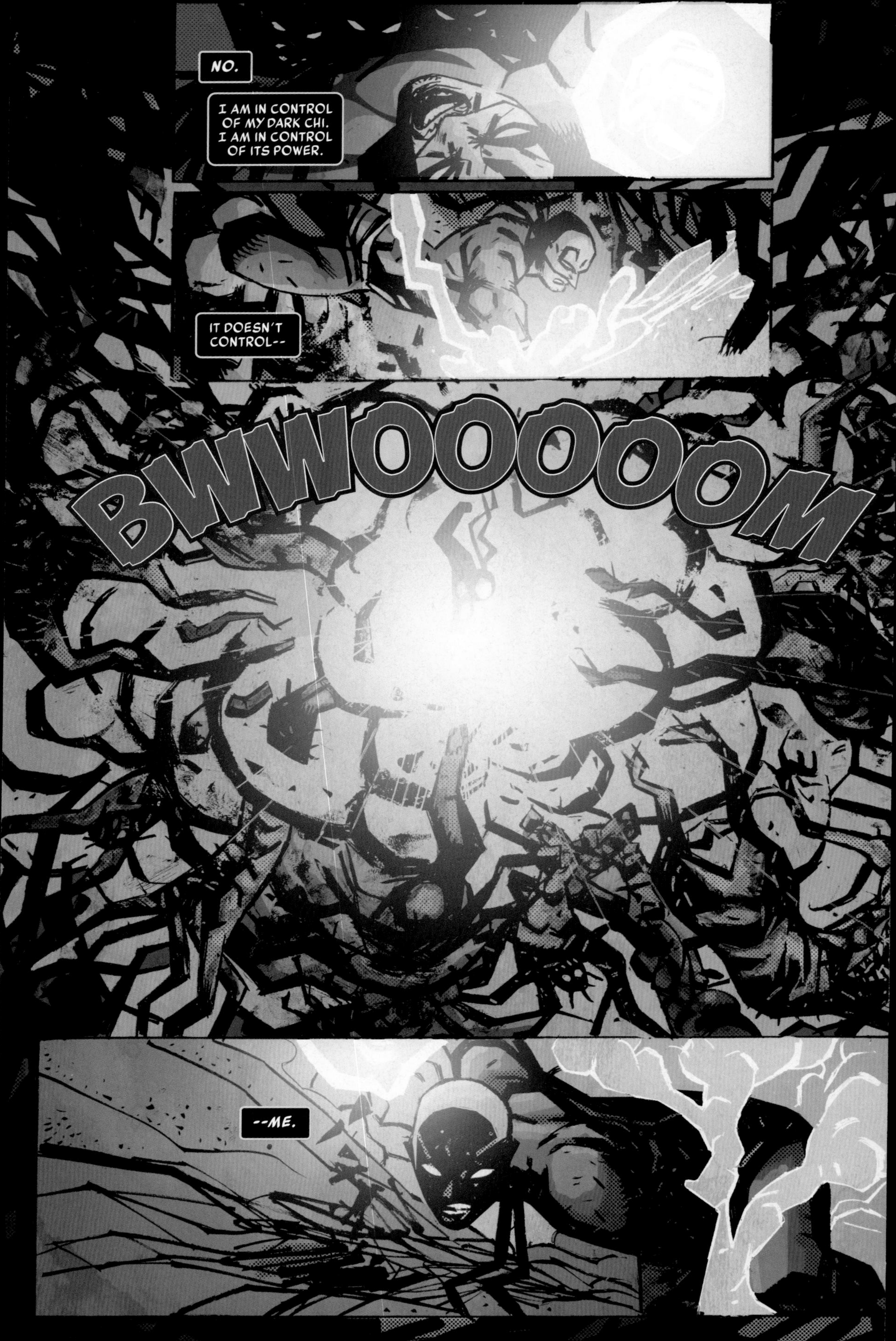

NO.
I AM IN CONTROL OF MY DARK CHI. I AM IN CONTROL OF ITS POWER.
IT DOESN'T CONTROL--
BWWOOOOOOM
--ME.

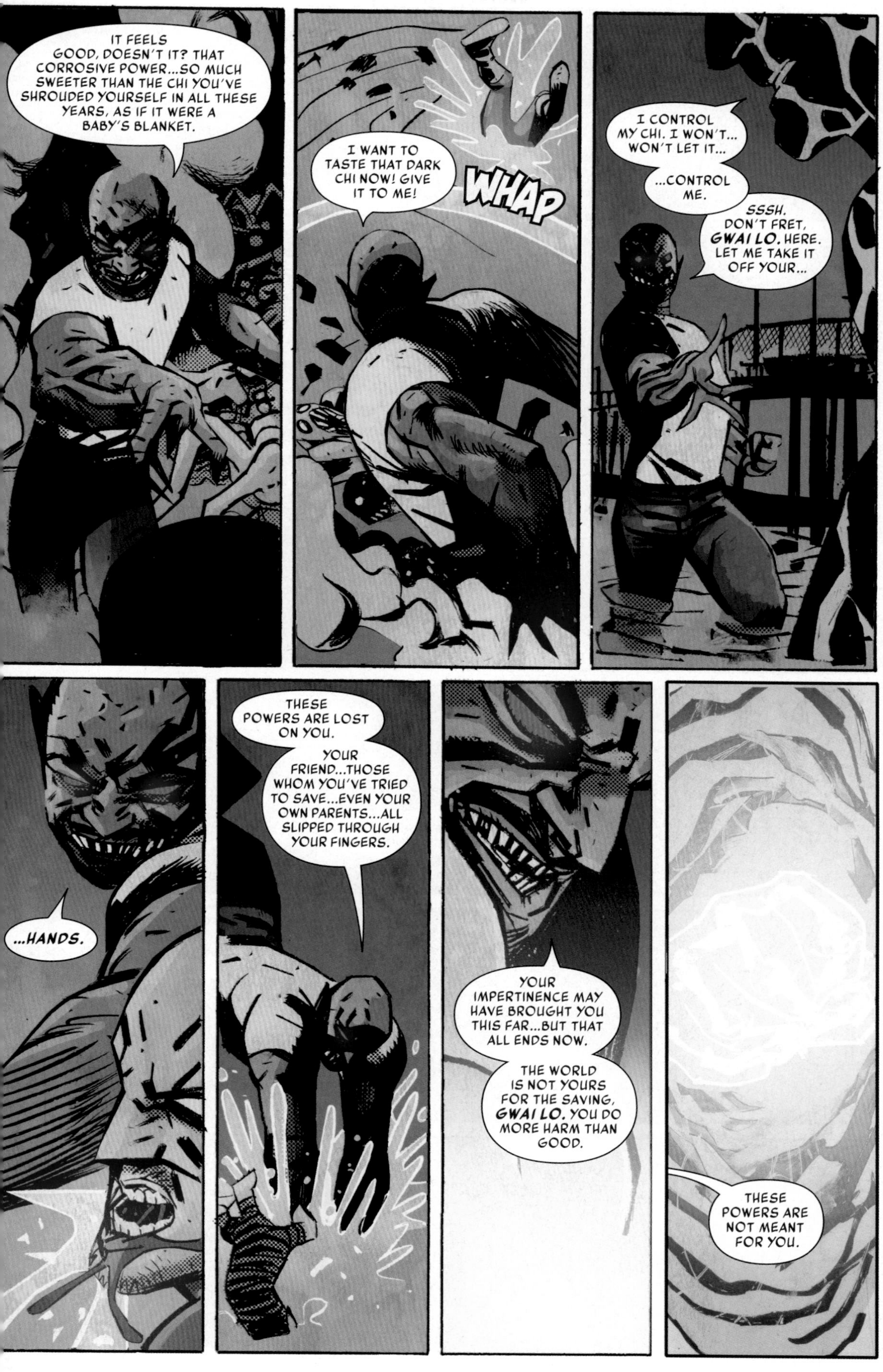
IT FEELS GOOD, DOESN'T IT? THAT CORROSIVE POWER...SO MUCH SWEETER THAN THE CHI YOU'VE SHROUDED YOURSELF IN ALL THESE YEARS, AS IF IT WERE A BABY'S BLANKET.
I WANT TO TASTE THAT DARK CHI NOW! GIVE IT TO ME!
WHAP
I CONTROL MY CHI. I WON'T... WON'T LET IT...
...CONTROL ME.
SSSH. DON'T FRET, GWAI LO. HERE. LET ME TAKE IT OFF YOUR...
...HANDS.
THESE POWERS ARE LOST ON YOU.
YOUR FRIEND...THOSE WHOM YOU'VE TRIED TO SAVE...EVEN YOUR OWN PARENTS...ALL SLIPPED THROUGH YOUR FINGERS.
YOUR IMPERTINENCE MAY HAVE BROUGHT YOU THIS FAR...BUT THAT ALL ENDS NOW.
THE WORLD IS NOT YOURS FOR THE SAVING, GWAI LO. YOU DO MORE HARM THAN GOOD.
THESE POWERS ARE NOT MEANT FOR YOU.

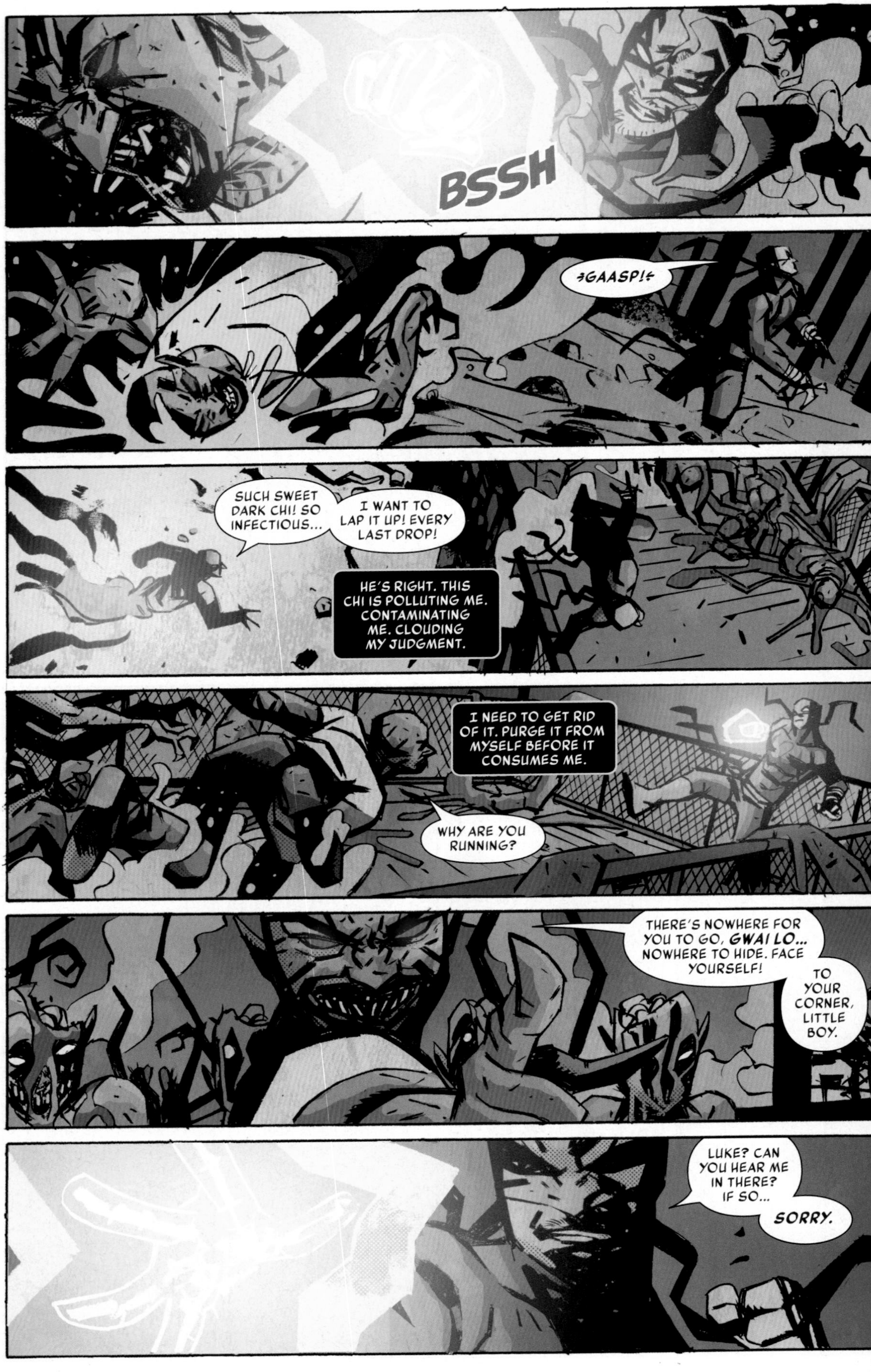
BSSH
ƷGAASP!Ƹ
SUCH SWEET DARK CHI! SO INFECTIOUS...
I WANT TO LAP IT UP! EVERY LAST DROP!
HE'S RIGHT. THIS CHI IS POLLUTING ME. CONTAMINATING ME. CLOUDING MY JUDGMENT.
I NEED TO GET RID OF IT. PURGE IT FROM MYSELF BEFORE IT CONSUMES ME.
WHY ARE YOU RUNNING?
THERE'S NOWHERE FOR YOU TO GO, GWAI LO... NOWHERE TO HIDE. FACE YOURSELF!
TO YOUR CORNER, LITTLE BOY.
LUKE? CAN YOU HEAR ME IN THERE? IF SO...
SORRY.

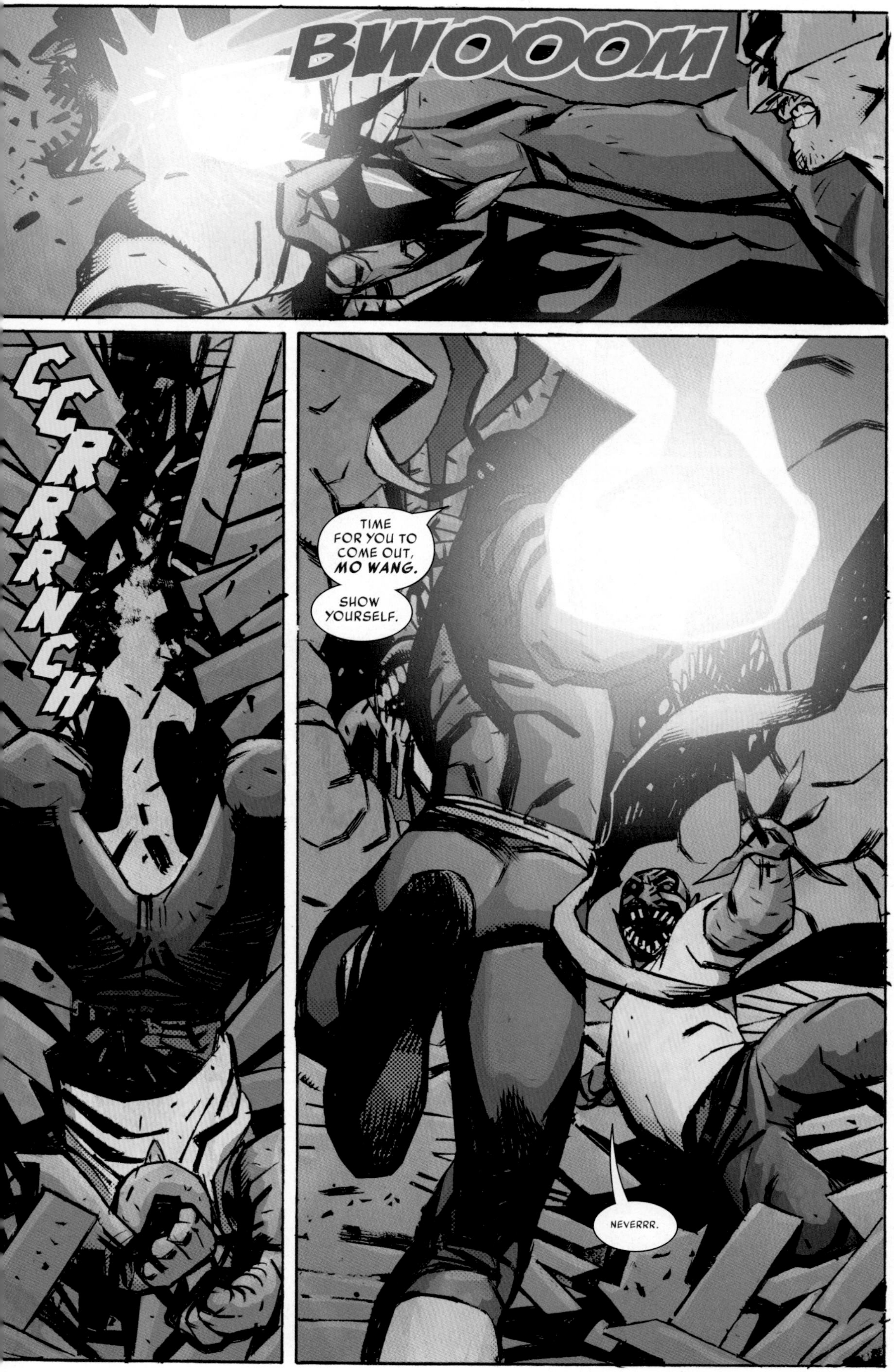
BWOOOM
CCRRRRNCH
TIME FOR YOU TO COME OUT, **MO WANG.**
SHOW YOURSELF.
NEVERRR.

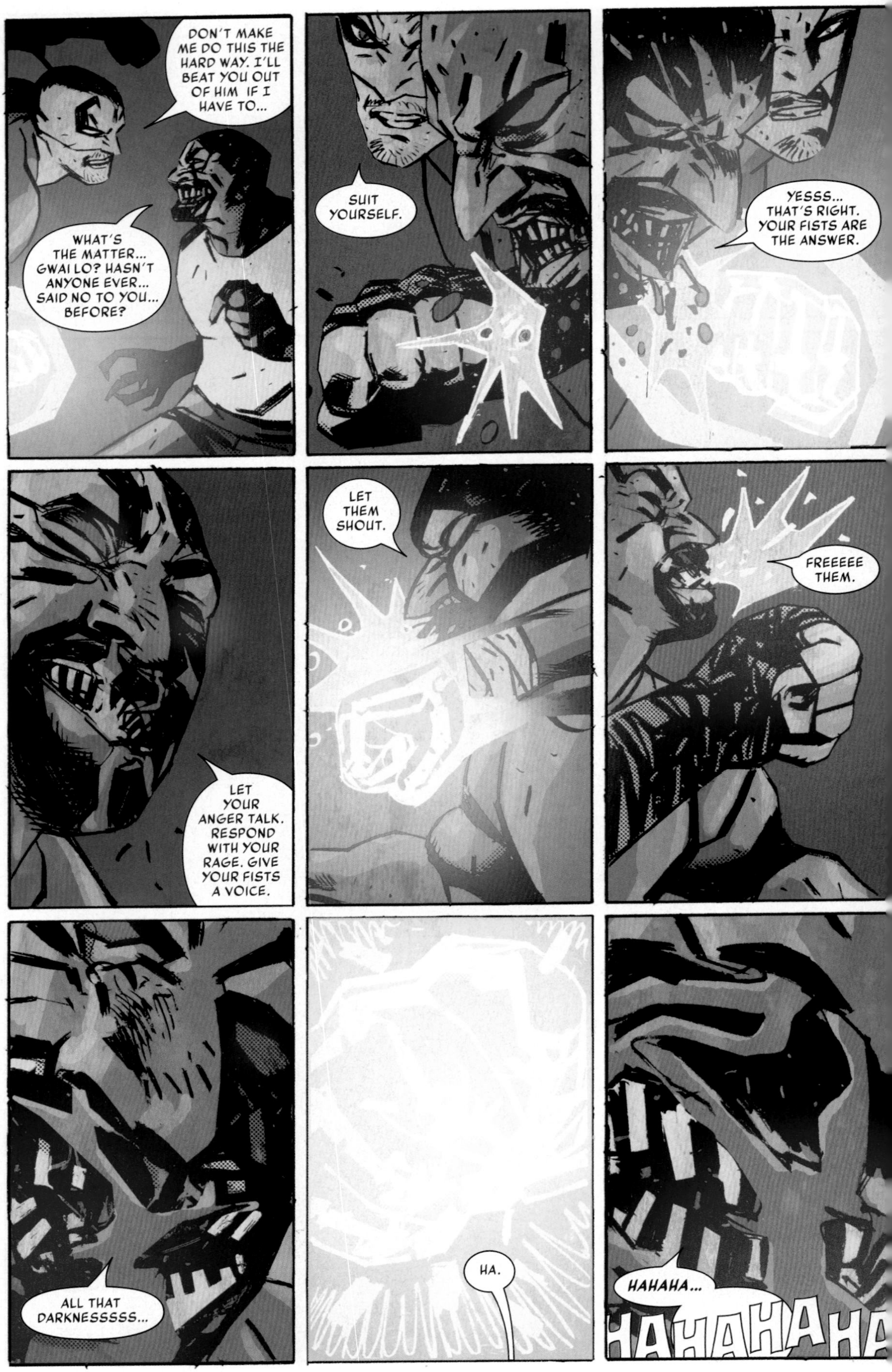
DON'T MAKE ME DO THIS THE HARD WAY. I'LL BEAT YOU OUT OF HIM IF I HAVE TO...
WHAT'S THE MATTER... GWAI LO? HASN'T ANYONE EVER... SAID NO TO YOU... BEFORE?
SUIT YOURSELF.
YESSS... THAT'S RIGHT. YOUR FISTS ARE THE ANSWER.
LET YOUR ANGER TALK. RESPOND WITH YOUR RAGE. GIVE YOUR FISTS A VOICE.
LET THEM SHOUT.
FREEEEE THEM.
ALL THAT DARKNESSSSS...
HA.
HAHAHA...
HAHAHAHA

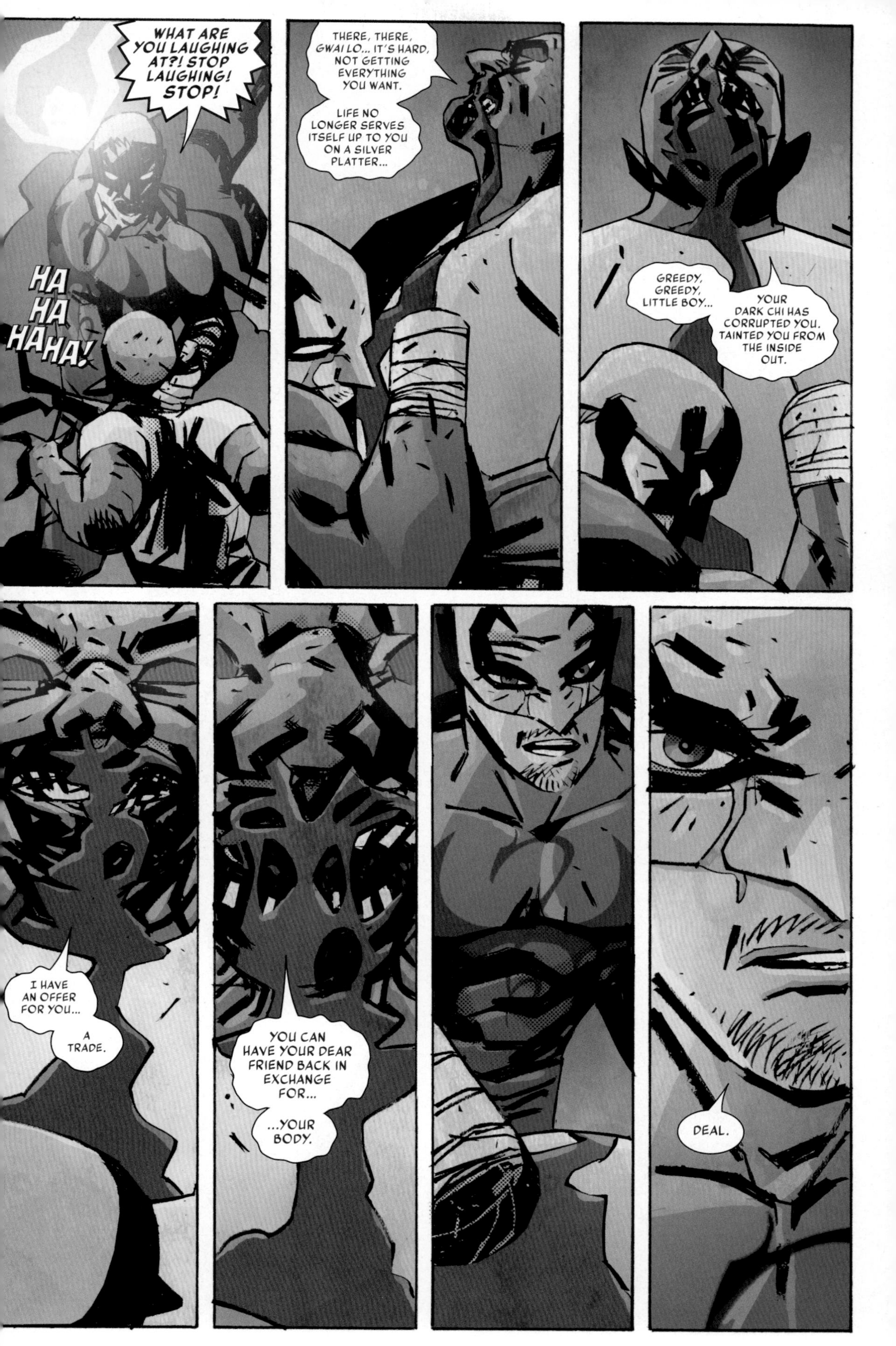

WHAT ARE YOU LAUGHING AT?! STOP LAUGHING! STOP!
HA HA HAHA!
THERE, THERE, GWAI LO... IT'S HARD, NOT GETTING EVERYTHING YOU WANT.
LIFE NO LONGER SERVES ITSELF UP TO YOU ON A SILVER PLATTER...
GREEDY, GREEDY, LITTLE BOY...
YOUR DARK CHI HAS CORRUPTED YOU. TAINTED YOU FROM THE INSIDE OUT.
I HAVE AN OFFER FOR YOU...
A TRADE.
YOU CAN HAVE YOUR DEAR FRIEND BACK IN EXCHANGE FOR...
...YOUR BODY.
DEAL.

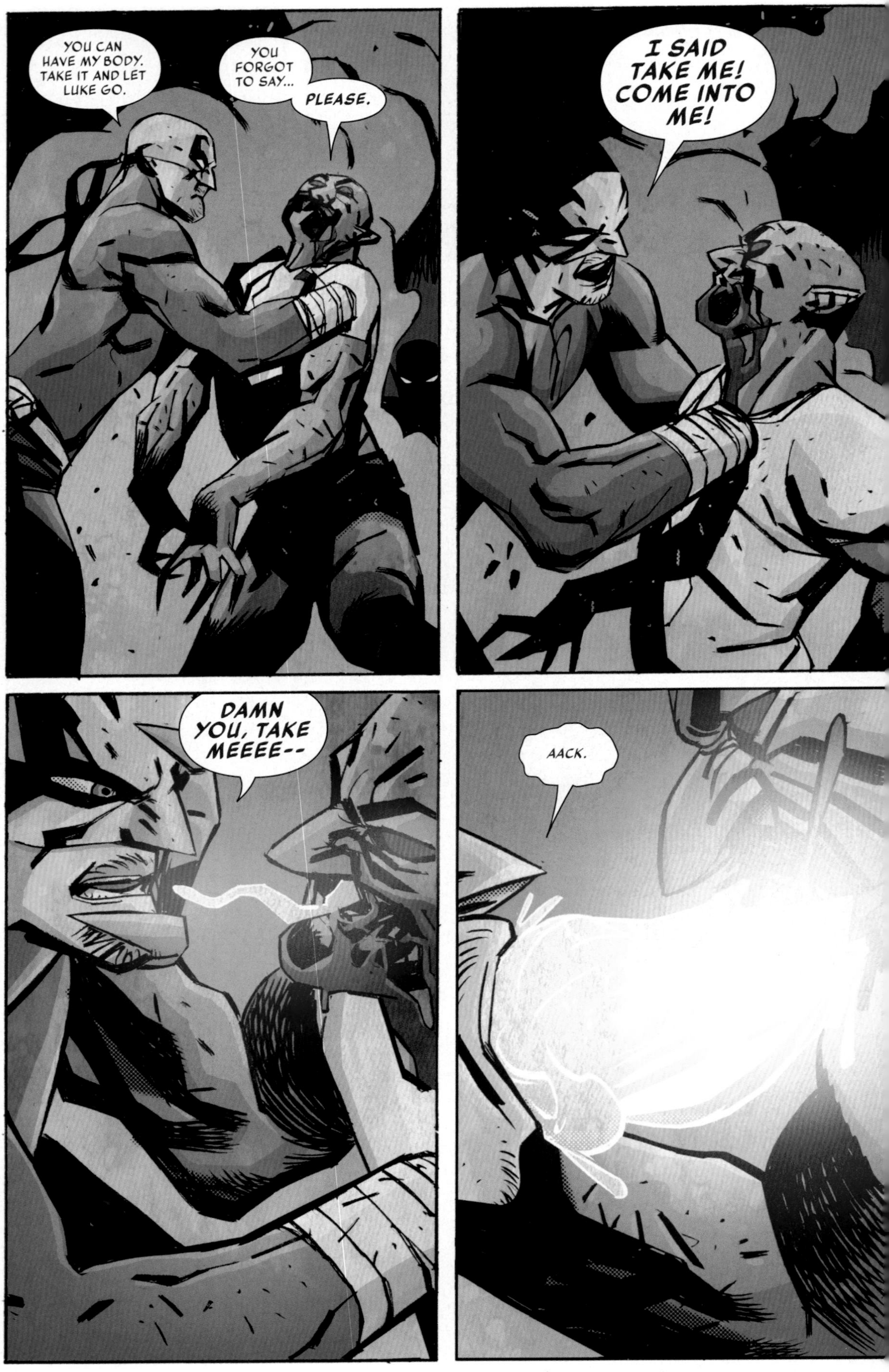
YOU CAN HAVE MY BODY. TAKE IT AND LET LUKE GO.
YOU FORGOT TO SAY...
PLEASE.
I SAID TAKE ME! COME INTO ME!
DAMN YOU, TAKE MEEEE--
AACK.

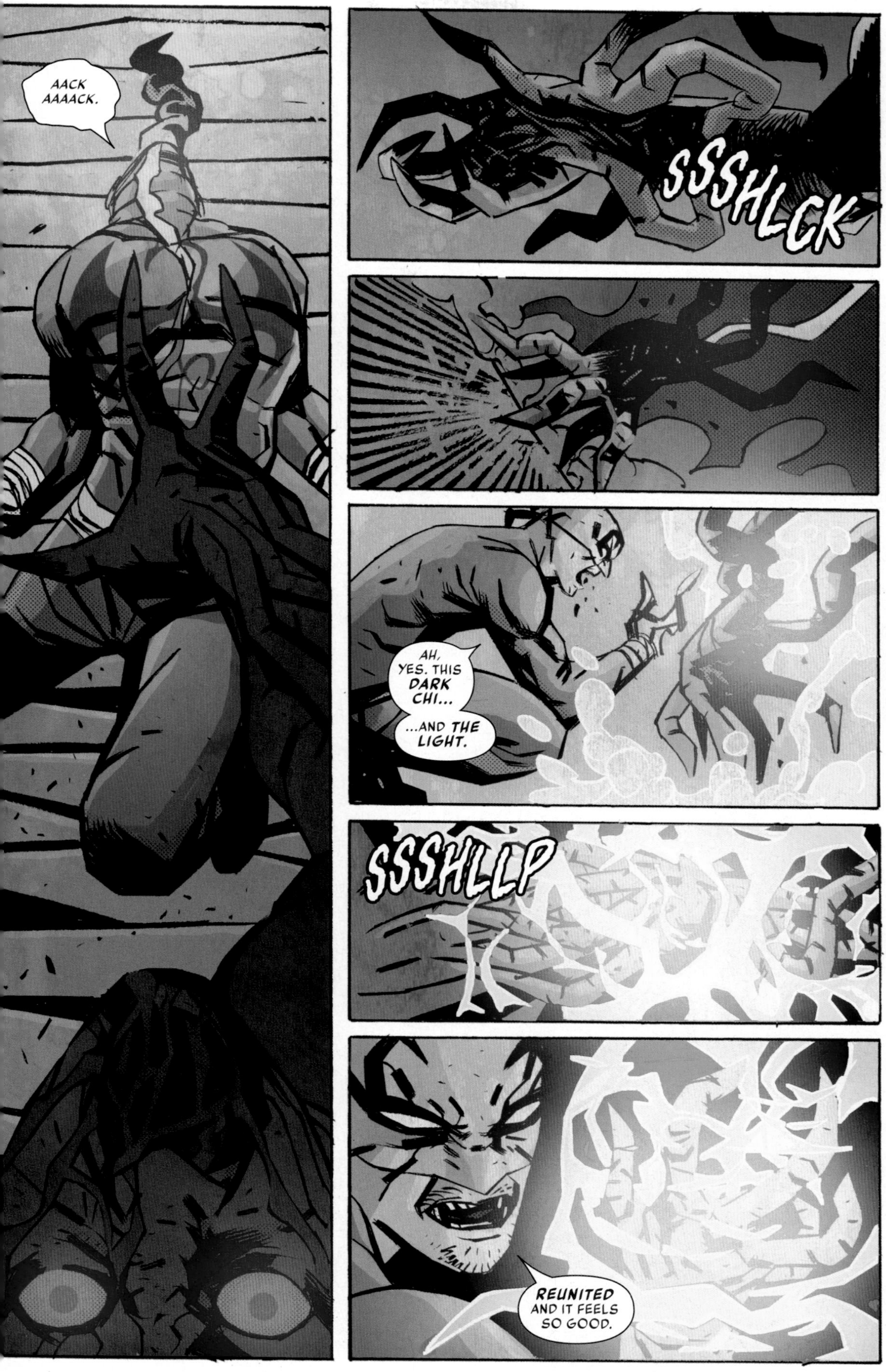
AACK AAAACK.
SSSHLCK
AH, YES. THIS DARK CHI...
...AND THE LIGHT.
SSSHLLP
REUNITED AND IT FEELS SO GOOD.

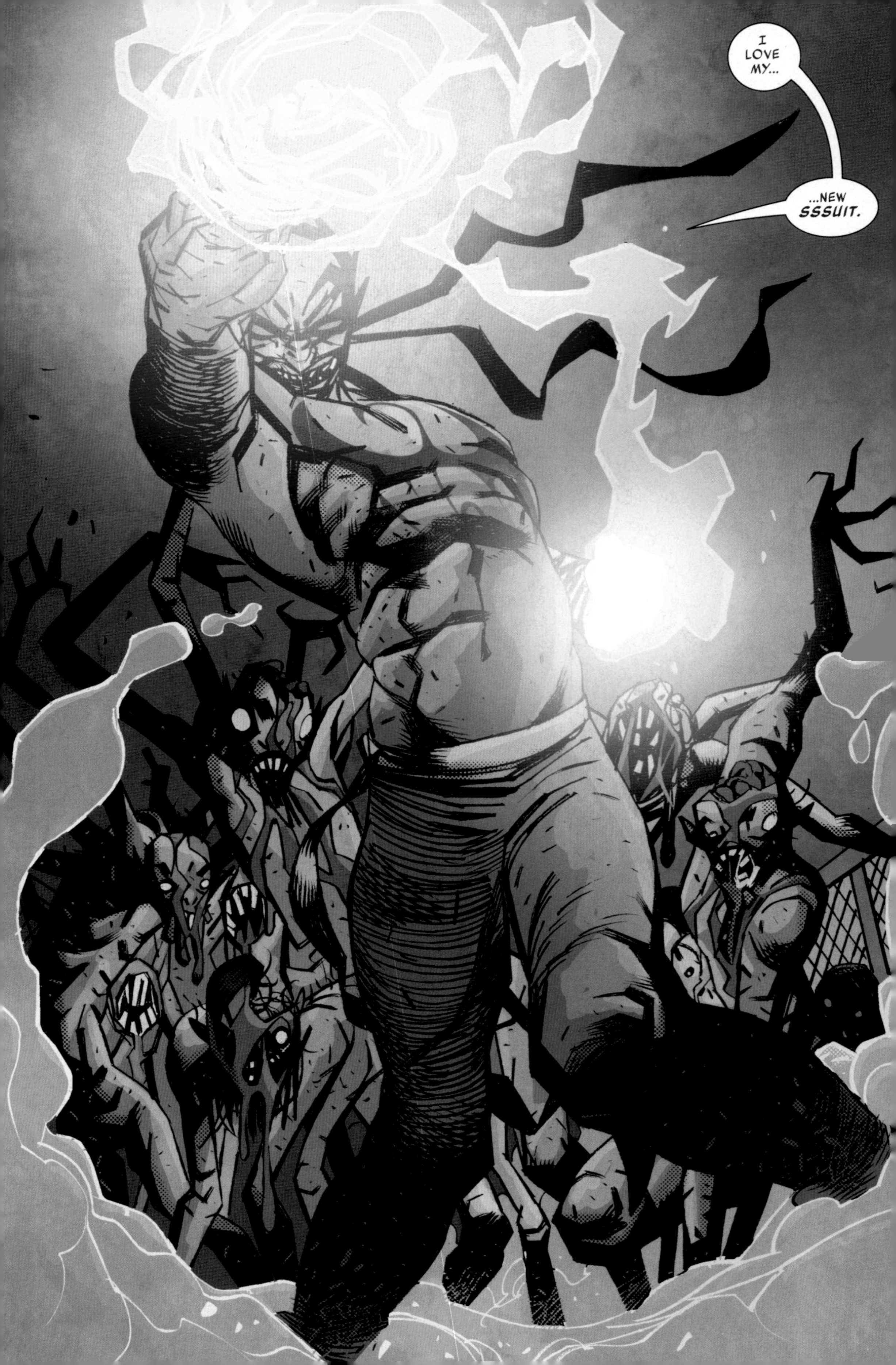
I LOVE MY...
...NEW SSSUIT.

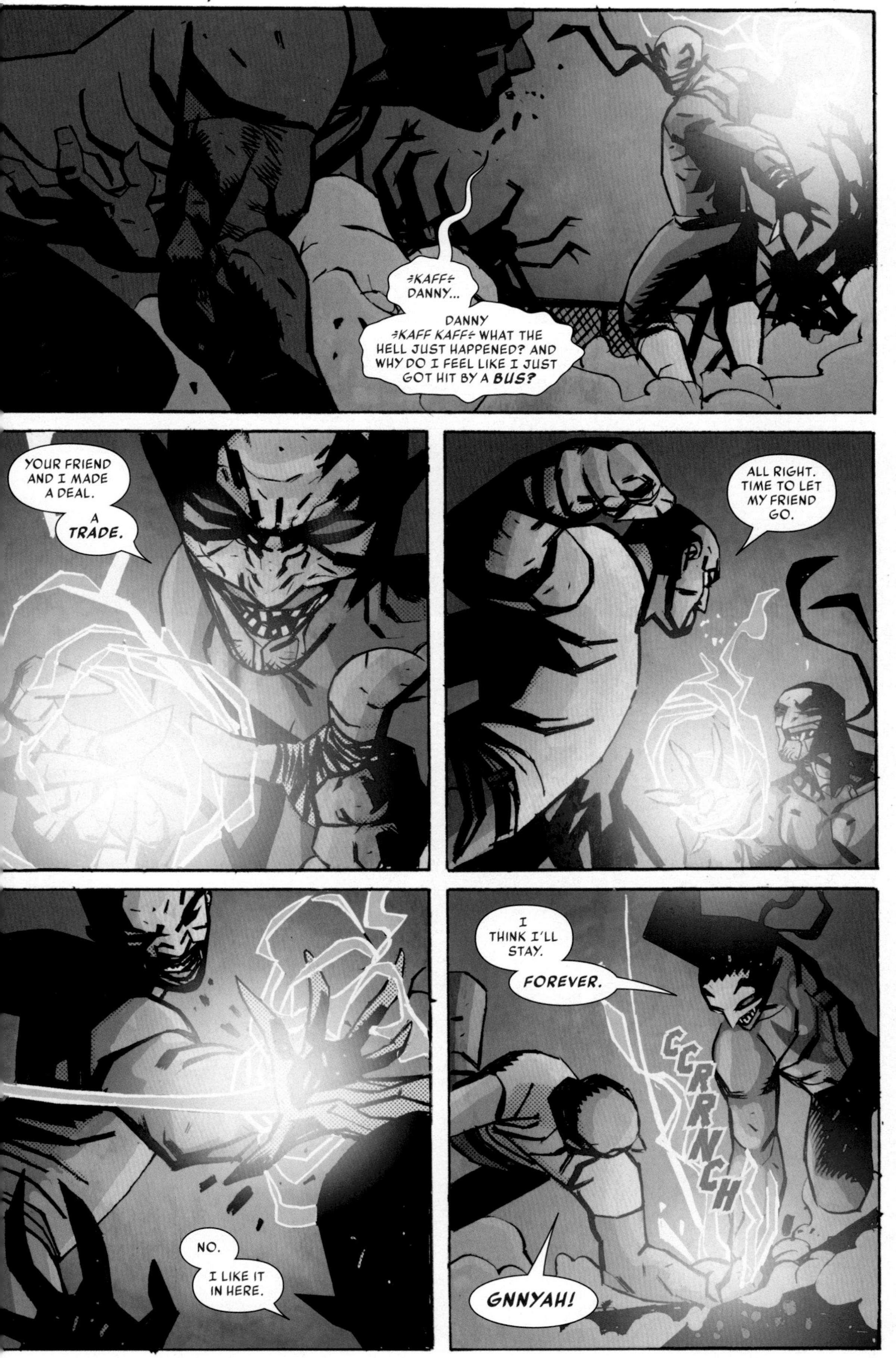

≠KAFF≠ DANNY...
DANNY ≠KAFF KAFF≠ WHAT THE HELL JUST HAPPENED? AND WHY DO I FEEL LIKE I JUST GOT HIT BY A BUS?
YOUR FRIEND AND I MADE A DEAL.
A TRADE.
ALL RIGHT. TIME TO LET MY FRIEND GO.
NO.
I LIKE IT IN HERE.
I THINK I'LL STAY.
FOREVER.
CCRRNCH
GNNYAH!

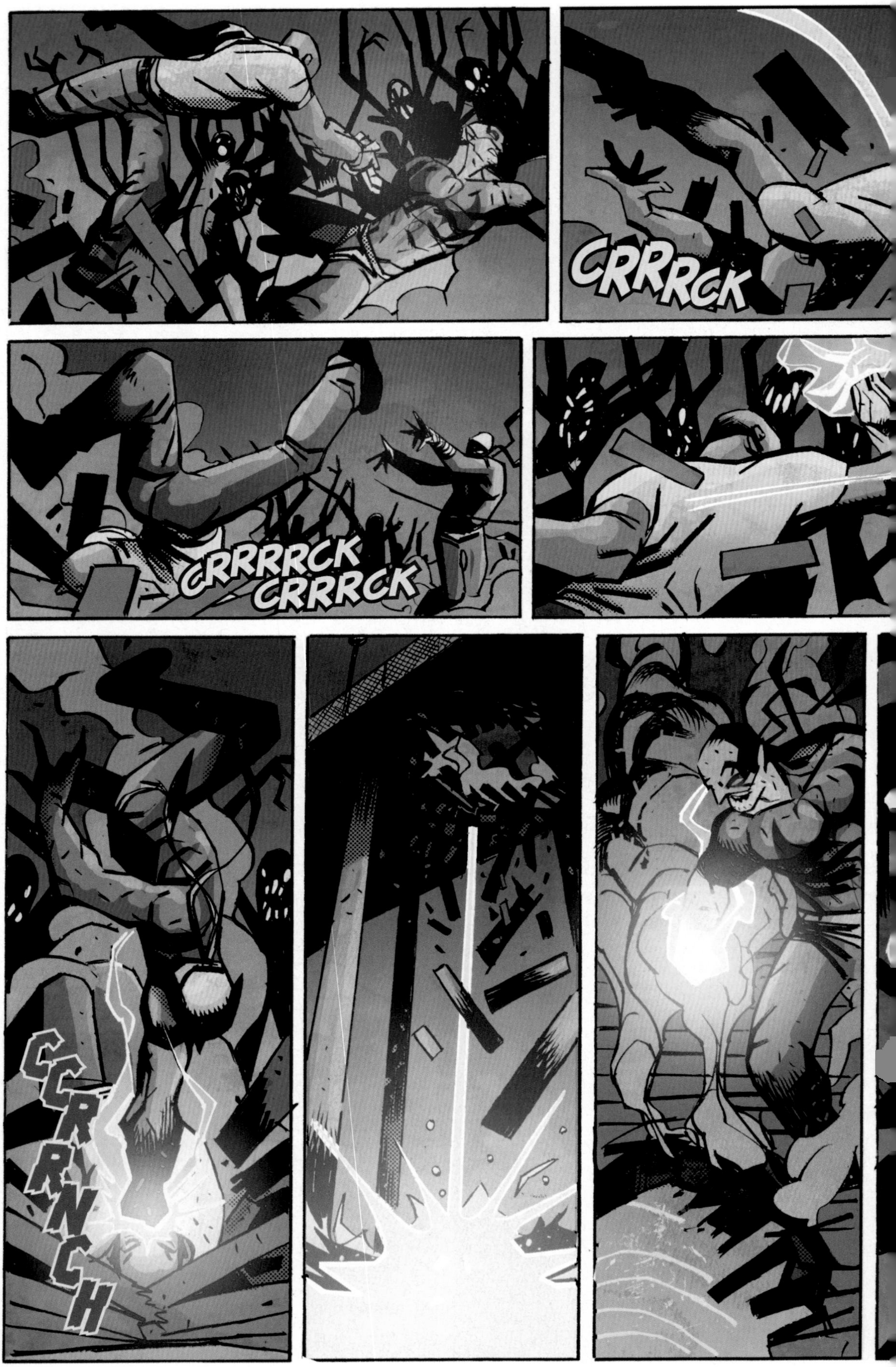
CRRRCK
CRRRRCK
CRRRCK
CCRRNCH

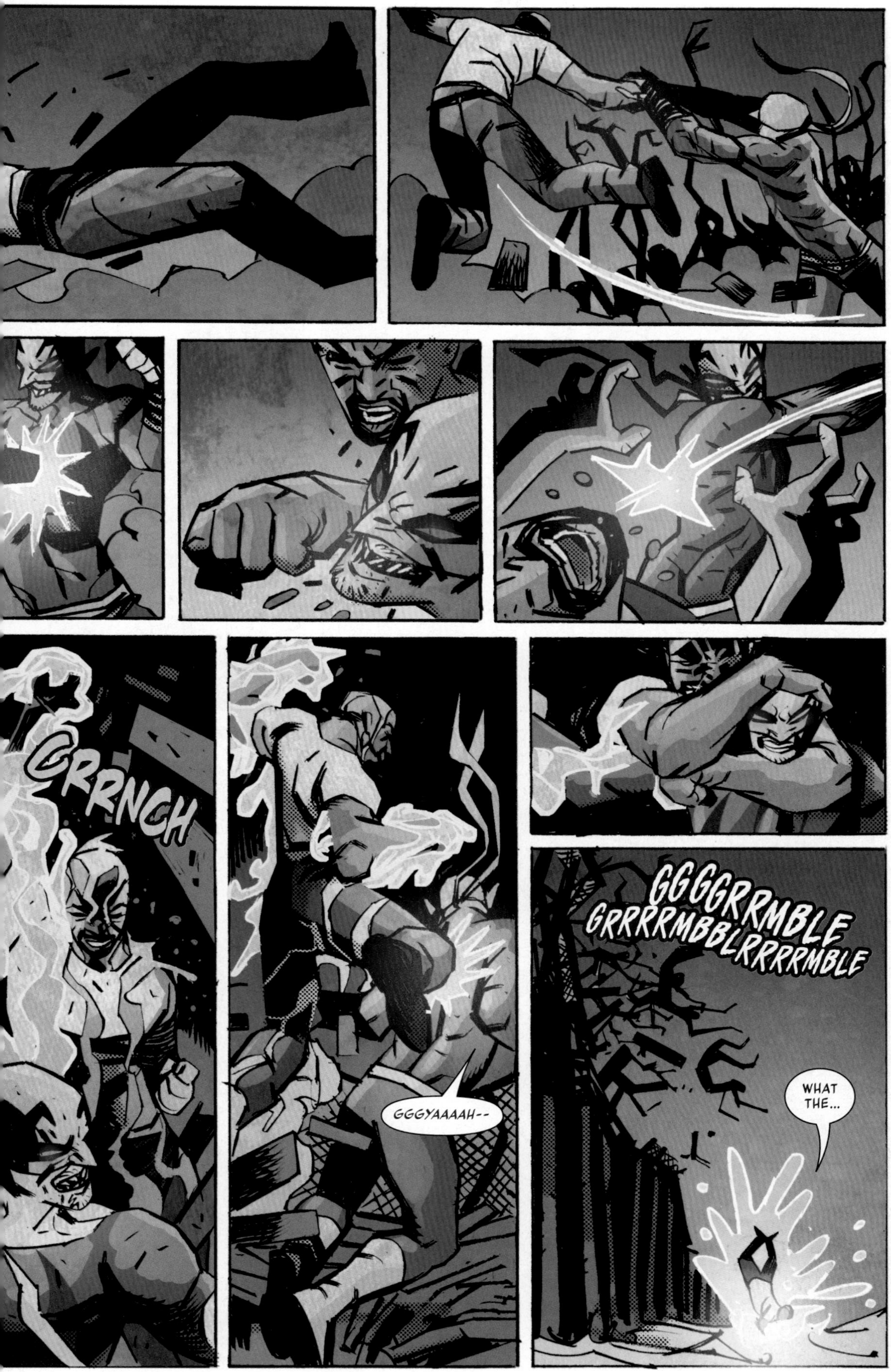
CRRNCH
GGGYAAAAH--
GGGGRRMBLE
GRRRRMBBLRRRRMBLE
WHAT THE...

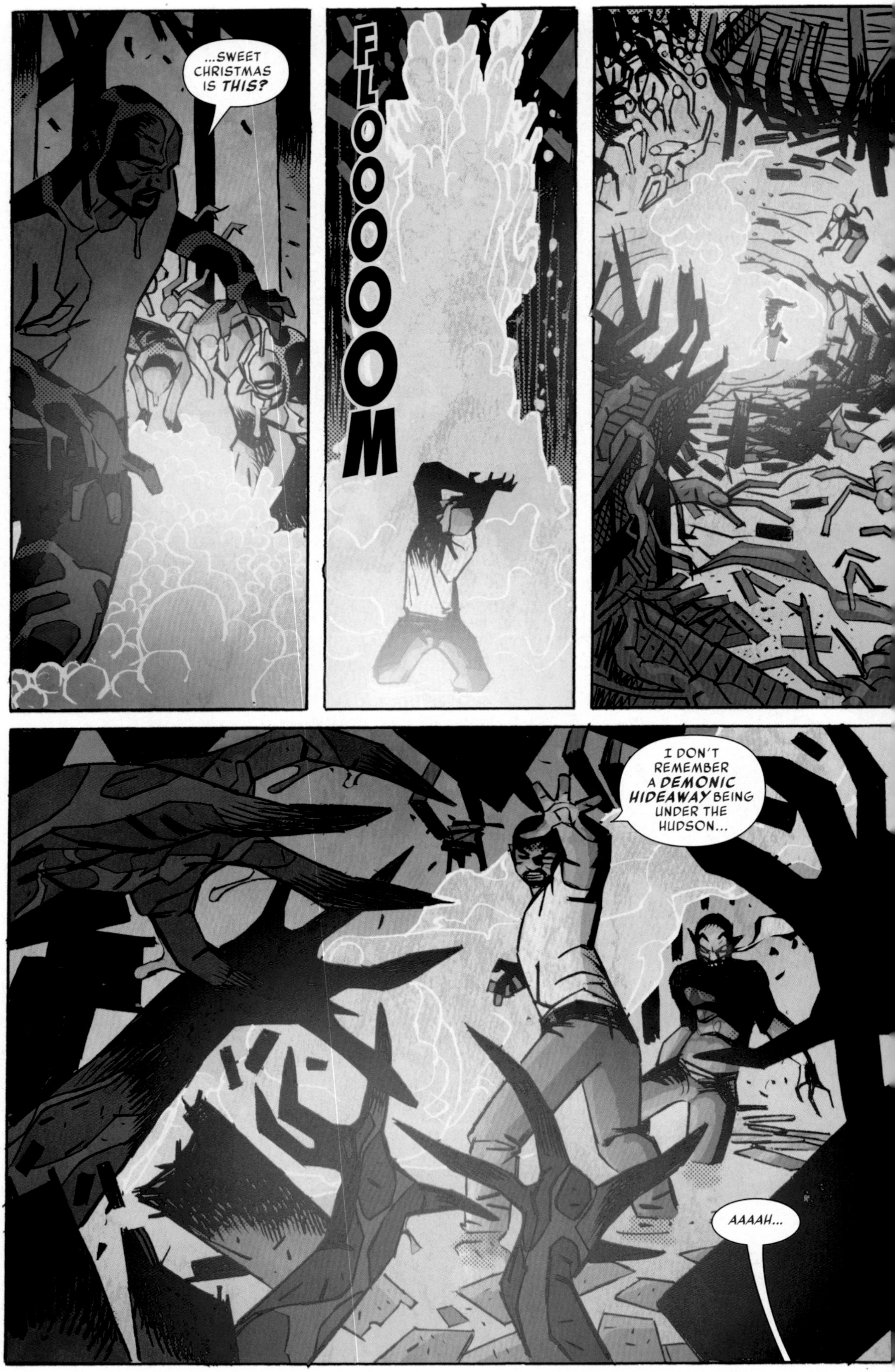
...SWEET CHRISTMAS IS THIS?
FLOOOOOOM
I DON'T REMEMBER A DEMONIC HIDEAWAY BEING UNDER THE HUDSON...
AAAAH...

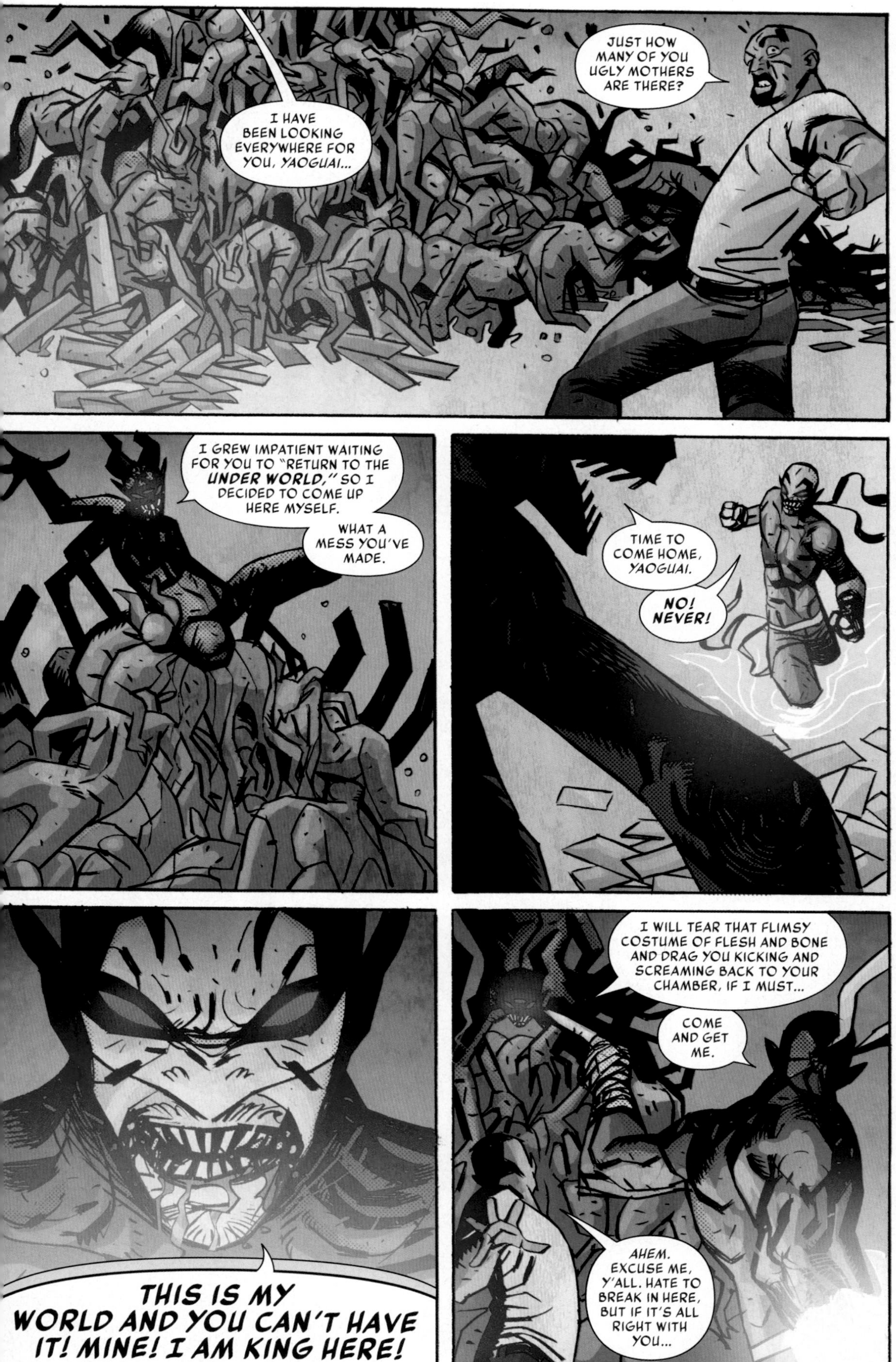
JUST HOW MANY OF YOU UGLY MOTHERS ARE THERE?
I HAVE BEEN LOOKING EVERYWHERE FOR YOU, *YAOGUAI*...
I GREW IMPATIENT WAITING FOR YOU TO "RETURN TO THE ***UNDER WORLD,***" SO I DECIDED TO COME UP HERE MYSELF.
WHAT A MESS YOU'VE MADE.
TIME TO COME HOME, *YAOGUAI*.
NO! NEVER!
THIS IS MY WORLD AND YOU CAN'T HAVE IT! MINE! I AM KING HERE!
I WILL TEAR THAT FLIMSY COSTUME OF FLESH AND BONE AND DRAG YOU KICKING AND SCREAMING BACK TO YOUR CHAMBER, IF I MUST...
COME AND GET ME.
AHEM. EXCUSE ME, Y'ALL. HATE TO BREAK IN HERE, BUT IF IT'S ALL RIGHT WITH YOU...

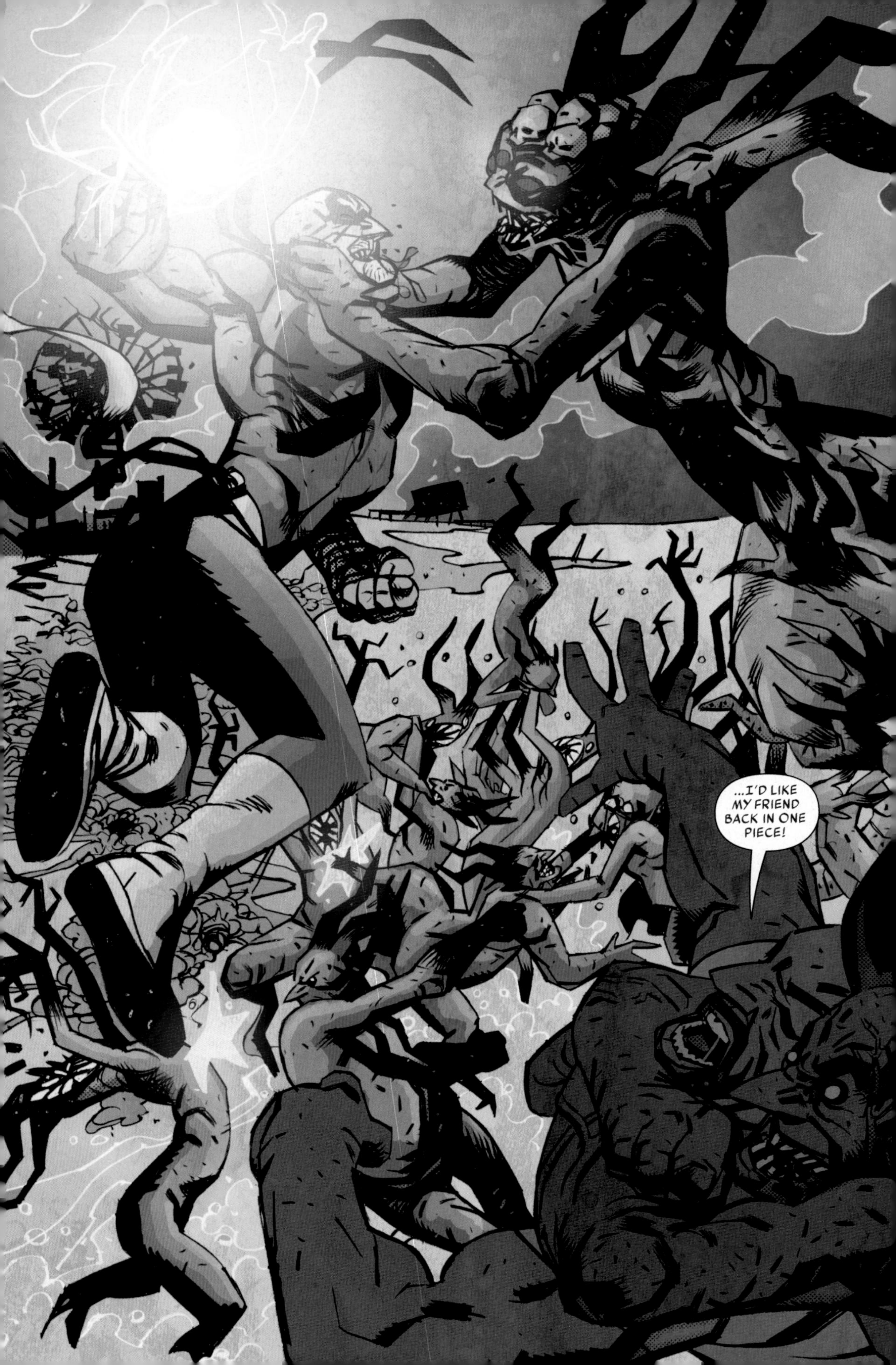
...I'D LIKE MY FRIEND BACK IN ONE PIECE!

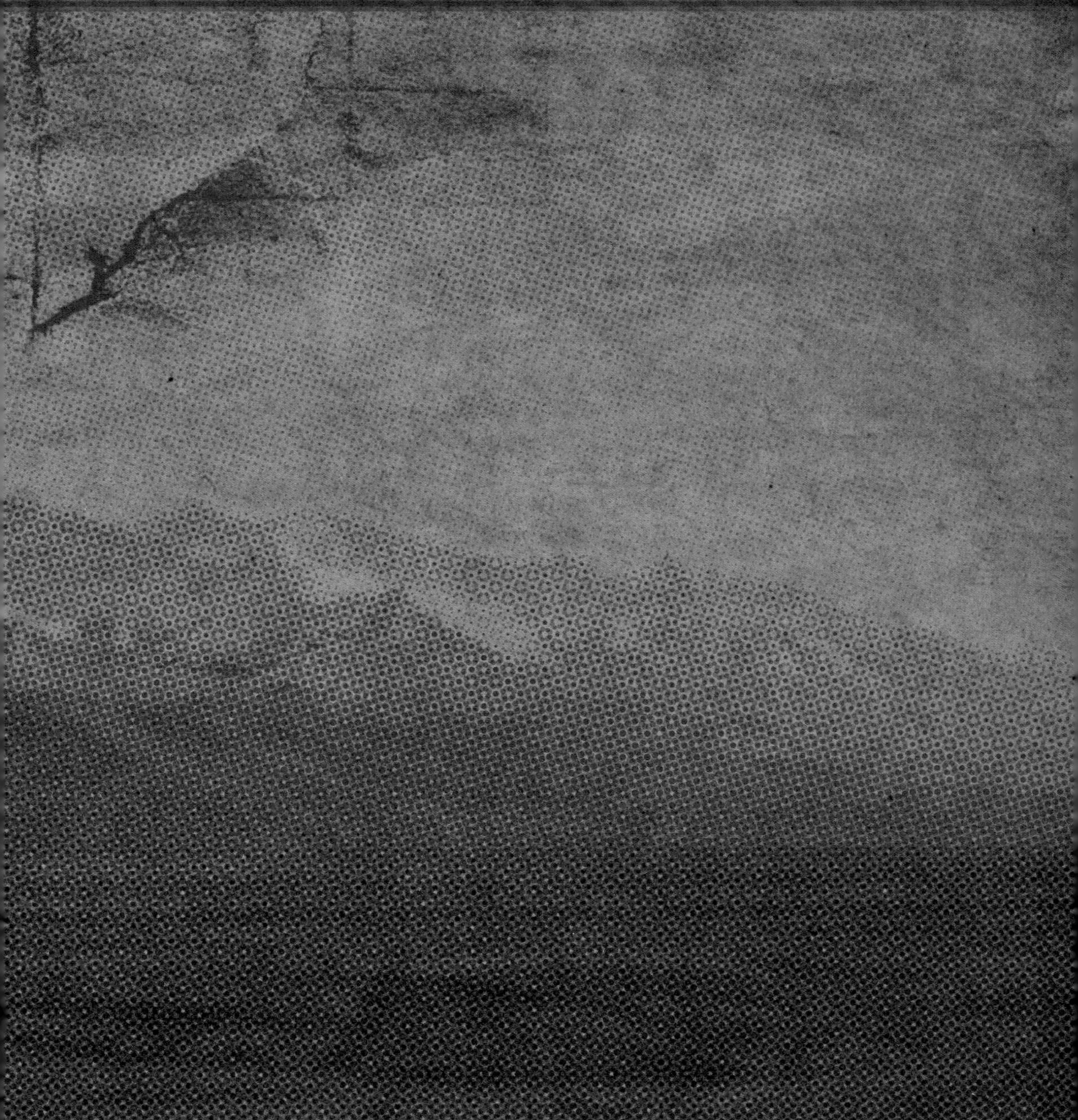

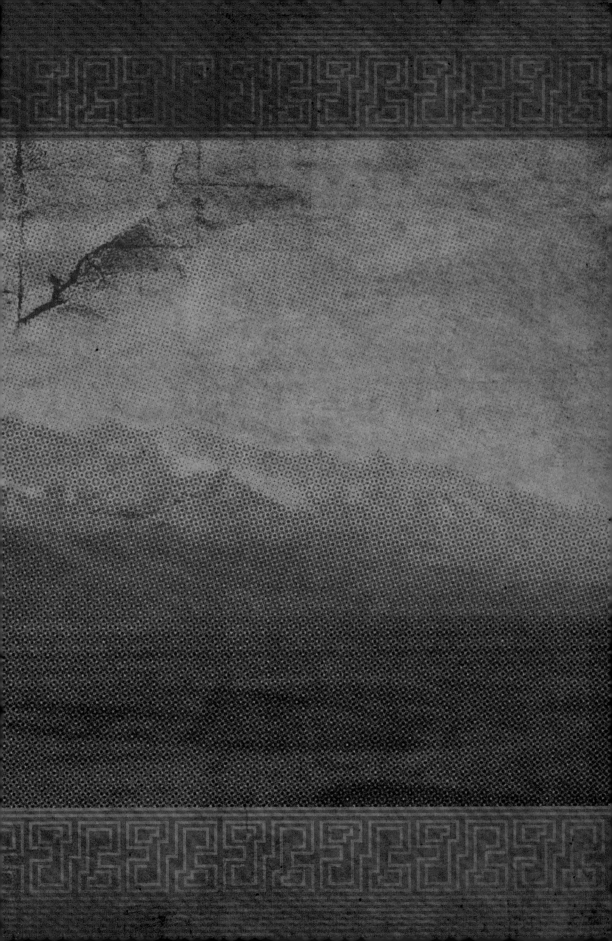

PHANTOM LIMB

CHAPTER 6

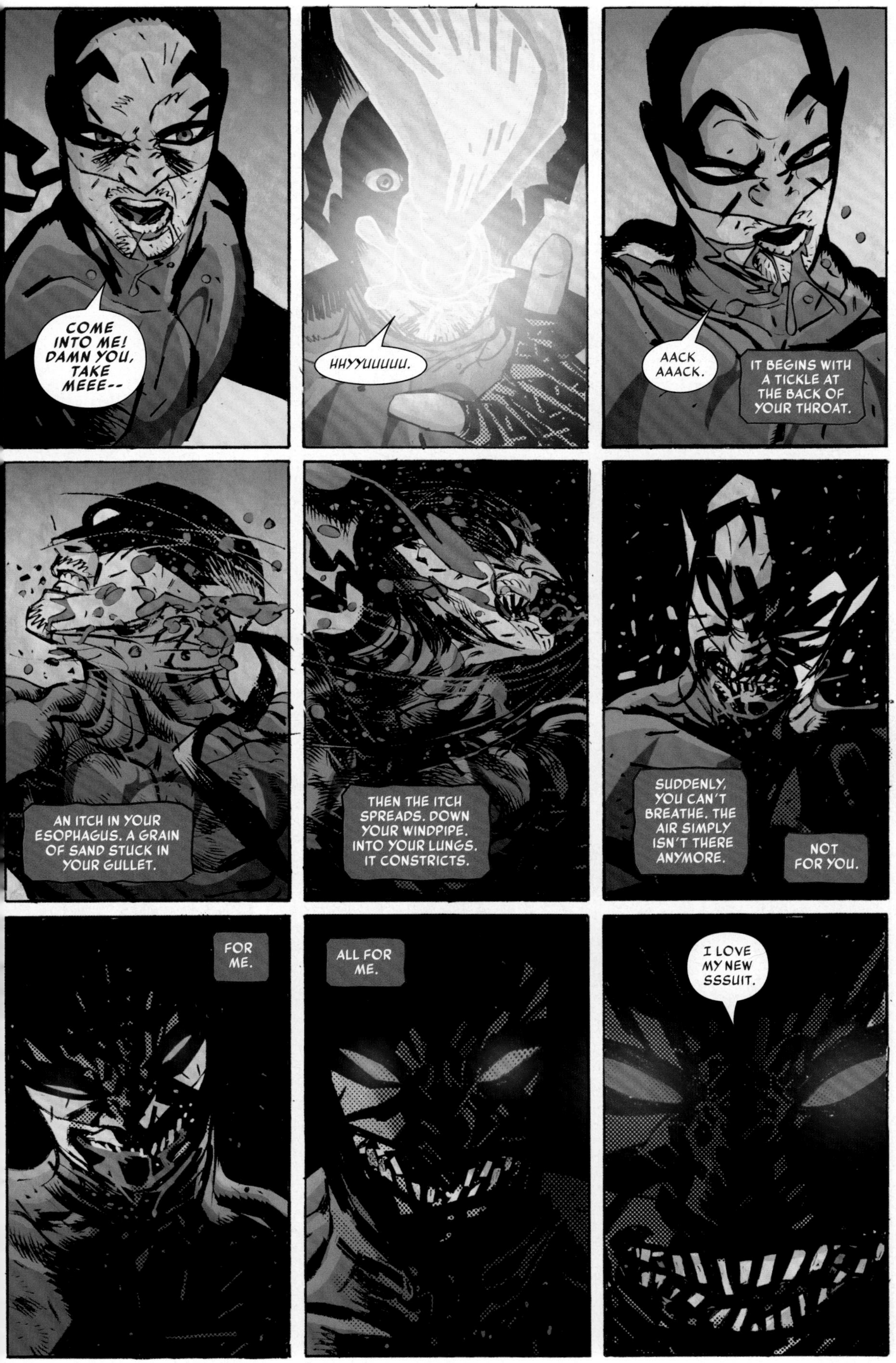

COME INTO ME! DAMN YOU, TAKE MEEE--
HHYYUUUUU.
AACK AAACK.
IT BEGINS WITH A TICKLE AT THE BACK OF YOUR THROAT.
AN ITCH IN YOUR ESOPHAGUS. A GRAIN OF SAND STUCK IN YOUR GULLET.
THEN THE ITCH SPREADS. DOWN YOUR WINDPIPE. INTO YOUR LUNGS. IT CONSTRICTS.
SUDDENLY, YOU CAN'T BREATHE. THE AIR SIMPLY ISN'T THERE ANYMORE.
NOT FOR YOU.
FOR ME.
ALL FOR ME.
I LOVE MY NEW SSSUIT.

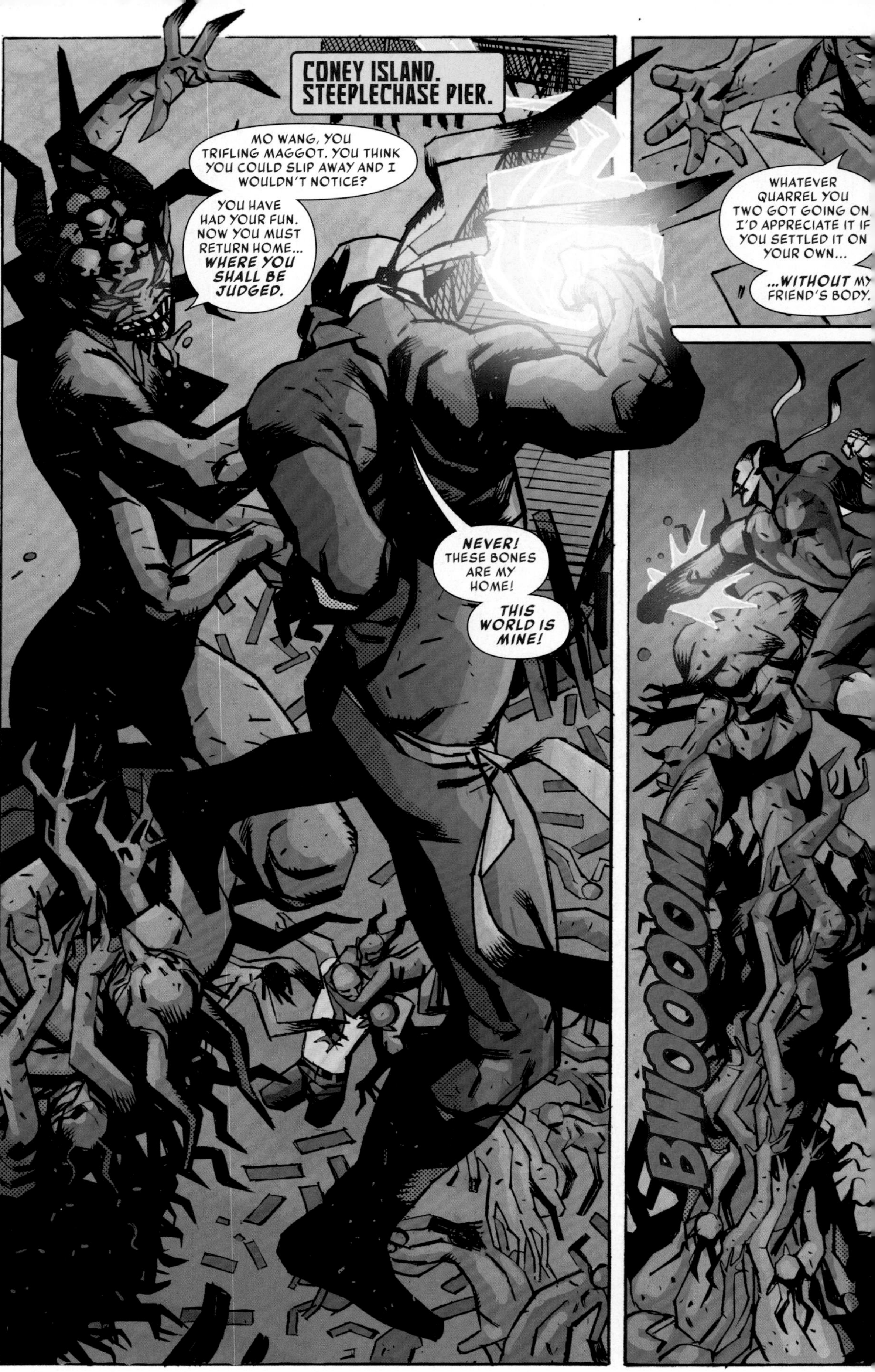
CONEY ISLAND. STEEPLECHASE PIER.
MO WANG, YOU TRIFLING MAGGOT. YOU THINK YOU COULD SLIP AWAY AND I WOULDN'T NOTICE?
YOU HAVE HAD YOUR FUN. NOW YOU MUST RETURN HOME... WHERE YOU SHALL BE JUDGED.
NEVER! THESE BONES ARE MY HOME!
THIS WORLD IS MINE!
WHATEVER QUARREL YOU TWO GOT GOING ON, I'D APPRECIATE IT IF YOU SETTLED IT ON YOUR OWN...
...WITHOUT MY FRIEND'S BODY.
BWOOOOM

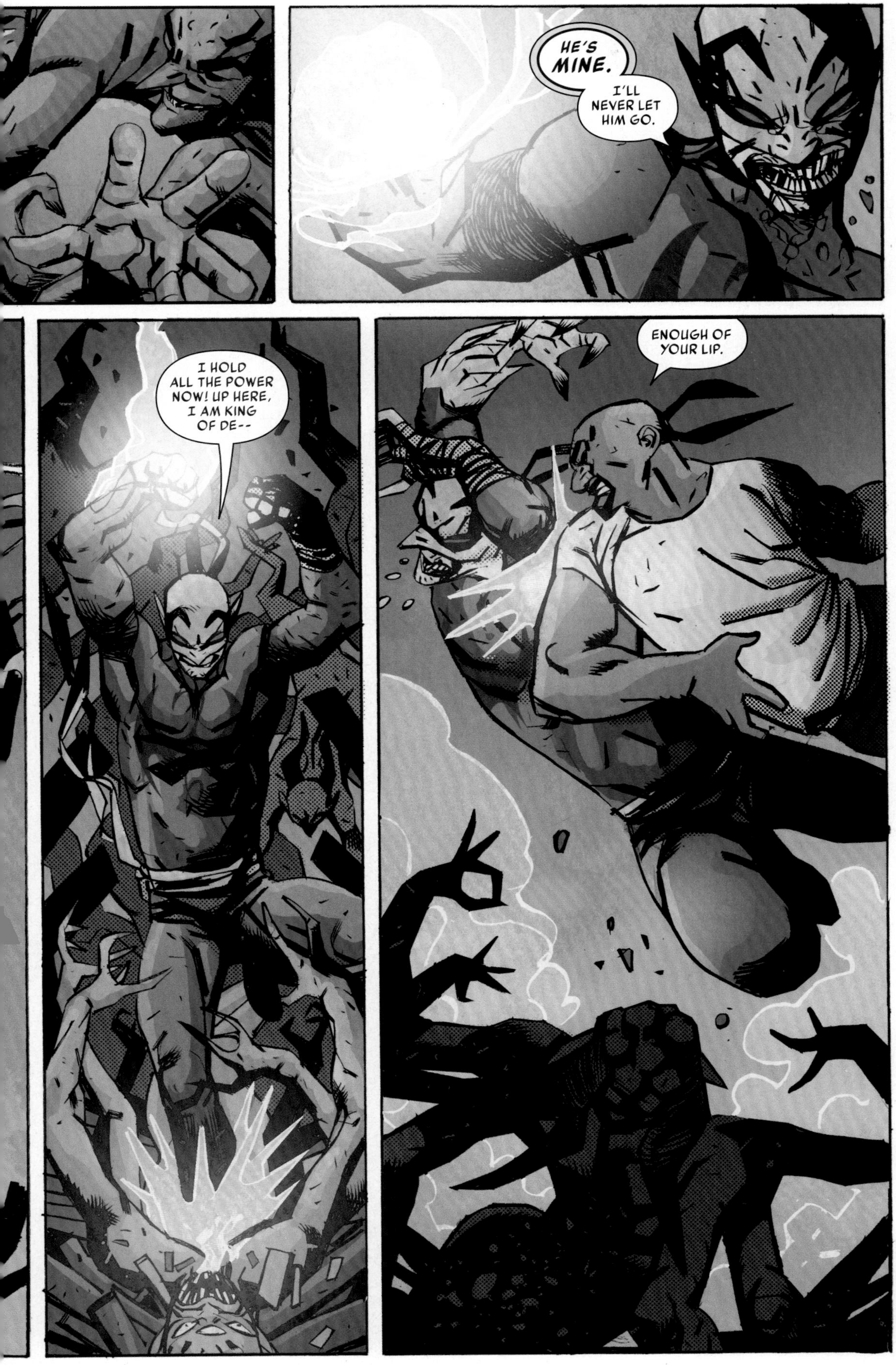
HE'S MINE.
I'LL NEVER LET HIM GO.
I HOLD ALL THE POWER NOW! UP HERE, I AM KING OF DE--
ENOUGH OF YOUR LIP.

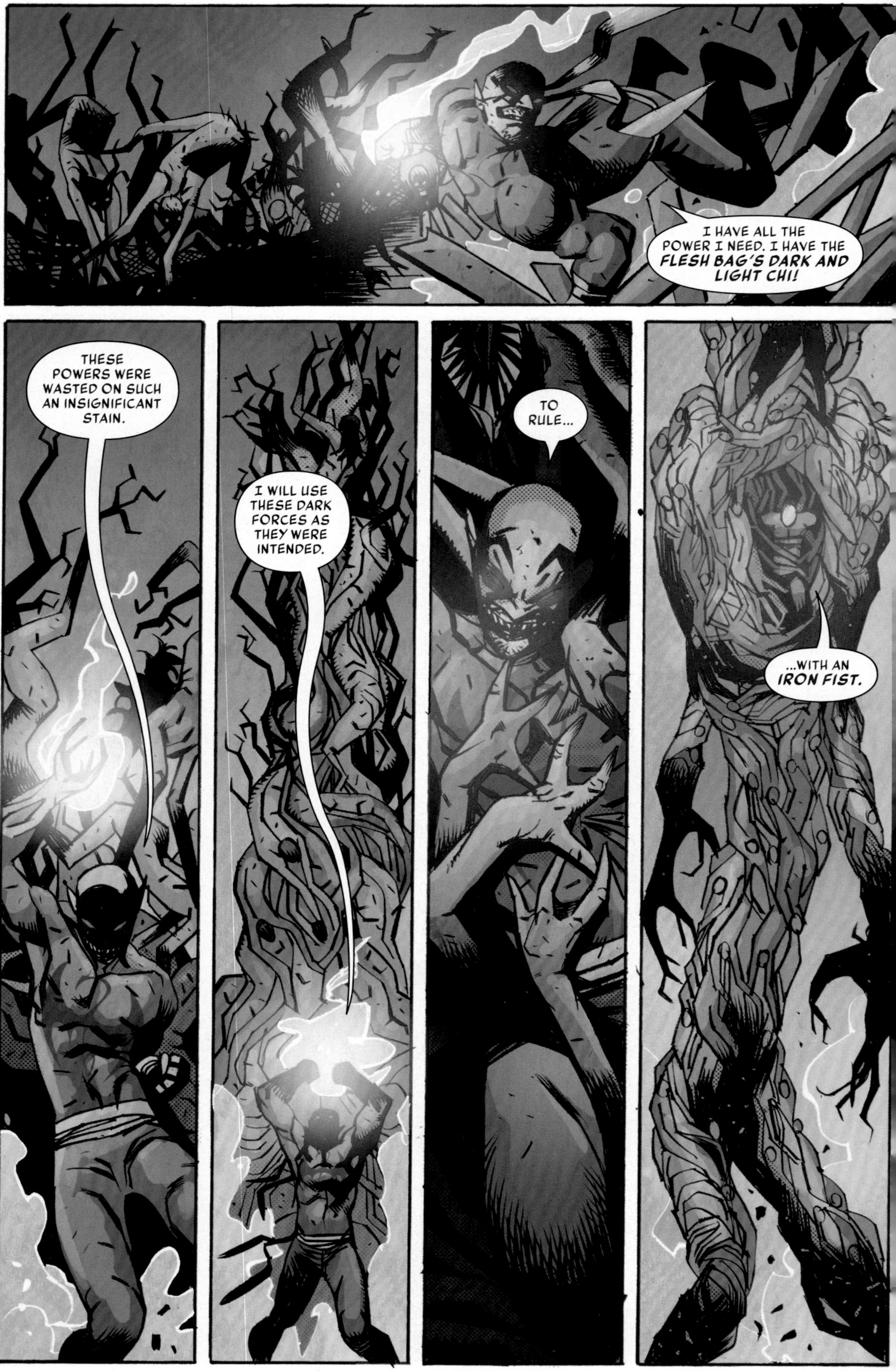
I HAVE ALL THE POWER I NEED. I HAVE THE FLESH BAG'S DARK AND LIGHT CHI!
THESE POWERS WERE WASTED ON SUCH AN INSIGNIFICANT STAIN.
I WILL USE THESE DARK FORCES AS THEY WERE INTENDED.
TO RULE...
...WITH AN IRON FIST.

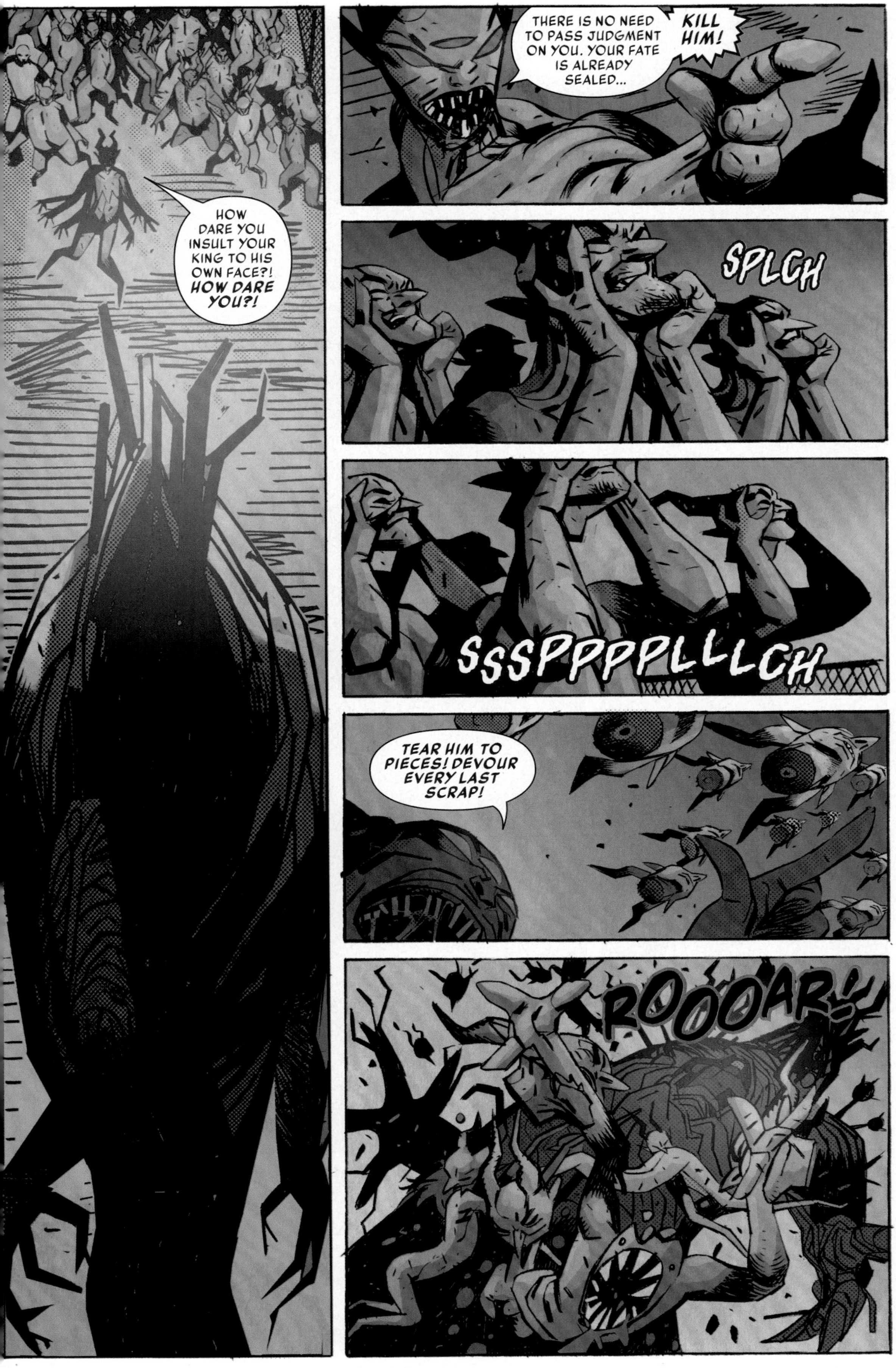
HOW DARE YOU INSULT YOUR KING TO HIS OWN FACE?! HOW DARE YOU?!
THERE IS NO NEED TO PASS JUDGMENT ON YOU. YOUR FATE IS ALREADY SEALED...
KILL HIM!
SPLCH
SSSPPPPLLLCH
TEAR HIM TO PIECES! DEVOUR EVERY LAST SCRAP!
ROOOAR!

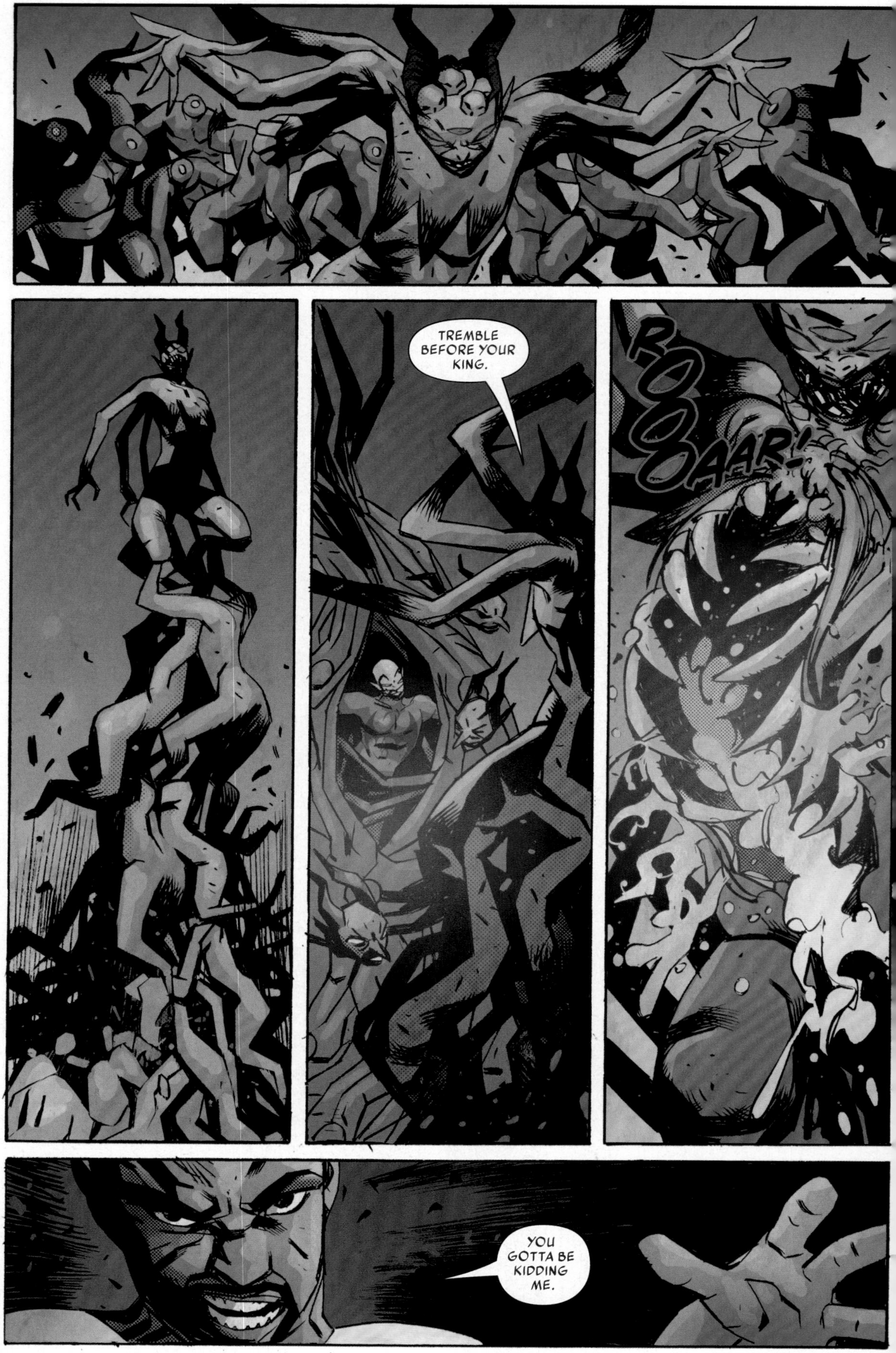
TREMBLE BEFORE YOUR KING.
ROOOAAR!
YOU GOTTA BE KIDDING ME.

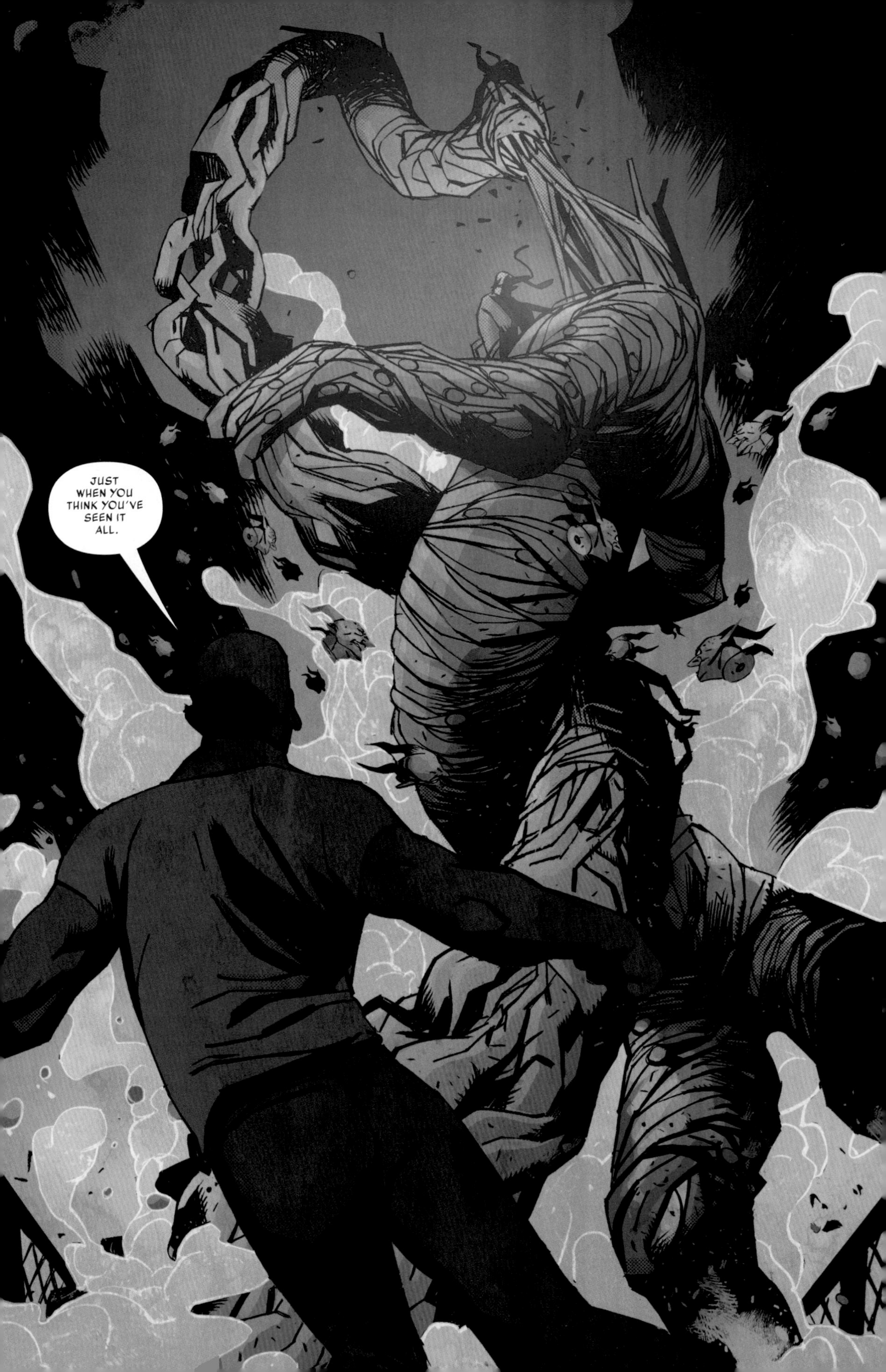
JUST WHEN YOU THINK YOU'VE SEEN IT ALL.

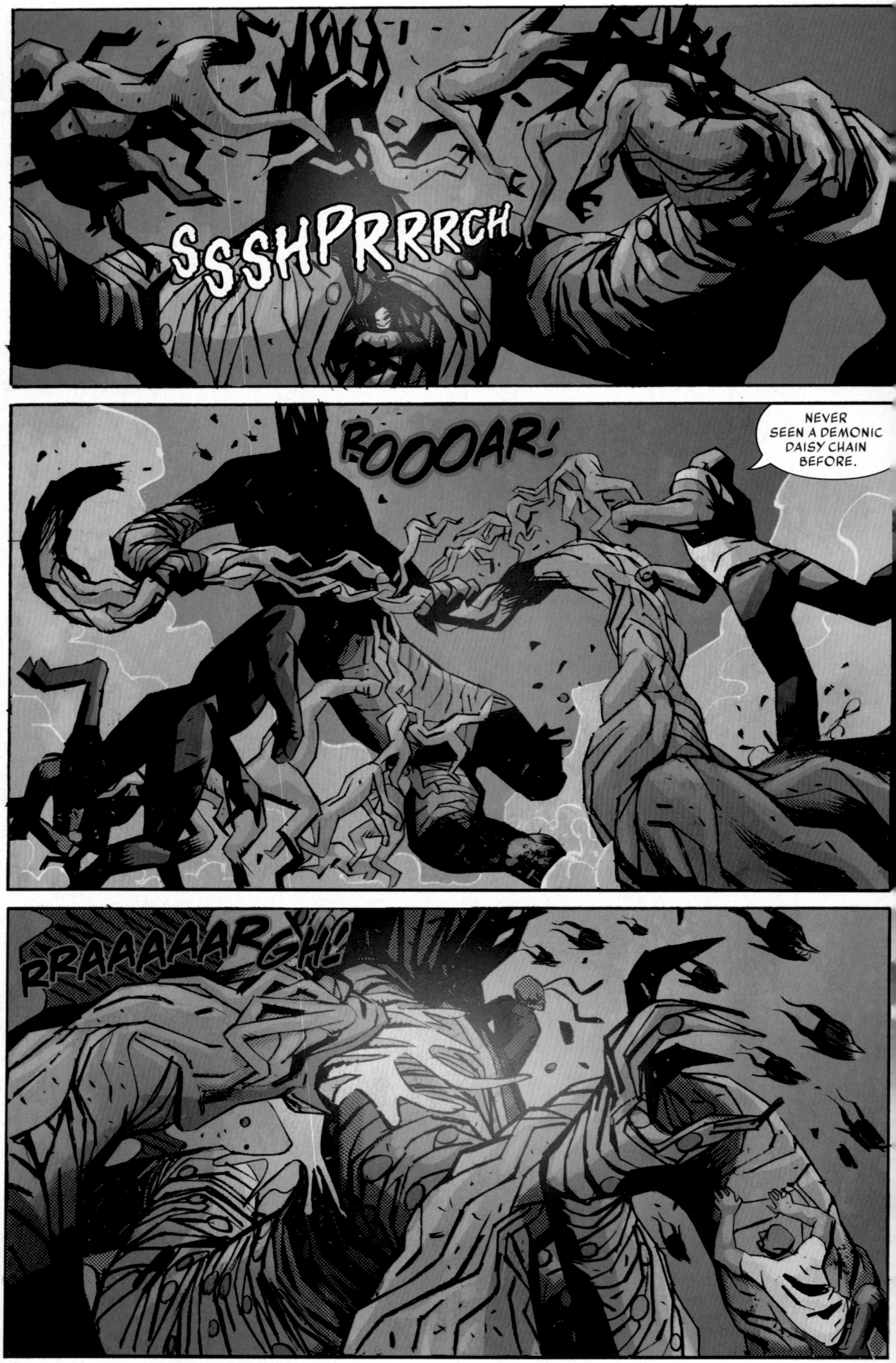
SSSHPRRRCH
ROOOAR!
NEVER SEEN A DEMONIC DAISY CHAIN BEFORE.
RRAAAAAARGH!

"DON'T BE ≠HNNGH≠ STUPID, DANNY. WHEN WOULD WE EVER NEED TO ROCK CLIMB?"

"WE MIGHT AS WELL FLUSH THE GYM MEMBERSHIP FEES DOWN THE CAN."

THERE'LL BE NO LIVING WITH HIM AFTER THIS...

DANNY?

HEY, YO, DANNY! CAN YOU HEAR ME IN THERE?

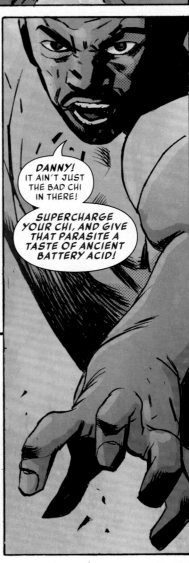

LISTEN TO ME, DANNY! YOU GOTTA FIGHT THIS THING... FLUSH HIM OUT!

KLLK

THESE BONES ARE MINE! THE CHI IS MINE!

DANNY! IT AIN'T JUST THE BAD CHI IN THERE!

SUPERCHARGE YOUR CHI, AND GIVE THAT PARASITE A TASTE OF ANCIENT BATTERY ACID!

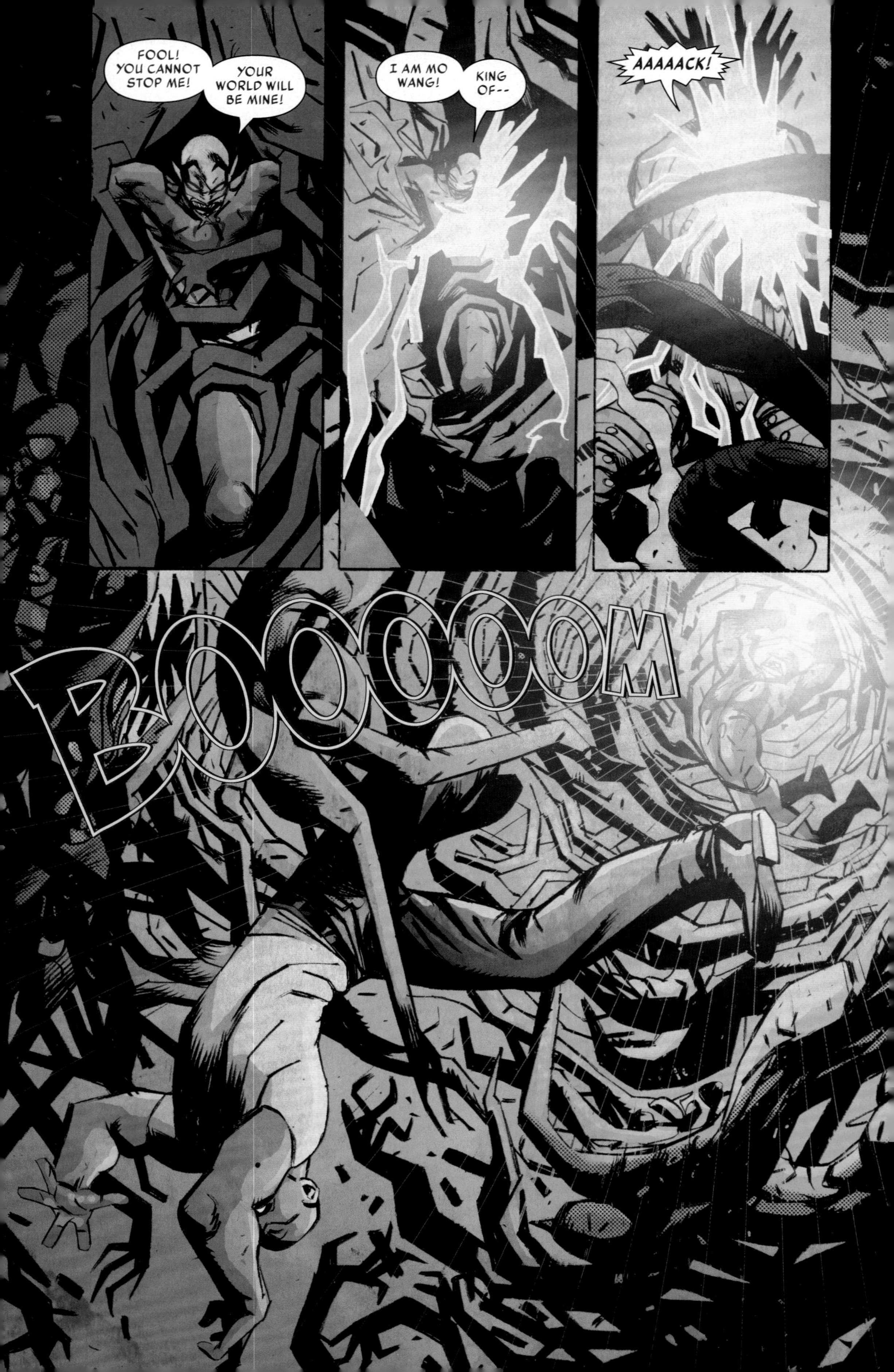

FOOL! YOU CANNOT STOP ME!
YOUR WORLD WILL BE MINE!
I AM MO WANG!
KING OF--
AAAAACK!
BOOOOOOOM

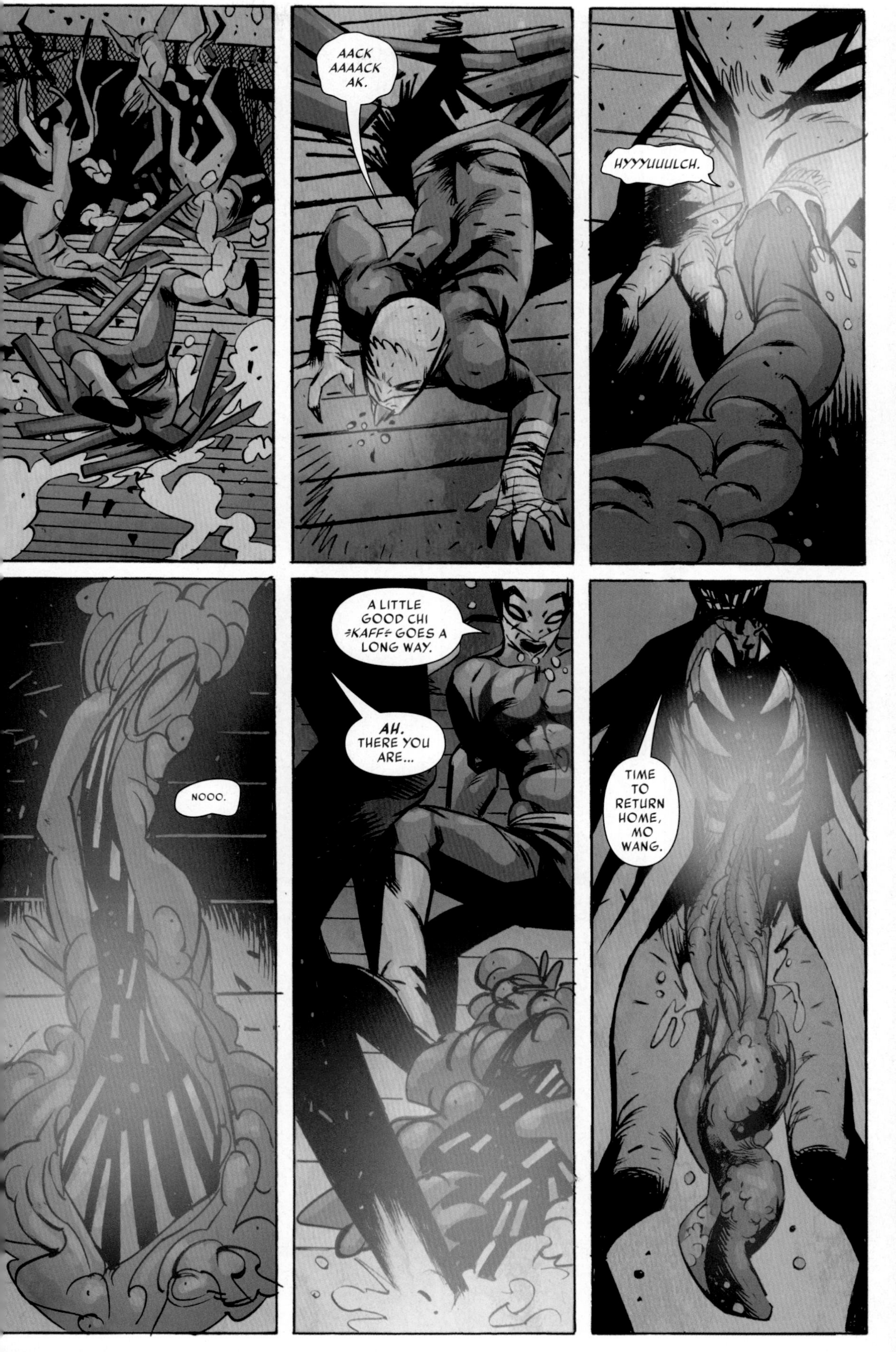
AACK AAAACK AK.
HYYYUUULCH.
NOOO.
A LITTLE GOOD CHI ≠KAFF≠ GOES A LONG WAY.
AH. THERE YOU ARE...
TIME TO RETURN HOME, MO WANG.

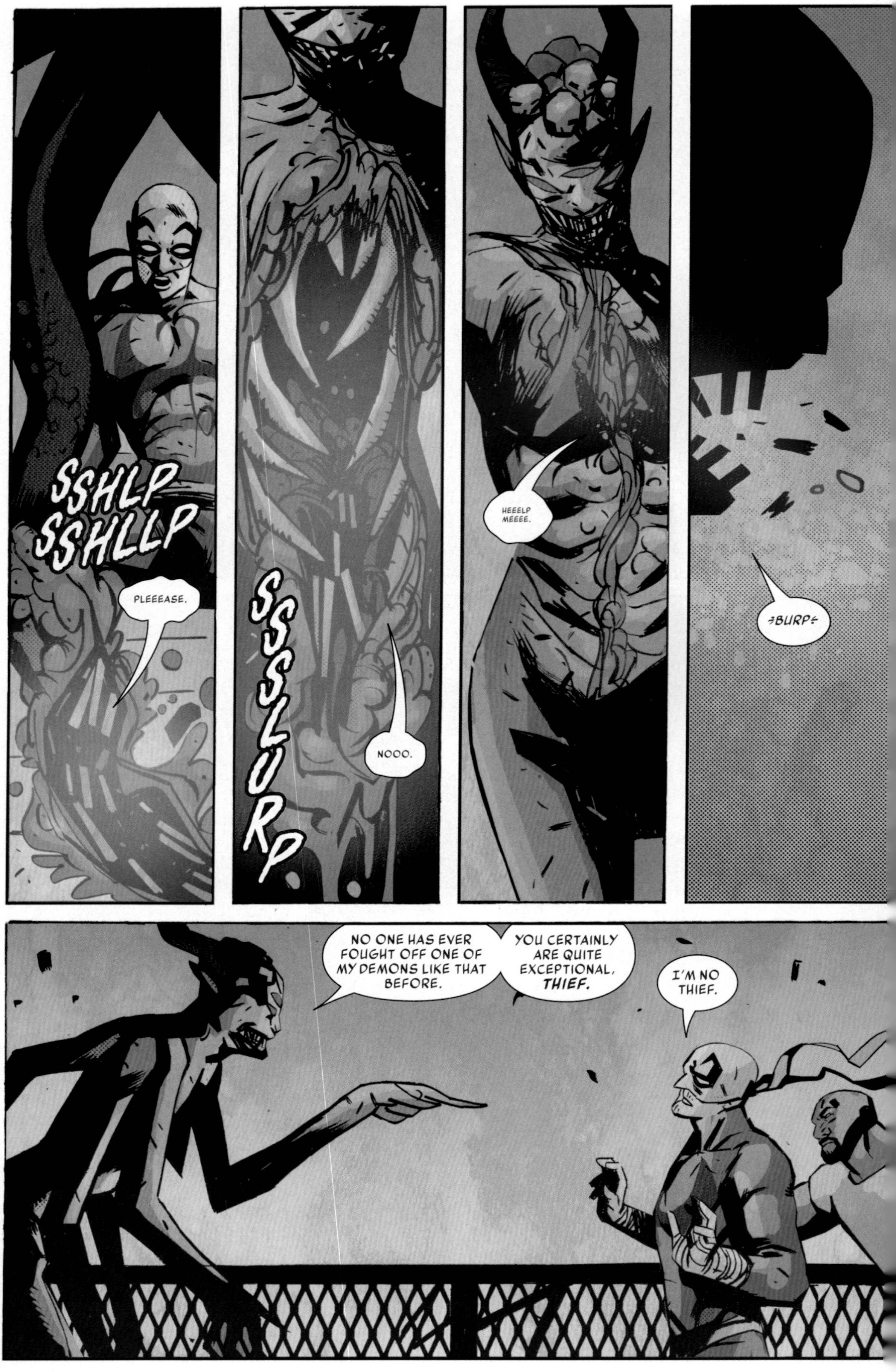
SSHLP
SSHLLP
PLEEEASE.
SSSLURP
NOOO.
HEEELP MEEEE.
BURP
NO ONE HAS EVER FOUGHT OFF ONE OF MY DEMONS LIKE THAT BEFORE.
YOU CERTAINLY ARE QUITE EXCEPTIONAL, *THIEF.*
I'M NO THIEF.

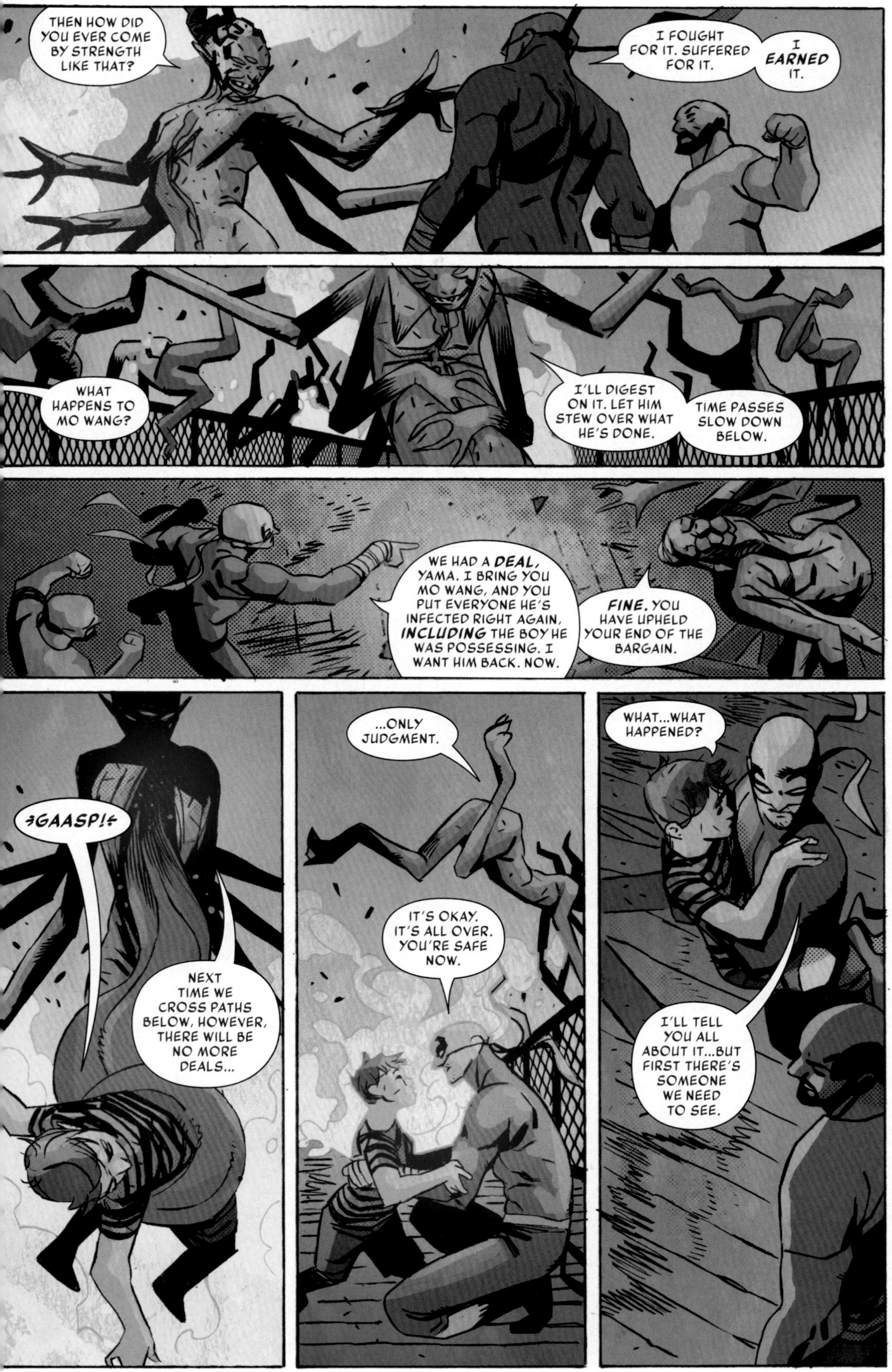
THEN HOW DID YOU EVER COME BY STRENGTH LIKE THAT?
I FOUGHT FOR IT. SUFFERED FOR IT.
I *EARNED* IT.
WHAT HAPPENS TO MO WANG?
I'LL DIGEST ON IT. LET HIM STEW OVER WHAT HE'S DONE.
TIME PASSES SLOW DOWN BELOW.
WE HAD A *DEAL,* YAMA. I BRING YOU MO WANG, AND YOU PUT EVERYONE HE'S INFECTED RIGHT AGAIN, *INCLUDING* THE BOY HE WAS POSSESSING. I WANT HIM BACK. NOW.
FINE. YOU HAVE UPHELD YOUR END OF THE BARGAIN.
GAASP!
NEXT TIME WE CROSS PATHS BELOW, HOWEVER, THERE WILL BE NO MORE DEALS...
...ONLY JUDGMENT.
IT'S OKAY. IT'S ALL OVER. YOU'RE SAFE NOW.
WHAT...WHAT HAPPENED?
I'LL TELL YOU ALL ABOUT IT...BUT FIRST THERE'S SOMEONE WE NEED TO SEE.

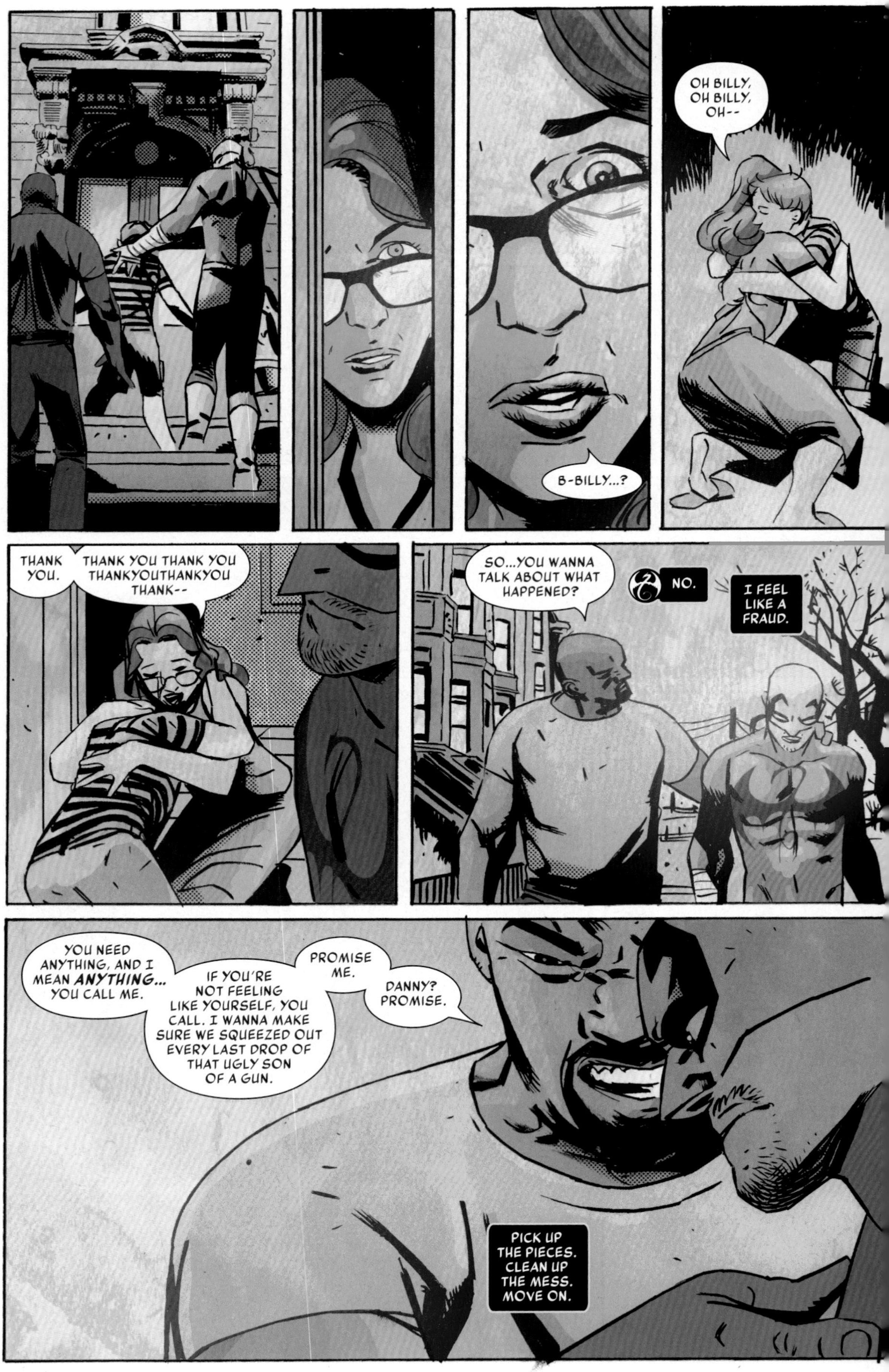
B-BILLY...?
OH BILLY, OH BILLY, OH--
THANK YOU.
THANK YOU THANK YOU THANKYOUTHANKYOU THANK--
SO...YOU WANNA TALK ABOUT WHAT HAPPENED?
NO.
I FEEL LIKE A FRAUD.
YOU NEED ANYTHING, AND I MEAN ANYTHING... YOU CALL ME.
IF YOU'RE NOT FEELING LIKE YOURSELF, YOU CALL. I WANNA MAKE SURE WE SQUEEZED OUT EVERY LAST DROP OF THAT UGLY SON OF A GUN.
PROMISE ME.
DANNY? PROMISE.
PICK UP THE PIECES. CLEAN UP THE MESS. MOVE ON.

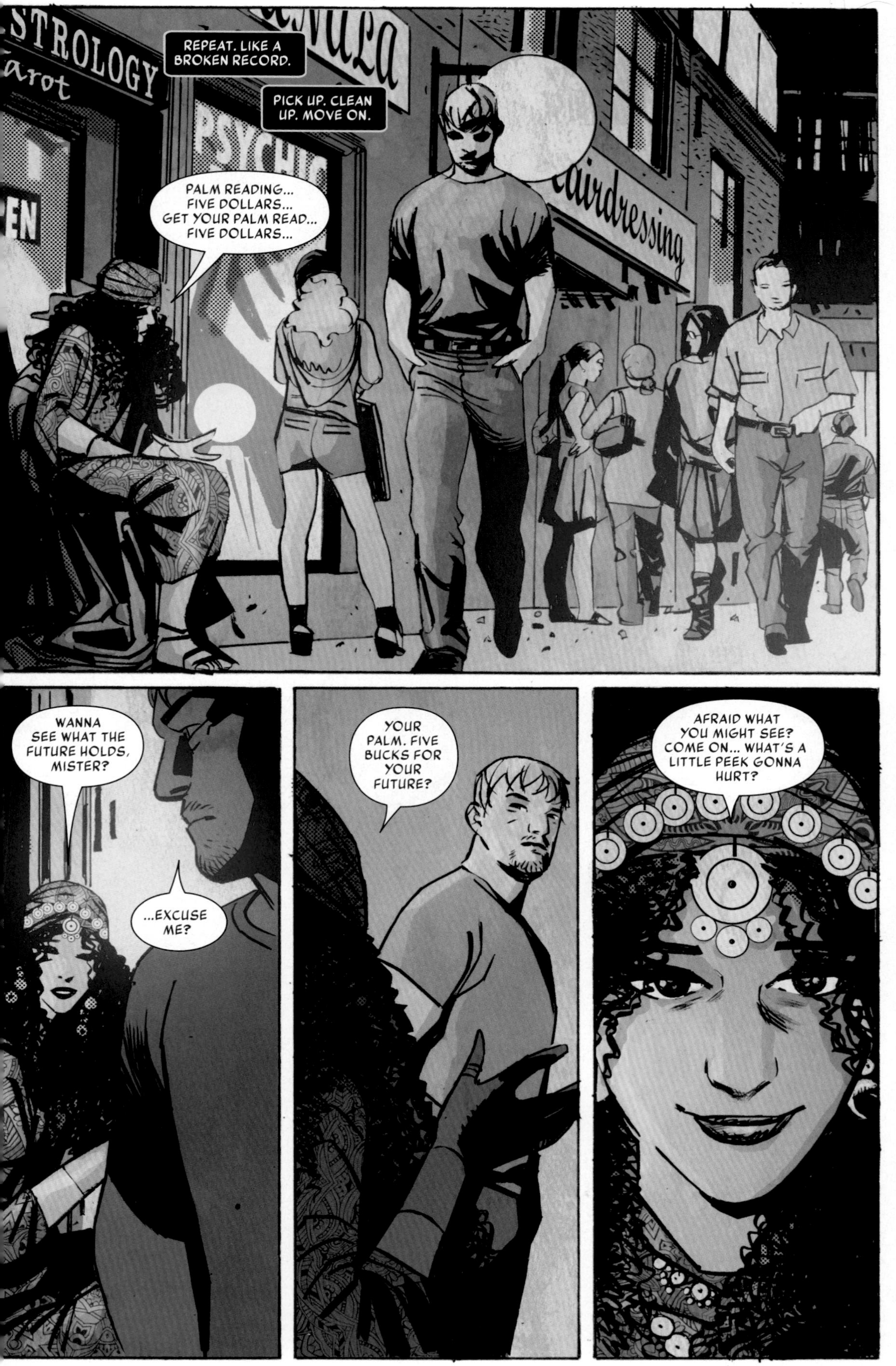
ASTROLOGY
Tarot
PSYCHIC
OPEN
REPEAT. LIKE A BROKEN RECORD.
PICK UP. CLEAN UP. MOVE ON.
Hairdressing
PALM READING... FIVE DOLLARS... GET YOUR PALM READ... FIVE DOLLARS...
WANNA SEE WHAT THE FUTURE HOLDS, MISTER?
...EXCUSE ME?
YOUR PALM. FIVE BUCKS FOR YOUR FUTURE?
AFRAID WHAT YOU MIGHT SEE? COME ON... WHAT'S A LITTLE PEEK GONNA HURT?

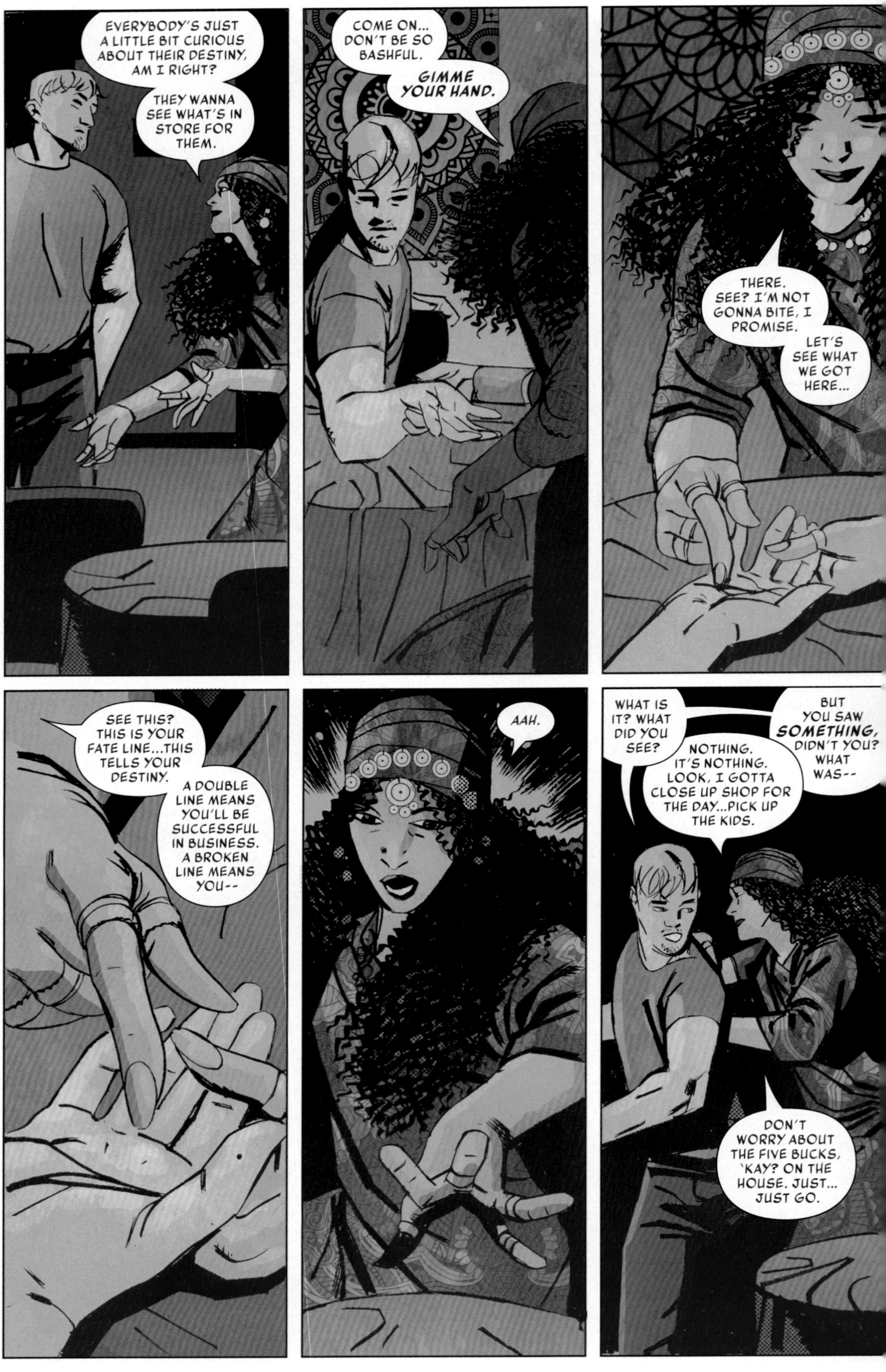
EVERYBODY'S JUST A LITTLE BIT CURIOUS ABOUT THEIR DESTINY, AM I RIGHT?
THEY WANNA SEE WHAT'S IN STORE FOR THEM.
COME ON... DON'T BE SO BASHFUL.
GIMME YOUR HAND.
THERE. SEE? I'M NOT GONNA BITE, I PROMISE.
LET'S SEE WHAT WE GOT HERE...
SEE THIS? THIS IS YOUR FATE LINE...THIS TELLS YOUR DESTINY.
A DOUBLE LINE MEANS YOU'LL BE SUCCESSFUL IN BUSINESS. A BROKEN LINE MEANS YOU--
AAH.
WHAT IS IT? WHAT DID YOU SEE?
NOTHING. IT'S NOTHING. LOOK, I GOTTA CLOSE UP SHOP FOR THE DAY...PICK UP THE KIDS.
BUT YOU SAW SOMETHING, DIDN'T YOU? WHAT WAS--
DON'T WORRY ABOUT THE FIVE BUCKS, 'KAY? ON THE HOUSE. JUST... JUST GO.

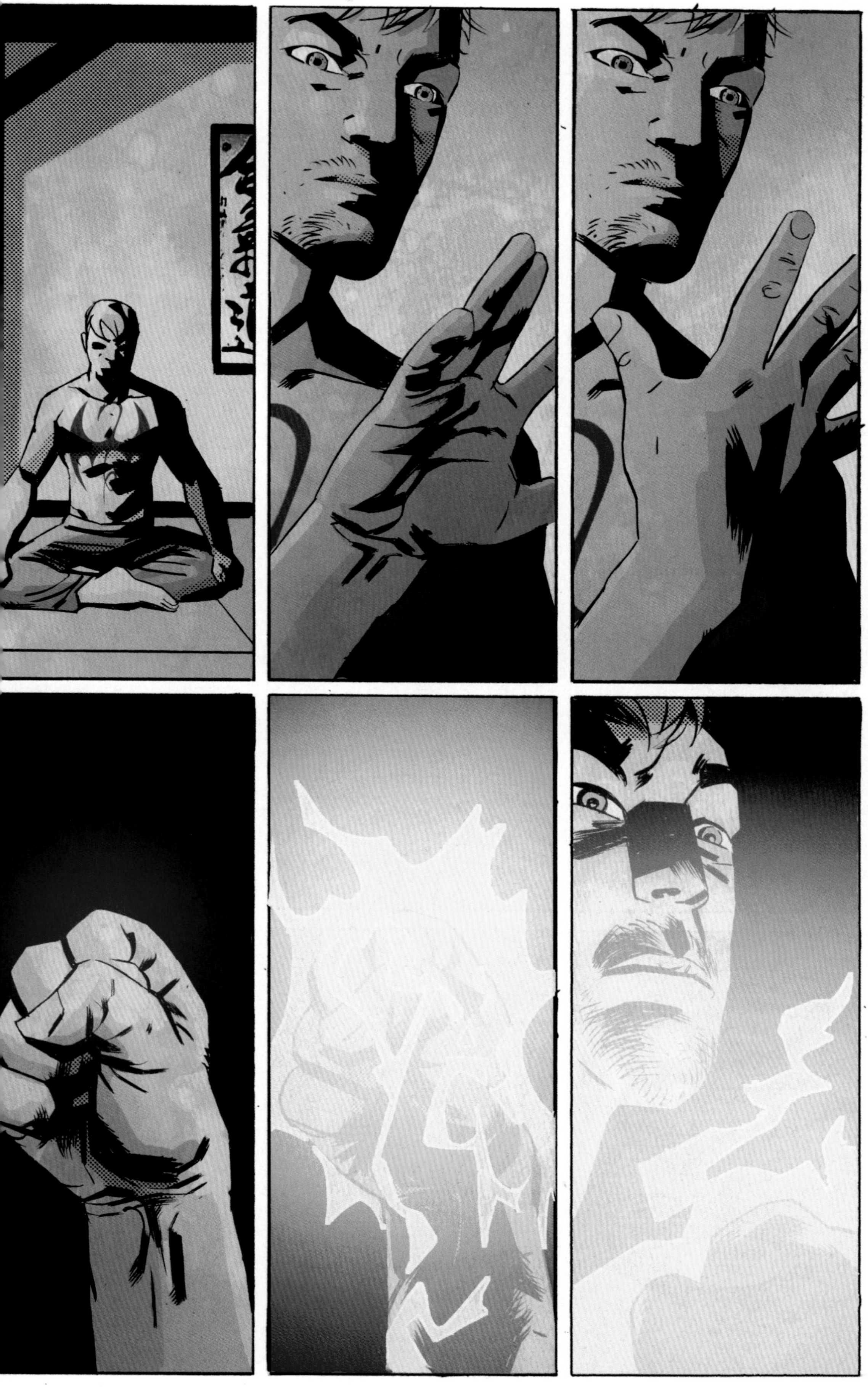

CRRRNCH

...LUKE?

HEY, UH... IT'S ME. DANNY.

CRNCH

I KNOW IT'S BEEN A WHILE, BUT...

LISTEN, I...I DON'T WANT TO BOTHER YOU.

CRRNCH

YOU MADE ME PROMISE I'D REACH OUT IF...

CRRRNCH

SO... THIS IS ME.

CRNCH CRNCH

REACHING OUT.

CRRNCH

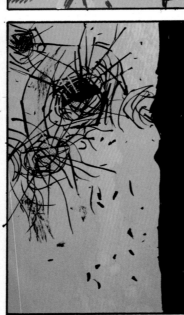

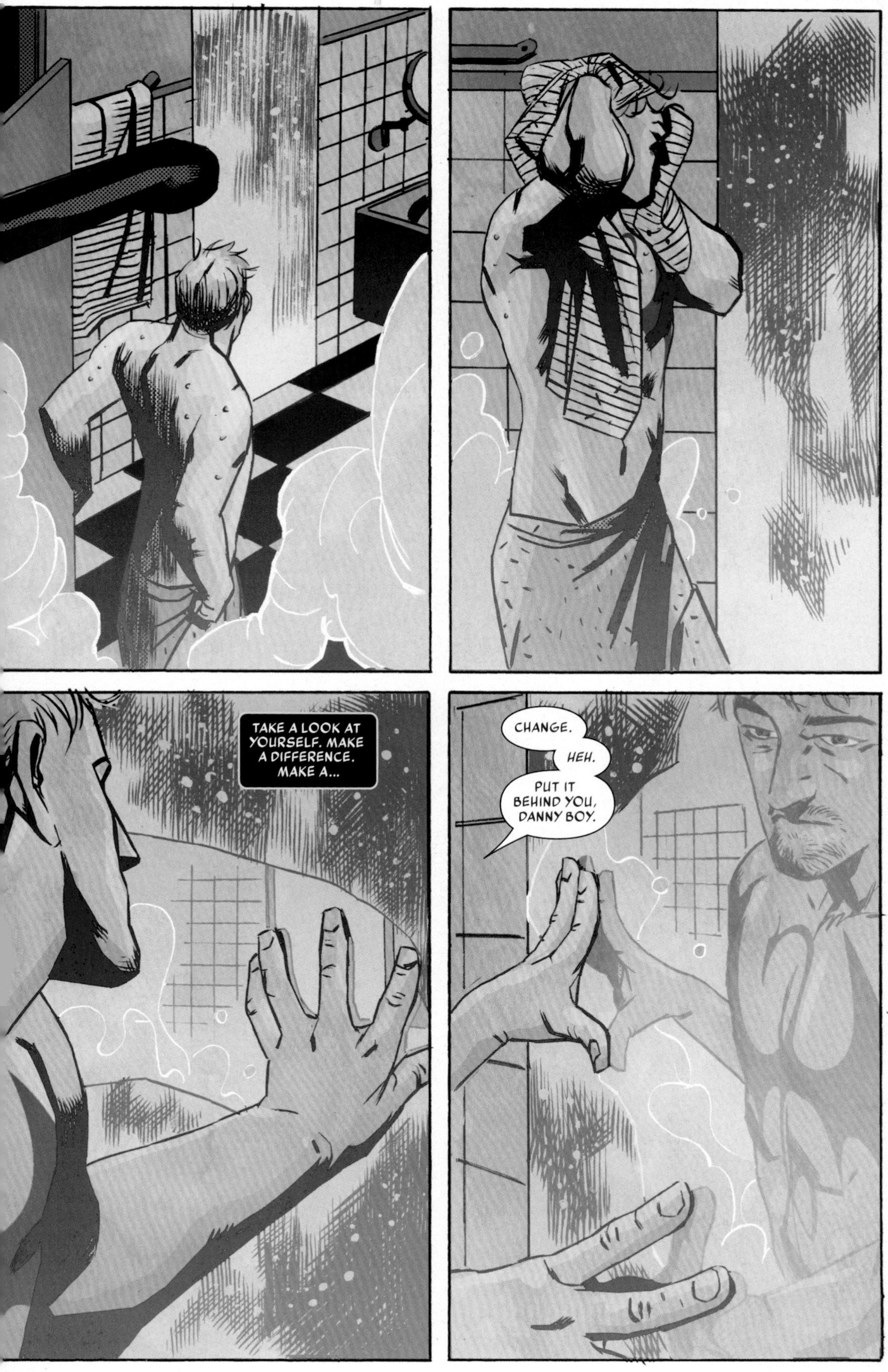
TAKE A LOOK AT YOURSELF. MAKE A DIFFERENCE. MAKE A...
CHANGE.
HEH.
PUT IT BEHIND YOU, DANNY BOY.

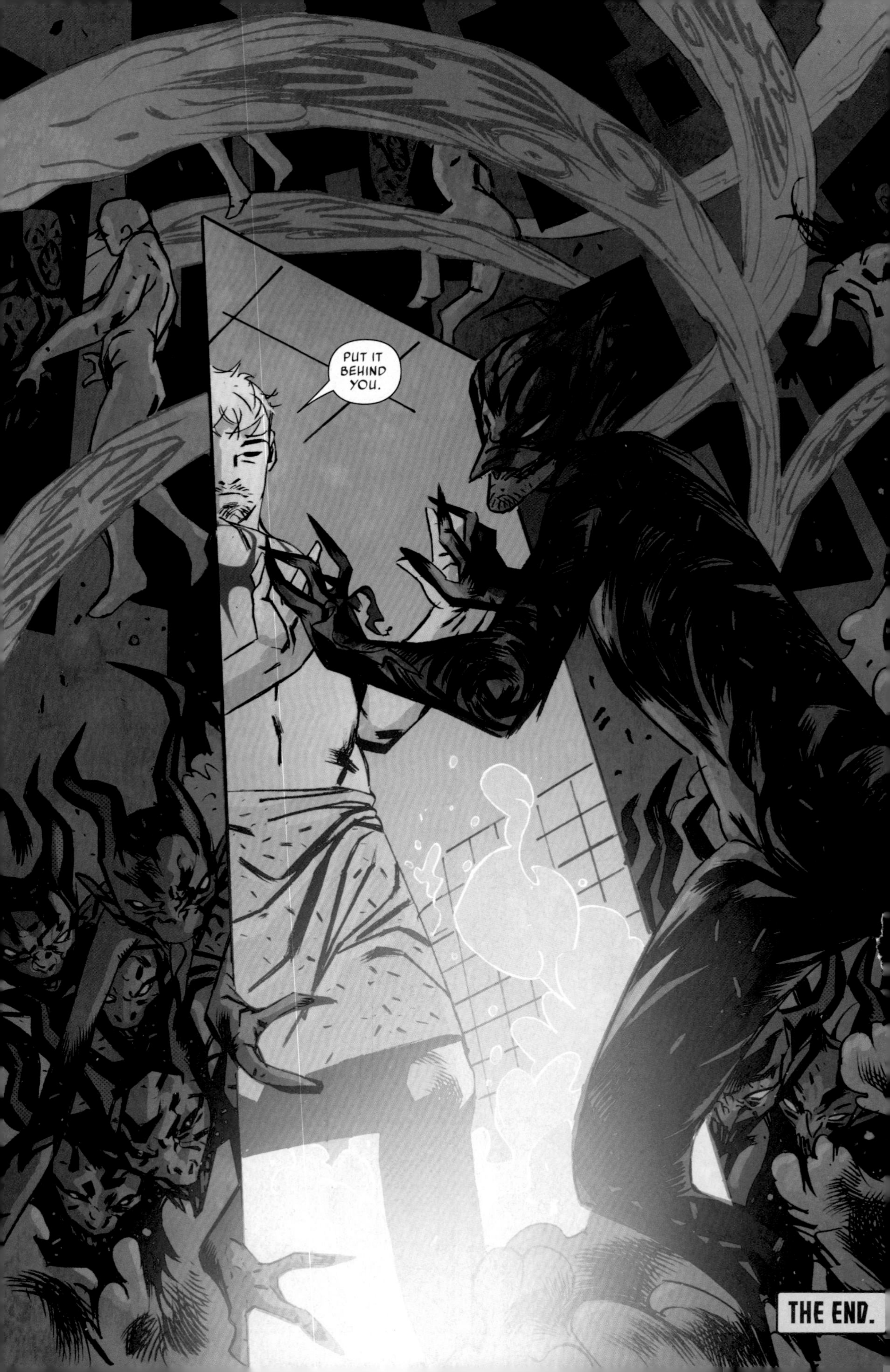
PUT IT BEHIND YOU.
THE END.

I'm not sure I was the right person to tell Iron Fist's story. When I was first invited to write Danny Rand, the news cycle was churning through an astounding amount of violence. It was everywhere. Violence was everywhere — real-world super villains in Hollywood, political tensions and one senseless tragedy after another. Very suddenly, we all had to reckon with "real world" stuff in a profoundly loud way.

I couldn't help but wonder if this was the right time to write about Danny. I saw his privilege and I found it difficult to know how to best access his heart. His nobility of spirit has always been an integral part of his character, what made Rand resonate throughout the decades…but the timing felt a wee bit off. Did the world need another problem solved with ANY fists, let alone an Iron one?

Then I got to thinking about *Evil Dead II*.

Dead by Dawn is a downright classic. I remember watching that pivotal scene where Bruce Campbell's Ash defends himself against his own demonically possessed hand and…for some reason, I knew this is where I wanted to go with Danny. I wanted to take his iron fist away.

The question I usually ask myself before I start writing is: What's the most inappropriate thing I can do here? Every writer has got to find their way into a story, and for me, I tend to begin by thinking of the wrong choices first… which, occasionally, leads to the right one, simply because it feels so, so wrong. Here it seemed like the most inappropriate thing to do to Iron Fist would be to cut his hands off. Symbolically speaking, who is Iron Fist without his, you know, fists?

Another guiding influence was the Rockbiter from *The NeverEnding Story*. I always think back to the scene where Atreyu stumbles upon that mountainous giant, slouched over, left alone to obsess over how his own hands failed to save his friends. To hold on. Here you have a character who identifies his sense of self by way of his strength—the strength of his hands—and yet that strength isn't enough. It's never enough. And when that strength fails him, the one thing he identified himself by is gone. He's left to question who he is. Who he ever was.

They look like big good, strong hands, don't they?

That line always echoed in my head… so I wanted Danny to ask himself the same question.

In all sincerity, I believe what lifts this story up to a higher level is the work by Guillermo Sanna and Lee Loughridge. Along with Travis Lanham's lettering and the covers by Khoi Pham and Chris Sotomayor, everybody took my doggerel and truly elevated it. Huge props need to go out to Devin Lewis and Lauren Amaro for assembling this dream team and letting me spin this yucky yarn.

Clay McLeod Chapman

Horror comics have been part of my life since childhood. I love to be scared from the safety of my bed. That's why I was very excited to be part of this story.

Like the rest of the team, I put a lot of effort and dedication into this comic. I hope the reader enjoys reading it as much as I did drawing it.

Guillermo Sanna

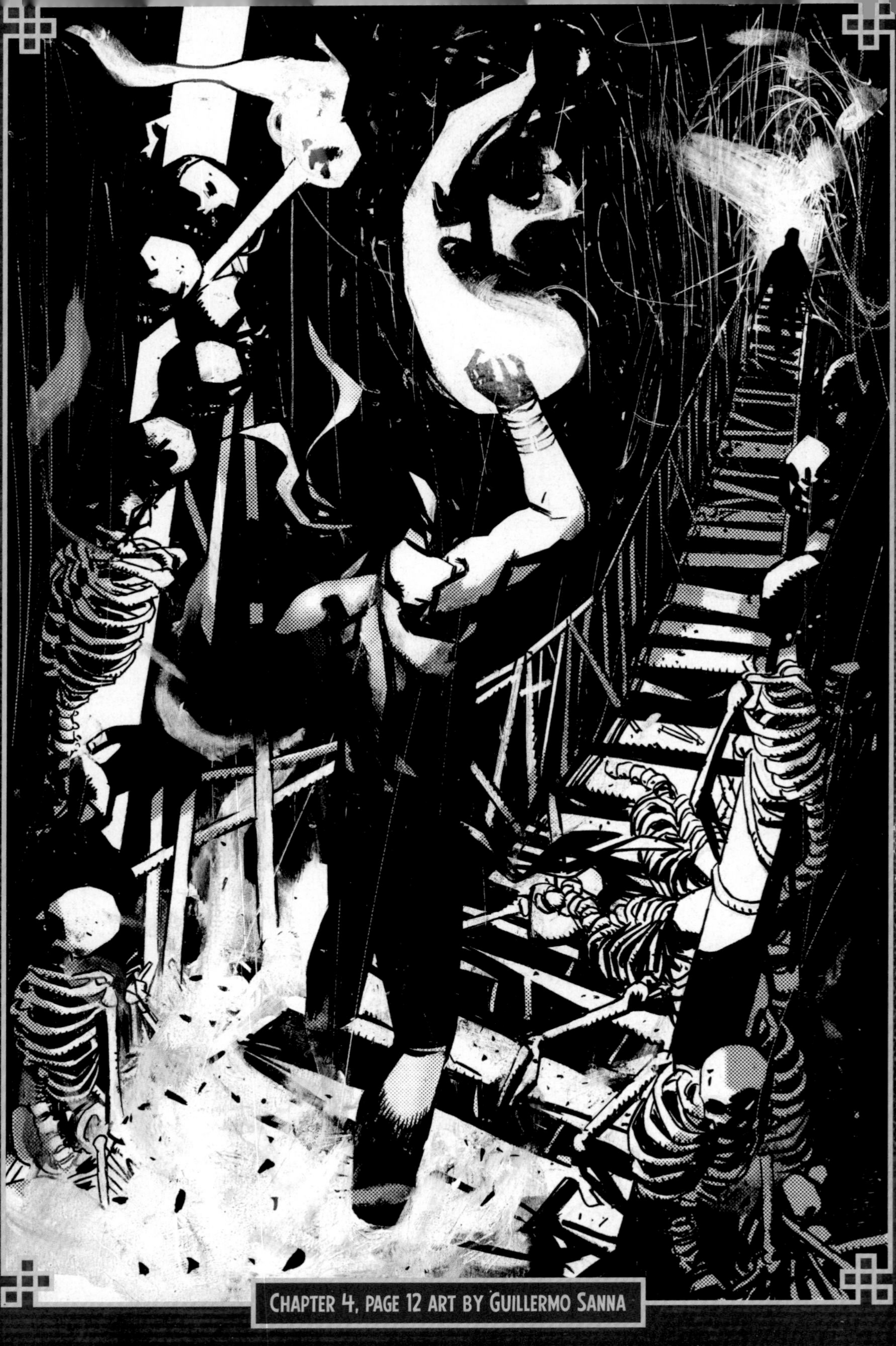

Chapter 4, page 12 art by Guillermo Sanna